Buddhist Trends in Southeast Asia

Buddhist Trends in Southeast Asia

Edited by

Trevor Ling

LSEAS Social Issues in Southeast Asia
INSTITUTE OF SOUTHEAST ASIAN STUDIES

Published by
Institute of Southeast Asian Studies
Heng Mui Keng Terrace
Pasir Panjang Road
Singapore 0511

Cataloguing in Publication Data

Buddhist trends in Southeast Asia / edited by Trevor Ling.
  1. Buddhism--Asia, Southeastern.
  2. Buddhism--Burma.
  3. Buddhism--Cambodia.
  4. Buddhism--Singapore.
  5. Buddhism--Thailand.
  I. Ling, Trevor.
BQ408 B92   1993   sls91-11870

ISBN 981-3035-80-3 (hard cover)
ISBN 981-3035-81-1 (soft cover)

Typeset by International Typesetters
Printed in Singapore by Stamford Press Pte Ltd.

Dedicated to the memory of
Professor K.S. Sandhu
Director of ISEAS, 1972–1992

Contents

Acknowledgements

The Social Issues in Southeast Asia (SISEA) programme has benefited greatly from the financial support provided by the Ford Foundation and the Rockefeller Brothers Fund for the Social Issues in Southeast Asia series, of which *Buddhist Trends in Southeast Asia* is a part. The Institute would like to record its appreciation of all such help and support and to express the wish that the various numbers of "Social Issues in Southeast Asia" will circulate widely amongst all concerned with the social dynamics of the region.

Introduction

TREVOR LING

Towards an Account of "Buddhisms" in Country-Specific Terms

The use of such a term as "Buddhisms" appears to be required as soon as it is acknowledged that there is more than one sort of Buddhism, even within Southeast Asia. The degree of plurality that can be found is such that the use of the word "Buddhism" in an unspecified sense has very little heuristic value and can be a source of confusion in comparative studies within the Southeast Asia region. (The same is true, of course, of certain other geographical areas where a variety of "Buddhisms" is found.) However, opposition to a more precise terminology is likely to come from modern Buddhists who are eager to fall in with ecumenical trends set by other religious traditions; for the purposes of the social and historical sciences, however, comparative analysis demands precise terminology that takes account of the various national forms of Buddhism, rather than simply distinguishing between "Theravada" and "Mahayana". For even *within* the Theravada, for example, comparison can be made in terms of complexity of historical and organizational tradition (as in Myanmar), compared with relative simplicity of historical and organizational tradition (as in Thailand). The indiscriminate approach is one which is sometimes followed by the "Buddhologist" (as the late Edward Conze used to describe himself), and it comes directly from the answer to the question: "In what language are the Buddhist scriptures which are used by these people: Sanskrit or Pali?" If they used what were basically Sanskrit texts, even though now translated into, say Tibetan, then these people are "Mahayanists", according to the Buddhologist. Similarly, if they use Pali texts they are simply, according to the Buddhologist, Theravadins.

Some social scientists seeking data on such "Buddhists" as have come under their scrutiny are likely to have resort to the Buddhologist by way of background reading. If the Buddhologist is not also equipped with a knowledge of the historical complexities of the Southeast Asian region, this will result, for example, in an initial identification of Myanmar Buddhists (because they use the Pali canon) as of "the same kind" as Sinhalese Buddhists. But the modern predominance of Pali Buddhism in both Myanmar and Sri Lanka, or in both Myanmar and Thailand, hides important historical, political, and organizational differences between the Buddhisms of Myanmar and Sri Lanka, and again, between those of Myanmar and Thailand, differences which may override the common element of Pali scriptures. The crude assumption which too often follows is that once a country's present form of Buddhism has been labelled in such simple terms as Pali or Sanskrit, Theravada or Mahayana, there is no need for further heuristic procedure; upon such misapprehension "social scientific" study of the Buddhist institutions and organizations will then proceed.

Buddhisms whose present-day canonical scriptures are of the Pali kind include Sinhalese, Thai, Myanmar, Indian, and Cambodian. Those whose present-day canonical scriptures are derived, in part at least, from the Sanskrit kind include, among others, Chinese, Japanese, and Tibetan. The *community* of Buddhisms allegedly represented by the use of Pali texts is no more impressive than might be any alleged community of Buddhisms based on Sanskrit texts. And yet such a form of commonality is not infrequently implied by social scientists making hasty surveys of the "characteristics" of the "Buddhism" of the area they are studying.

One has to return therefore to the basic position that "Buddhisms" are many and various. To this must be added, in order to elucidate the matter further, that Buddhisms are in most cases "country-specific". This can hardly be surprising to a social scientist with even a little historical consciousness. In any case, he or she is not likely to proceed very far with the analysis of the "Buddhist" characteristics of the society concerned before encountering aspects of this *particular* country's "Buddhism" that do not conform to the ideal type described in the works of Buddhologists.

Thus it may well be that the Buddhologist tells us that the Buddhism of country X is "like" the Buddhism of country Y. The sociological investigator in country X, having read the description of Buddhism in country Y is, however, unlikely to proceed very far with field-work before finding that there is a great deal in the "Buddhism" of country X that is significantly different from the "Buddhism" of country Y. This is understandable, since the Buddhologist has started from a priori assumptions about the nature and character of a certain general type of Buddhism and its adherents, whereas the sociological investigator is concerned with the empirical character of the Buddhism practised by the social actors in the country concerned. The former tends to give the ideal version of the "Buddhism" of the area while the latter tends to notice the realities which disagree with the ideal version. In the ideal version there is *one* form "found" in countries X, Y, and Z. The realities suggest that there are three fairly clear forms, related to some extent and in certain respects, but each form being country-specific in quite important ways.

Moreover, where some *regularities* in Buddhist polity and Buddhist social action *are* found in a given cultural region these *may* have to be accounted for, not simply by their being ascribed to one Buddhist tradition (Theravada, for example) but by similarities of social organization and culture within the region. So also the differences within the one Buddhist tradition in that region may need to be accounted for in country-specific terms. It is important that the *Buddhist* factors are given due weight; so also the *non-Buddhist* factors.

A question which might be asked, however, is "Why *country-specific?*" That is to say, why should it be at that particular level of localization or organization that one form of Buddhism becomes identifiably different from other forms? It is fairly clear that major differentiations do occur at national levels, that is, at the level of the various countries or *political* units of Southeast Asia (as they do elsewhere). From the earliest period of Buddhism's history, that is, from the days of the Buddha, it appears that a certain tension existed between Buddhist practitioners and political rulers. The relations between the Buddha and the rulers of the various territories of north India of that period appear to have varied from fairly cordial to positively hostile.

In the Pali canon, certainly, monarchy is presented on the whole in a bad light, with one or two notable exceptions. The (Pali) *Maha Parinibbana Sutta* represents the attitude of the Buddha towards the new *monarchies* as having been distinctly unfavourable. His sympathies are regarded as having been decidedly in favour of the older *republican* form of government. Nevertheless, monarchy, it seemed, had to be accepted "as a necessary evil in a degenerate period of history", as A.K. Warder observed (Ling 1981, pp. xvii f.); however, some individual monarchs of the Buddha's day are represented favourably in the Buddhist literature. It appears to be much the same today: governments vary one from another in their attitudes and policies towards Buddhists within their realms, and this is reflected in the nature and constitution of the Buddhism found there. The political factor is not, of course, the only one that has to be taken into account when considering the varieties of Buddhist practice and institutions in a region such as Southeast Asia; on the other hand, it is a factor that should certainly not be ignored when accounting for such variety as is found.

A Buddhist in Malaysia will have a different context in which to practise and profess Buddhism from that enjoyed by a Buddhist in Thailand. Different from both of these may be the experience of a Myanmar Buddhist. And a Singapore Buddhist may well face quite different problems from all of them.

Apart from political factors there are others which have been mentioned, and which are also responsible for the variety which is observable in the Buddhism of Southeast Asia: historical, linguistic, geographical, or environmental, the nature of the terrain and the difficulty of travel, and, not least, economic and developmental, including the nature and the extent of general educational development. In all of these ways the countries of mainland Southeast Asia show a considerable variety: so also does the Buddhism, varying in form and nature from country to country.

It is clear then that it is not enough to say in passing concerning the "Buddhism" of such and such a country in Southeast Asia that it is of the "Theravada" type or the "Mahayana", the Pali type or the Sanskrit. We need to know more than that in order to begin to understand and appreciate what is the position of Buddhism in that country, why "Buddhists" in that country react so differently in matters such as public events, social relationships, natural disasters, political oppression, and so on, from Buddhists elsewhere, even in another Southeast Asian country. In other words, we need to be aware that "Buddhism" is an ideological abstraction, since "Buddhists" and their Buddhist traditions are everywhere country-specific, and that Buddhism, in real terms, has from the earliest days been pluralistic.

No doubt the Buddhist philosopher will claim that Buddhist philosophy remains the same in whatever country it may be, and that Buddhist teachings are universal in nature. Nevertheless, Buddhist teachings, as any other philosophical or religious ideas and teachings, have to be applied in real situations, and then it is at the level of *application* that local or national conditions have their effect.

It is with some of these, the major national or local *variant* forms of Buddhism in Southeast Asia that the present work is concerned. Four such local variants are dealt with here: Myanmar, Thailand, Cambodia, and Singapore. These, of course, are not the only countries in Southeast Asia where there is a Buddhist presence: others are Laos, Vietnam, and Malaysia. But these four happen to be areas in which Buddhism is found that are best known to the writers. And, as it happens, these four countries represent between them a considerable variety of historical, political, and cultural contexts within which the various "Buddhisms" have developed; also, not surprisingly, they exhibit considerable differences in the trends within their various "Buddhisms" at the present time.

REFERENCE

Ling, Trevor O. *The Buddha's Philosophy of Man: Early Indian Buddhist Dialogues*. London: J.M. Dent, 1981.

CHAPTER TWO

Sangha Reforms and Renewal of Sasana in Myanmar: Historical Trends and Contemporary Practice

TIN MAUNG MAUNG THAN

Introduction

According to legends Buddhism reached the shores of Myanmar even during the Buddha's lifetime when two Mon merchants brought back some hair relics from the Buddha Himself and enshrined them in a small temple which was the precursor of the famous Shwedagon Pagoda (Maung Htin Aung 1967, p. 5; Tin Hla Thaw 1969). It is also believed that during the reign of the Indian Emperor Asoka (*c.* 310 BC) religious missionaries sent by this Buddhist king who was also the convenor of the Third Buddhist Synod came to the Mon land of Suvannabhumi and established a Theravadin monastery at Kelasa Hill near the city of Thaton (Maung Htin Aung 1970, p. 28; Ray 1946, pp. 7–13). Archaeological and historical evidence suggest that elements of Theravada Buddhism existed during the Pyu period (200 BC to the ninth century AD) in the central and southern regions of Myanmar (Tin Hla Thaw 1969; Maung Htin Aung 1967, pp. 11, 12, 14; Ray 1946, pp. 18–73; Than Tun 1964, pp. 40, 49–52; Aung-Thwin 1985*a*, pp. 17–20). However, only in the eleventh century AD, with the prominence of Pagan as a power centre, did Theravada Buddhism as such take root in the Myanmar culture and became the *de facto* state religion for the successive dynasties of the Myanmar nation-state (Maung Htin Aung 1967, pp. 32–37; Maung Htin Aung 1970, pp. 29–31; Than Tun 1964, pp. 197–237; Aung-Thwin 1985*a*, pp. 30–46).[1]

The continuity of the Buddhist tradition in Myanmar for the past millennium (at least) would not have been possible but for the role played by the *sangha* (monks or *rahan*) in perpetuating Buddha *sasana* (the teachings and doctrines of the Buddha; His religious legacy) throughout the dynastic cycles of the nation-states, under the British rule and in post-independence Myanmar. Both as a tangible embodiment of the sacred "triple gems", and as an instrumental social class in the state-society nexus the Myanmar *sangha* could be said to have transcended its traditionally attributed role of merely being a conveyor of the *dhamma* (laws or teachings of the Buddha). For, institutionally as well as individually, it has always been a potent force in the socio-political processes throughout the history of Myanmar (Sarkisyanz 1965; Maung Htin Aung 1967; Bechert 1972; Smith 1965; Spiro 1982; Von der Mehden 1961; Aung-Thwin 1979, 1985*b*).

Sectarianism and the Myanmar *Sangha*

According to Ling (1989), Buddhism in Myanmar is clearly sectarian in sociological terms and as such consists in the prominence and importance of *gaing* or "sects" as the characteristic form of religious structure.[2] The existence of "schisms" or "orders" or "factions" or "branches" or "fraternities" in the form of *nikaya* or *gana* in the monastic history of Myanmar is well documented (Mendelson 1975; Spiro 1982; Dhammagawtha U Maung Maung 1981; Ikumo 1987; Than Tun 1981–85). Many scholars have contended that "sect" is not the most appropriate term for the *nikaya* or *gaing* since the existence of different *gaing* has not resulted in the development of separate doctrines (Spiro 1982, pp. 315–16; Mendelson 1975, pp. 40–41, 86; Kemper 1980, p. 27, n. 6; Bechert 1980, pp. 33–34; Ferguson 1978, p. 73). For all practical purposes, a *sangha gaing* in Myanmar may be identified by the following principal characteristics: a distinctive monastic lineage amongst its leaders identified with the founder through educational or organizational patronage; some form of hierarchical organizational structure; separate rules, rituals, and behavioural practices based on a particular interpretation of *vinaya* rules of conduct; affiliation which transcends local boundaries in an attempt to assume a national or even international character; and some recognition by the secular authorities (Ferguson 1978, p. 73; Kemper 1980, pp. 30–32).[3]

The branching out of monastic groupings into *gaing* may be a phenomenon as old as the order of monks in Myanmar itself. After King Anawrahta embraced Theravada Buddhism and endorsed the followers of Shin Arahan as the orthodoxy (*c.* eleventh century AD) at Pagan, the *sangha* remained united for less than a century. In the closing years of the eleventh century a Myanmar monk who had returned from Sri Lanka formed an exclusive order with four of his Sinhalese companion monks. Thus Pagan's *sangha* split into *purimagana* (earlier *gaing*) and *paccagana* (later *gaing*); a harbinger of the long waves of sectarianism that threatened the unity of the order of monks in Myanmar.[4]

After the fall of the Pagan dynasty in the last decades of the thirteenth century the *sasana* waned in Upper Myanmar. Nevertheless, it was ascendent in Lower Myanmar — the land of the Mons — known as Ramannadesa, where six *gaing* were known to have flourished in the early fourteenth century. Buddhism was revived in Upper Myanmar at Pinya as the new dynasty took root. The remnants of the two Pagan *gaing* became integrated during the reign of King Uzana, who offered royal patronage to the unified *sangha*. Yet again it split into forest-dwellers and town-monks while the Ari Gaing which was banished by King Anawrahta resurfaced after nearly three centuries of ignominy. When Inwa became the power centre for Upper Myanmar in the fifteenth century the town-dwellers obtained royal patronage and dominated the *sangha* polity. Meanwhile, in Lower Myanmar King Dhammaceti of Bago enforced unity among monks by subscribing to the admonishments of Sinhalese-ordained monks of the Mahavihara order and enforcing the re-ordination of all monks at the hands of the returnees from Sri Lanka (*c.* 1480).

In the sixteenth and seventeenth centuries the *sangha* in Lower Myanmar lapsed into a state of confusion and laxity as regards adherence to the *vinaya* and unorthodox *gaing* which engaged in worldly activities proliferated. Descendants of the town-monks characterized by their distinctive headgear became influential in the late Inwa period and it was reported that by the last decades of the seventeenth century three different *gaing* had established themselves in and around Inwa as well as at Toungoo (in Central Myanmar, which became the power centre for the Bamar in the mid-sixteenth century as Inwa came under Shan influences).

In the closing years of the seventeenth century, as the centre of power returned to Inwa with the eclipse of the restored Toungoo dynasty, a controversy developed among the Myanmar *sangha* in Inwa which embroiled the resulting two *gaing* into acrimonious debate for the next century or so. The cleavage between the so-called Ton Gaing and Yon Gaing, which centred around the manner of wearing the robe in public, involved not only the monks but also the lay followers, and inevitably successive monarchs of both the late Toungoo and early Konbaung dynasties were drawn into the rivalry by way of royal patronage to one party or the other.[5] This was further complicated by the attempts of the proponents of the headgear-wearing *gaing* to influence the reigning monarch. Finally, in the year 1782 King Bodawpaya intervened and ended the controversy by restoring the orthodox practice favoured by Yon Gaing. Apparently, from the sectarian viewpoint at least the Myanmar *sangha* appeared to have become united under the Konbaung dynasty for about seven decades, until the advent of the Shwegyin Gaing which initiated a further round of sectarianism in the Myanmar *sangha*.

Historically, the roots of the Shwegyin Gaing may be traced to the forest-dwelling movement of reformist monks in the late 1840s which greatly influenced U Jagara, who hailed from Shwegyin village, and who later founded the *gaing*. King Mindon, who ascended the throne in 1853, succeeded in persuading U Jagara to come to the capital in about 1860 and became the patron of the monk whom he greatly admired for his thorough knowledge of the *vinaya*, and for his ascetic nature. One condition that prompted U Jagara to come and reside at the royal capital was believed to be the King's promise that he and his followers would be allowed to remain separate from all other monks. In fact this was tantamount to having *gana vimutti*, or an independent entity, from the very beginning of his residence in Mandalay. If this is interpreted as an official sanction for the Shwegyin group to assume a separate identity, then the year 1860 could be taken as the point in time when the Shwegyin Gaing was established.[6] Apparently, the institutionalization of the *gaing* gradually developed during the next twelve years. Meanwhile, the rest of the *sangha* who remained under the purview of the Thudhamma Assembly (or Council) came to be known as Thudhamma monks and this "silent majority", perhaps by default, came to constitute the Thudhamma Gaing under the tutelage of the *thathanabaing* (supreme patriarch, appointed by the monarch) of the time.

Around 1855, Okpo Sayadaw (presiding in Okpo, a town in Lower Myanmar under British rule) initiated a "puritan" movement with his strict interpretation of the *vinaya*. He and his followers refused to associate themselves with Thudhamma monks in the locality on account of the controversy regarding the purity-cum-legitimacy of a local *udakkukkhepa sima* (ordination hall built over water) which was in physical contact with the *gamakhit* (village land). The Okpo faction came to be known as the Dwaya Gaing by virtue of its insistence on emphasizing the *dvara* or *dwaya* (mediating sources of interaction) as opposed to *kan* (action, deed).[7] This *gaing* eventually cleaved into Anaukchaung Dwaya (*c.* 1900) and Mula Dwaya (*c.* 1918) due to disputes involving leadership succession and regionalism.[8]

The last of the so-called Mindon sects (Mendelson 1975, pp. 84 ff.), popularly known as Hngettwin Gaing, developed around the end of the nineteenth century. Led by Hngettwin Sayadaw, who apparently subscribed to the forest-dwellers' tradition, it stressed meditational practices and the *paramat* (ideal, absolute) interpretation of Buddhist doctrine and though originating in Upper Myanmar became more popular in the south.[9]

Three other *gaing* which evolved between 1875 and 1900 in the south were distinguished by their gradual establishment over time through cumulative association of followers around its leaders, rather than as cleavages resulting from personality clashes or *vinaya* disputes. Mahayin Gaing's popular title has its roots in the honorific of its founder (whose lay name was Maung Yin) who came to Myanmar from Thailand to preside over a monastery in Mawlamyine district. He was revered by Mon in the region and the official title of the *gaing* formally known as Dhammayuttika Nikaya was derived from the Thai Dhammayuttika movement (patronized by King Mongkut *c.* 1840) which in turn was reputedly inspired by the Mon Buddhist tradition. The so-called Gado (Kudo) Gaing's origin could be traced to the conferment of the *ganavimut* permission by the *thathanabaing* to the founder U Indavamsa in view of the latter's desire to strictly practise *vinaya* rules as an ascetic in the forest-dwellers' tradition near Gado village in Dawei district (the southernmost tip of Myanmar). In January 1897 he was granted permission to seek exclusivity not only for himself but also for his followers, hence the formal title "Ganavimut-Gado Gaing". The establishment of a teaching monastery in Bahan ward of Yangon by U Pandhavamsa around 1897 led to his prominence as the Weiluwun Sayadaw with reference to the bamboo groves (Weiluwun in Pali) and bamboo buildings of his monastery. In the following years he established more teaching monasteries in Yangon and in other towns in Lower Myanmar and attracted followers sympathetic to his scholastic tradition. Those subscribing to the Weiluwun network of monastic schools held a convention at Myanaung in 1919 for a combined recitation of Buddhist canons and formally instituted the Weiluwun Nikaya by electing a Maha-Nayaka-Dipitti (Supreme President of the Order).[10]

These nine *gaing* were the officially acknowledged sects at the time when the state-sponsored "Congregation of the Sangha of All Orders" was convened in May 1980 in a successful attempt to form a unified *sangha* organization with a national character (Tin Maung Maung Than 1988).[11] As far as these nine *gaing* are concerned one may generalize that they all represent *vinaya*-centred cleavages.[12] Strong personalities initiated these *gaing* and their fortunes were more or less dictated by the extent of royal patronage (as in the case of Shwegyin, Thudhamma, and Dwaya in the Konbaung period) under Myanmar kings and the changing socio-political environment under colonial rule. By the time Myanmar gained independence in 1948 all these nine *gaing* were institutionally well established though perhaps only Thudhamma and Shwegyin can assume a national character in terms of geographical representation. Institution-wise Shwegyin seems to be most advanced with its strict hierarchical organization and well-defined rules and regulations (Mendelson 1975, pp. 161–63, 224–27; Panditta 1988; Than Tun 1981–85). All other *gaing* do have hierarchical organizational structures though these may be relatively sluggish or even dormant rather than dynamic in their *modus operandi*.

The demographic strength of each *gaing* may have fluctuated throughout the decades of their existence, more or less, depending upon the dynamism and influence of the supreme leader and the leading *sayadaw* as well as the propensity of the external environment in the form of lay supporters and the ruling élite to favour one faction or the other — either with respect to the four main material requirements of the *sangha* traditionally identified as food, the yellow robe or *thingan*, shelter, and medicine, or through moral support and legitimacy accorded by way of secular traditions in Myanmar political culture.[13] Lack of time series data (if at all) on *gaing* membership among the Myanmar *sangha* prevents one from ascertaining trends in the corporate strength of these *gaing* even for the past four decades of post-independence rule as a modern nation-state. Table 1 shows the membership affiliations of the total *sangha* population at the time of the convening of the "Congregation of the Sangha of All Orders (Gaing) for Purification, Perpetuation, and Propagation of the Sasana" (hereafter referred to as "the Congregation") in May 1980. This illustrates the overwhelming majority enjoyed by Thudhamma over the other *gaing*. Thudhamma monks constituted over 88 per cent of the total monk population and outnumbered its nearest rival, the Shwegyin, by a ratio exceeding 12:1.[14] Although numbers alone do not accurately reflect either the importance of a particular *gaing* or its impact upon the *sasana* as a whole in relation to the Buddhist polity of Myanmar, they do indicate the human resources available to each *gaing* at a particular point in time and may throw some light on the question of the sustainability of the *gaing* in question, especially if accurate membership figures for a sufficient period of time are available. Unfortunately, except for Shwegyin, such data are not available in a systematic manner for meaningful analysis and to draw unequivocal conclusions. As for Shwegyin Nikaya its membership of monks (apart from *samanera* or novices) grew from around 1,000 monks in the mid-1860s to 4,620 in 1931 and remained steady at over 5,600 in the decade 1935–45. Apparently, World War II diminished its ranks and its strength dipped to nearly 4,000 in 1952. It recovered its pre-war strength only after more than a decade when it registered around 5,500 in 1963. It seems to have rapidly increased its membership in the following seventeen years to 7,730 in early 1980 (Than Tun 1982, pp. 37, 39). Comparable figures for other groups are not available and even data on the total *sangha* population over the past fifty years are few and far between. Censuses of 1931, 1973, and 1983 give aggregated figures which included not only monks but also novices, other religious workers, and priests in different combinations so that one can only infer to some limiting values on the estimated *sangha* population. Such an exercise revealed that the monk population between 1931 and 1973 increased by only about 42 per cent while the Shwegyin Gaing registered a 40 per cent increase between 1931 and 1975. Given the degree of uncertainty associated with the former figure,[15] it appears that during the four decades from the

TABLE 1
Sangha Membership by *Gaing*, c. 1980

Gaing	No. of Members	Percentage of Total*
Thudhamma	96,614	88.6
Shwegyin Nikaya	7,730	7.1
Dhammanudhamma Mahadwaya Nikaya	1,621	1.5
Weiluwun Nikaya	1,155	1.1
Dhammavinayanuloma Muladwaya Nikaya	867	0.8
Dhammayuttika Nikaya Mahayin	326	0.3
Catubhummika Mahasatipatthana Hngettwin	316	0.3
Ganavimut Gado	286	0.3
Anaukchaung Dwaya	117	0.1
Total	109,032	100.0

* Figures may not add up to 100 because of rounding.

SOURCE: Than Tun (1982), p. 38.

1930s to the early 1970s the rate of growth of Shwegyin Gaing deviated very little from the national average as such. Records from Weiluwun Nikaya's annual conventions showed a stable membership roster of around 1,100 members in the period between early 1980 and mid-1985. It is quite likely that the other five *gaing* with membership of less than 1,000 have had similar experiences with regard to *gaing* membership. If such a generalization can be made, it means that post-1980 increases in the total *sangha* population (see Table 2) reflected membership gains in the main-stream establishment comprising Thudhamma and Shwegyin adherents.[16]

Sangha Reforms in Myanmar

In the *Shorter Oxford Dictionary*, one of the many definitions of the word "reform" is given as "to amend or improve (an arrangement, state of things, institutions, etc.) by removal of faults or abuses".[17] Past attempts in the history of Myanmar to purify the *sasana* through *sangha* reforms involved a return to the orthodoxy in the practice of *vinaya* rules and/ or a reorganization of the order of monks in an attempt to achieve *sangha*

TABLE 2
Sasana Membership Register, Annual

Year[a]	Census Figures		Records Presented	
	Rahan	*Samanera*[b]	*Rahan*	*Samanera*
1980/81	113,445	114,242	n.a.	n.a.
1981/82	116,927	139,359	99,723	61,122
1982/83	119,247	136,410	111,184	99,123
1983/84	121,193	132,129	115,421	103,283
1984/85	124,319	188,532	115,421*	103,283*
1985/86	133,167	162,687	128,270	109,137
1986/87	134,218	164,040	131,356	112,768
1987/88	134,258	164,165	132,437	114,164
1988/89	135,325	164,077	133,879	118,124

n.a. — Not applicable, owing to time lag in implementation.
* The presentation was probably freezed or suspended due to preparations under way for the "Second Congregation" in May 1985.
[a] The years correspond to the Burmese calendar used by the *sangha* organization.
[b] The number of novices fluctuated widely over the years because a substantial number (at times up to one-third of them) are novices on a temporary basis; there might also have been under-reporting in the early years.
SOURCE: Various reports of the State Central Working Committee of the Sangha.

unity. In conformity with the traditional Myanmar concepts of kingship and authority such actions were, more often than not, initiated by the ruler or the ruling élite.[18]

Reification of the teachings of the Buddha into what is commonly accepted as Buddha *sasana* have placed the *sangha* in a unique position of practitioners and upholders of the faith embracing both mundane and supra-mundane realms. Bounded by *vinaya* rules of conduct and inspired by the ideals of *arahatship* (an enlightened one who has attained perfect insight leading to *nibbana*), the *sangha* as an individual inevitably has to reconcile the need for isolation and renunciation with the incessant demand for interaction with the secular world with its ample opportunities for corruption and deviance.[19] Theoretically, perceptions of the ruler and the ruled on how successful the *sangha* as a whole managed to operationalize such a reconciliation would seem to be a logical reason for *sangha* reform but in practice the motivations and intentions of those initiating such reforms are probably much more complex and mundane.[20]

Whatever the reasons behind them, *sangha* reforms have been carried out under the rubric of *"sasana* reforms" to purify and perpetuate Buddha *sasana* which could become extinct if

1. there are adulterations in the scriptures which contain the teachings of the Buddha;
2. there are no more students learning Buddhist texts;
3. there are no more prominent teachers to explain the teachings of the Buddha;
4. there are widespread contraventions of *vinaya* rules and material gains are pursued; and
5. there are many cleavages among the *sangha,* resulting in quarrelling and sectarianism.

Sangha reforms apparently serve to forestall the extinction of the *sasana* by way of the last two causes among the five causes cited above. In a wider context the remaining three causes are neutralized by holding a *sangayana,* collation and revision of textual material by royal sanctions, patronage of the centres of learning, and maintenance of the well-being of the *sangha* through provision of basic needs.

The Myanmar regard Anawrahta of Pagan (*c.* eleventh century) as the first of a long lineage of monarchs who reify the concept of *dhamma raja* (the righteous king) by reforming the order of monks and extending royal patronage to the Theravadin orthodoxy (Aung-Thwin 1983, 1985*a*).

For the next eight centuries almost every ruler of the Myanmar kingdoms of Pagan, Pinya, Inwa, Toungoo, Amarapura, and Mandalay in Upper Myanmar and the Mon kingdom of Bago in Lower Myanmar tried to emulate the *dhamma raja* ideal by proclaiming to be the protector, promoter, and perpetuator of the *sasana* as well as the patron and benefactor of the "orthodox" *sangha.* Attempts (at least symbolic) were made to introduce *vinaya*-centred reforms and/or unification of the *sangha* which had persistently exhibited sectarian tendencies. However, most attempts fell short of reforms proper and did not outlast the reign of a particular monarch.[21]

The fifteenth century Mon King Dhammaceti of Bago, himself an ex-monk, introduced reforms to purify the *sangha* and *sasana* by strictly enforcing *vinaya* rules and allowing only those re-ordained in the Sinhalese Mahavihara tradition to remain in the order (*c.* 1480). He seemingly set the pattern for later reforms and reaffirmed the role of the ruler *vis-à-vis* the *sangha* in the Asokan tradition (Mendelson 1975, pp. 50–53, 63; Ray 1946, pp. 182–92; Aye Chan 1988, pp. 92–93). Nearly four centuries later King Mindon attempted to achieve the ultimate accolade as a *sasana dayaka* (supporter of religion) by convening the Fifth Buddhist Synod or Sangayana in 1871 where the whole of the *Tipitaka* (literally, "three baskets", with reference to the three parts of the Theravada Pali canon: *Vinaya, Abhidhamma,* and *Sutta*) was recited by learned monks and the "orthodox" version thus reaffirmed was inscribed on marble slabs (known as Mandalay Inscriptions). Fifteen years prior to this undertaking King Mindon issued a royal order called Dhamma Vinaya for the purification of Buddhist religion by endorsing the rule of law according to the *vinaya*. This was reminiscent of the Dhamma Vinaya Order of King Dhammaceti (also known as Rammadipitti)[22] and it delineated twenty-one acts of *alajji* (illicit, corrupt) among the *sangha* which could lead to the waning and destruction of the *sasana*. The last Myanmar king, Thibaw, persuaded the *thathanabaing* and other leading senior monks to admonish the *sangha* against laxity in observing *vinaya* rules and the prevalence of *alajji* acts among them. Between 1883 and 1885 — when the British finally annexed the whole of Myanmar exiling the monarch to India — three edicts were issued by the then *thathanabaing* Taungdaw Sayadaw which contained, respectively, thirty-four points, nine points, and seven points describing *alajji* acts and worldly practices which were to be avoided on pains of punishment.[23] All these appeared to be rearguard actions against the waning influence of the *thathanabaing* and spreading infringements of *vinaya* rules among the *sangha* which could have resulted from instability in the hierarchy of *sangha* leadership during the late Konbaung dynasty.[24] They did constitute prerequisites for *sangha* reforms but the ruling élite failed to take the initiatives to carry through the entire process of reforms by effectively utilizing the state's resources and power in conjunction with a clear consensus among the leading monks on its means and ends. Moreover, the cleavage produced by the advent of the Mindon sects was probably too deep to institute effective reforms amongst the divided *sangha* polity.

During the nearly sixty years of British colonial rule the "hands off" policy of the colonial government left a void in the state-*sangha* relationship which suffered from the loss of traditional continuity in terms of patronage and legitimation (Smith 1965, pp. 38–57; Mendelson 1975, pp. 179–96). The absence of state-sponsored *vinaya*-centred reforms and the rising nationalist sentiment among the *sangha*, however, was somewhat tempered by the strict enforcement of internal discipline by the *gaing* which stressed the importance of *vinaya* (Mendelson 1975, pp. 224–30).

Organizational reforms which attempted to unify the *sangha* since the formation of the General Council of Sangha Sameggi (GCSS) in 1922 were mainly for political purposes and in spite of the rising groundswell of militant nationalism, more or less, failed to attract the majority of the *sangha*.[25] Even the GCCS itself was politically motivated and though it instituted *vinicchaya* committees to adjudicate *sangha* disputes it was not able to function as a unified *sangha* organization dedicated to *sangha* affairs *per se* and soon became embroiled in the local politics of the day leading to further cleavage into factions along the lines of fissures occurring in its lay counterpart, the General Council of Buddhist Associations (GCBA).[26]

During the Japanese occupation (1942–45) the Japanese-sponsored government of Dr Ba Maw initiated the formation of the Gaing-baungsoan Maha Sangha Ahpwe-Gyoke (GMSA, Grand Council of the Sangha of All Orders), which was supposed to unify all monks in Myanmar transcending sectarian boundaries. Shwegyin Gaing refused to co-operate and the scheme as envisaged by the Ministry of Religious Affairs — created for the first time by the Ba-Maw government — fell through as the fortunes of the Japanese occupiers waned in the closing years of World War II. After the British re-occupation of Myanmar in 1945, GMSA was revived by leading *sayadaw* of Lower Myanmar but it could not overcome the sectarianism of various *gaing*, and with the gaining of independence in January 1948 was quickly superseded by the more militant semi-political organizations patronized by the various political leaders and factions vying for power during the parliamentary democracy period (1948–62). Even the Buddhist revival of the 1950s sponsored by the Union government of Premier U Nu failed to introduce effective reforms in spite of the institutionalization of Buddhism within the state superstructure and notwithstanding the holding of the Sixth Buddhist Synod in 1954.[27] The twelve-point Dhammavinaya Order endorsed by the participants of the Synod and promulgated in 1956 upon its conclusion also failed to have significant impact upon the *sangha* polity due to the lack of institutional support and the absence of *anaset* (secular authority for enforcement). U Nu's misguided attempt in 1961 to legislate Buddhism as the state religion failed to materialize as his government succumbed to a military coup within a year after a compromise bill was adopted as an amendment to the state's constitution (Tin Maung Maung Than 1988, pp. 26–27). This was followed by an eighteen-year hiatus in which the state (ruled by a military "Revolutionary Council") withdrew to secular isolation leaving the *sangha* alone as regards purely religious affairs (ibid., pp. 28–35).[28]

Institutionalization of *Sangha* Reforms: The 1980 Convention and Its Aftermath

The adoption of the (new) constitution of 1974 by an overwhelming majority in a national referendum on 3 January 1974 ended nearly a dozen years of military rule in Myanmar. A socialist republic with a unicameral "People's Assembly" representing a one-party state was proclaimed. Preceded by a relaxation of the strict *dirgiste* policies of the 1960s, the return to constitutional government seemed to have created a political climate conducive to the formulation of a positive state-*sangha* relationship leading to *sangha* reforms which so far had eluded the successive governments of post-independence Myanmar. During the preceding decade two deviant strands gained ground among the urban Buddhist polity which were increasingly noticed with concern by the orthodox leading monks as well as the secular authorities. Esoteric cults in the form of mystic *gaing* led by charismatic lay *bodaw* and monks who claimed supernatural powers held sway over important sections of urban society: their clientele included rich merchants, civil servants, the educated middle class, and perhaps even some members of the state's power structure. On the other hand, the proliferation of various interpretations of *vipassana* (insight knowledge or intuitive under- standing of the path to salvation) doctrine with their attendant commentaries and idiosyncratic meditational techniques led to the emergence of controversial interpretation of the Buddha's teachings which because of their novel and unorthodox methods seemed to have more appeal to the uninitiated than the traditional ones.[29] Apart from these two disturbing trends the more expansive mood prevalent in the private economic sector led to exploitation and commercialization of many aspects of the *sasana* which reinforced the sense of foreboding among the conservative clergy as well as the state authorities who probably viewed the increasing influence of cult leaders as a challenge to state power and the maintenance of regime stability.[30]

Although the state reaffirmed its secular orientation with the provisions written into the new constitution, it has, since the early days of the Revolutionary Government, always maintained that the separation of state and religion does not amount to leaving the *sangha* and *sasana* open to exploitation by undesirable elements. At the same time, however, it has also maintained that this separation by no means precludes the state from honouring those in the *sangha* to whom honour is due simply because of the state's secular orientation. Hence, in the closing years of the 1970s, the leaders of the state, having consolidated the legislative, judicial, and executive structures of the nation which was apparently undergoing moderate economic growth, turned their attention towards the elusive tasks of uniting the *sangha* and purifying the *sasana*.

The Council of State (the highest executive body in the republic), after a detailed study, issued a notification in July 1978 concerning provisions for the conferring of titles and awards in the name of the state to all persons worthy of such honours and in these provisions there was included a class of titles for members of the *sangha*. These titles, namely, Abhidaja Maha Rattha Guru and Agga Maha Pandita (in descending order of eminence) were not coined anew but were honorifics which were instituted before the revolutionary days.[31] At the first presentation ceremony on 9 June 1979, held in Yangon, the Minister of Home and Religious Affairs explained that the main objective of presenting the titles to the *sayadaw* was to ensure the perpetuation, purity, and propagation of Buddha *sasana*. This recognition of the outstanding achievements of members of the monastic order was a harbinger of the state's new approach towards Buddha *sasana*, which ostensibly avoided direct sponsorship of Buddhism as such. Instead, it was an approach which created, on the one hand, an environment conducive towards the perpetuation and self-purification of the *sasana* by its adherents, whether lay devotees or monks (Kelasa 1980, p. 5), and, on the other hand, projected the power and authority of the state in such a way as to rid the *sasana* of unscrupulous elements as well as dubious doctrines and to act as a deterrent against further encroachments by undesirable elements.[32]

In line with this new approach which emphasized the symbolic dimensions of "self-help" and "self-discipline" and mindful of the failure of previous attempts by the state to achieve a unified monastic order with proper membership registration, the Ministry of Home and

Religious Affairs (which was responsible for implementing the task of assisting the monastic order in developing unified efforts towards upholding the traditions of the *sasana*) spared no effort in impressing upon the leading *sayadaw* of the various *gaing*, the much-belated need to set upon themselves the task of unifying the *sangha* into an organized and disciplined body dedicated to the purification, perpetuation, and propagation of the *sasana*. The Ministry, drawing upon the resources of the Department of Religious Affairs, during the last quarter of 1979 laid the groundwork for the forthcoming grand assembly of monks with the co-operation of State and Divisional People's Councils.[33] It was decided that a sixty-six-member "Working Committee" of monks be formed to make preparations for the holding of the congregation and the guiding rule for representation would be based on *gana* quotas while regional representation would be applied within each order.[34] On 15 December 1979, the Minister of Home and Religious Affairs launched a concerted effort to submit to the patrons and elder monks of the various *gaing*, "supplications" (that is, representations) asking them to supervise the election of representatives to the proposed Working Committee. He issued a statement "supplicating" the patrons and distinguished elders of all *gaing* on matters relating to the selection of representatives to the Working Committee as well as the forthcoming congregation of the *sangha*. In the several weeks that followed, the Minister, Deputy Minister, executives from the State and Divisional People's Councils, and responsible personnel from the headquarters as well as from state and divisional offices of the Department of Religious Affairs submitted the Minister's written supplication to leading patrons of the *sangha* at various assemblies held in state and divisional capitals as well as towns throughout the nation and facilitated the election of regional representatives.

The Working Committee deliberated on a four-point work programme consisting of the following:

1. fixing procedures and rules for the selection of *sangha* representatives and their number and qualifications;
2. drafting basic organizational rules for the proposed *sangha* organization at different levels;
3. drafting of procedures for handling ecclesiastical disputes in concordance with the *vinaya*; and
4. preparing and drafting a record of the membership of the *sasana*.

Various sub-committees related to the tasks in hand were formed as well as advisory bodies consisting of Abhidaja Maha Rattha Guru Sayadaw and the three Tipitakadhara Dhamma Bandagarika Sayadaw (bearers of the three *Pitaka* and keepers of the *dhamma* treasure).[35] The Working Committee then obtained feedback on the drafts in two series of field trips taken in March and May 1980 where meetings with the local members of the *sangha* were held to explain and discuss the proposed drafts.[36]

The Working Committee concluded the third session of meetings on 17 May 1980 after approving the final versions of the working papers on the proposed themes and procedural matters relating to the convening of the congregation in the following week. Meanwhile, letters of invitation to the *sangha* representatives to attend the congregation were sent out on 6 May 1980 together with the relevant draft proposals. Travel arrangements for them to attend the congregation (by public transport) were also made by the People's Councils at various levels and the Ministry of Home and Religious Affairs.

The Working Committee also prescribed the number of representatives of the *sangha* to be elected from each *gaing* and each township to attend the Congregation. Altogether 1,235 *sangha* representatives (officially called *"sangha samutiya* representatives") were listed to attend the Congregation which was to be held during 24–27 May 1980. Including the four Abhidaja Maha Rattha Guru, the thirty-six Agga Maha Pandita, the fifty-eight members of the Working Committee, and the three Tipitakadhara Dhamma Bandagarika title holders — all of whom became ex-officio representatives — altogether 1,219 *sangha* representatives were finally chosen to attend the Congregation: 1,076 representing forty-nine base areas in the seven states and seven divisions of the country and 143 representing the eight *gaing* exclusive of the Thudhamma majority.[37]

At the Congregation, the *sangha* representatives chose liaison monks according to *gaing* and regional representation (at the state and divisional levels), and these liaison monks met on 23 May 1980 to co-ordinate work relating to matters to be tabled at the forthcoming plenary session. At this co-ordination meeting, the list of candidates for the 300-strong State Central Working Committee of the Sangha and the 33-member State Sangha Maha Nayaka Committee as well as nominees for the presidency of the State Sangha Maha Nayaka Committee were discussed and a consensus was arrived at with respect to these electoral proposals.

The first meeting of the State Central Working Committee of the Sangha was held on the third day of the Congregation, and the plenary session of 299 members (with a 100 per cent turn-out) duly elected the president, who then proposed the nominations for the two vice-presidents, the secretary, and the two joint-secretaries. The nominations were unanimously accepted by the members who then went on to elect the rest of the members of the State Sangha Maha Nayaka Committee.[38]

On the same day the State Sangha Maha Nayaka Committee convened its first meeting and approved the list of eighty-one members for the State Ovadacariya Sayadaw Committee (a purely advisory body composed of patrons and elders who did not have to be present at the Congregation), which was then ratified at the plenary session of the State Central Working Committee of the Sangha.

After deliberating for four days, the Congregation was successfully concluded on 27 May 1980 with the passing of three documents, four resolutions, and the election of three important central bodies.[39] The three documents were the Fundamental Rules of the Organization of the Sangha of the Socialist Republic of the Union of Burma; the Procedures for Settling Vinaya Conflicts; and the Membership Register of the Sangha. The four resolutions comprised (1) revising the *Pariyatti* examinations so that *rahan* (monks) and *samanera* (novices) could master Pali as well as Myanmar in their course of studies, enhancing and developing their wisdom and knowledge, and to regulate their conduct according to the highest ideals of the *sasana*; (2) requesting the relevant authorities to prohibit the use of photographs of images of the Buddha and *chetiya* (pagodas) on the covers of calendars, books, and cassette tapes, and the publication of photographs of the three objects of worship (that is, the Buddha, *dhamma*, and *sangha*) contrary to the Buddhist scriptures; (3) removing permanent residents, including women, from monasteries and monastic compounds where the *sangha* reside, with the exception of parents who have no one to support them; and (4) removing bogus and undisciplined monks from the *sasana* to purify, perpetuate, and propagate the *sasana*.

The Council of State proclaimed a general amnesty pardoning those who had been found guilty of political offences and insurrection against the state and reducing the sentences of those involved in other offences. This amnesty order was promulgated "as a token of joyously honouring the successful conclusion of the First Congregation . . . and thereby to promote the unity and peace".[40]

With the adoption of the draft of the fundamental rules for the organization of the *sangha* by the Congregation, the means of systematizing the order of the *sangha* was achieved. A system of guidance and control of the *sangha* by members of the *sangha* for the removal of wayward or improperly ordained monks as well as for encouraging bona fide members of the *sangha* to abide by the *vinaya* was now in place. The fundamental principle adopted thus provided for only one *sangha* organization representing the community of monks of all *gaing* in Myanmar, which automatically incorporated all Theravada *rahan* residing in the nation; accordingly, no individual monk or novice could remain independent of the *sangha* hierarchy. The nine *gaing* in existence as of February 1980 and on the record of the Department of Religious Affairs at that time were recognized as such, but the establishment of new *gaing* from then on was prohibited. The existing *gaing* would, however, be allowed to merge with one another should they wish to in the future. The three national level central organs formed during the Congregation were entrusted with different tasks to pursue the general objectives of purifying, perpetuating, and propagating the *sasana*. Members of the Ovadacariya Committee at the central level were to individually or collectively "admonish and provide guidance to all members of the *sangha* through the central level Sangha Maha Nayaka"; the central level State Central Working Committee was to be "responsible for all the members of the *sangha* of the country" and to give guidance to and supervise the Sangha Maha Nayaka; and the central level Sangha Maha Nayaka was to be responsible to the State Central Working Committee for carrying out the day-to-day duties of centrally administering the different levels of *sangha* organization ("Draft Fundamental Rules for Sangha Organizations Presented", *Working People's Daily*, 26 May 1980; see also Department of Religious Affairs, Myanmar [1985a]). At the central level committees the members once elected were to act in unity irrespective of their *gaing*. On the other hand, the regional organizations to be formed below the central level could be constituted according to *gaing* at three different levels: that is, the state/division, township, and ward/village-tract (parallel to the national administrative structure of People's Councils with which they would liaise through the respective regional offices of the Department of Religious Affairs). Similar to the functions of the bodies at the central level, these regional organizations were to be set up as elected Working

Committees which at each level would form Sangha Nayaka Committees with executive functions to run the day-to-day affairs of the
respective communities of monks within their purview.[41] The overall
structure of the *sangha* organization is depicted in Figure 1.[42]

By the end of 1981, 36,072 Ward/Village-Tract Sangha Nayaka
members were elected and 3,777 Sangha Nayaka Committees were
formed at the basic level. Altogether, 19,026 Township Working Committee
members were elected, out of which 3,662 *sayadaw* were chosen to form
499 Sangha Nayaka Committees at the township or base area level. At the
provincial level 10,098 State/Divisional Working Committee members
were elected whereas 287 State/Divisional Sangha Nayaka *sayadaw* were
selected to form thirty-nine State/Divisional Level Sangha Nayaka
Committees (*Encyclopaedia Burmanica Yearbook, 1982*, p. 244).

The basic organizational rules of the *sangha* organization require
that all *rahan* and *samanera* residing in Myanmar shall hold identification
papers. The draft of the "record of membership of the *sasana*" adopted
by the Congregation was meant to provide for the scrutiny of individuals entering the monkhood and to systematically control and
supervise members after their admission into the monkhood. In
presenting the draft record to the Congregation, the following points
were cited as benefits which would accrue from the adoption of
"membership identity cards" (which are actually booklets with the cover
in the colour of the *sangha*'s yellow robe):

1. being able to prevent the *sasana* from the danger of those entering
   monkhood without proper ordination;
2. being able to prevent members of the *sangha*, those who have
   been ordained, from doing acts contrary to the *vinaya*;
3. enabling the members of the *sangha* to have complete faith and
   trust in dealing with [one] another — between teachers and
   pupils, between those belonging to the same monastery, and
   between teachers and lay disciples; and
4. it greatly contributes towards the members of the *sangha*
   performing their religious duties and holding of congregations
   such as this one.

                              (*Working People's Daily*, 26 May 1980)

The record is divided into two sections; the first pertaining to
novicehood and the second related to monkhood. Both sections for the
samanera (to be issued on attaining the age of twelve years) and the

rahan have provisions for the record's serial number and the photograph of the individual as well as information on seventeen points with respect to the personal history of the record holder.[43] The record also contains a form to be signed by the presiding abbot of the monastery concerned to the effect that the information provided by the record holder is correct and this has to be scrutinized and attested by the respective Township Sangha Nayaka Chairman *sayadaw* whose signature is also required. It has to be countersigned by the Head of the Immigration and Manpower Department's township office. There is also a final tabular section for recording the change of residence.[44] *Rahan* and *samanera* who are not on temporary refuge are required to carry this record at all times and can neither transfer the record to another person nor make any change in it. There must be only one record for each *rahan* or *samanera* and if it becomes indistinct or is lost the person concerned must report the matter to the corresponding Township Sangha Nayaka Committee. If the person concerned dies, the record must be returned to the corresponding Township Sangha Nayaka Committee. On the event of reverting to layman the record must be submitted to the Township Head of the Immigration and Manpower Department to facilitate the issuance of the national or foreigner's registration card. Hence the *sasana* membership record seems to be a most comprehensive documentation on the personal history of a *rahan* or *samanera* and is an extremely effective instrument for distinguishing genuine members of the *sangha* from the riff and raff.[45]

On the settling of *vinaya* disputes arising from conflicts within the *sangha*, the Congregation adopted the "Procedures for Solution of Cases and Conflicts in Accordance with the Rules of the Order", which defined the coverage and spelt out the procedures for solving cases according to the *vinaya* through the formation of ecclesiastical courts or *vinicchaya* committees composed of elected *vinayadhara sayadaw* at township level. The elections of *vinayadhara sayadaw* are to be based on numerical representation within the same *gaing*. Members of the Township Sangha Nayaka Committees and other higher *sangha* organizations were, however, barred from becoming *vinayadhara*.[46]

Compared with the abortive attempt in 1965 to carry out *sangha* reforms through reorganization of the *sangha* polity, the Congregation of 1980 was an unqualified success. This was mainly due to two factors: there were no longer any organized factions of political monks; and the secular authorities had carefully thought through, planned, and

FIGURE 1
Structure of the *Sangha* Organization in Myanmar, 1980–88

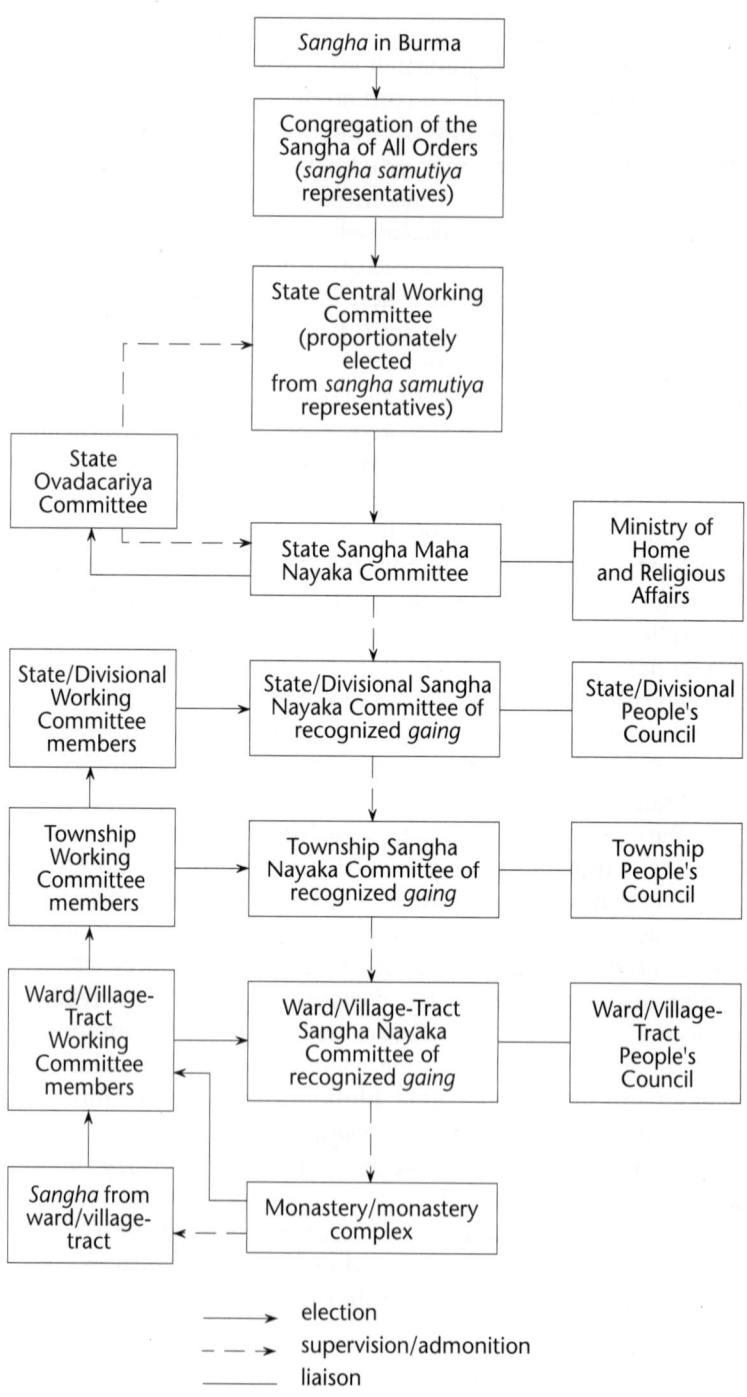

SOURCE: Adapted from Dhammagawtha U Maung Maung (1984, p. 317).

thoroughly executed a strategy to gain the confidence and consensus of the influential leading *sayadaw* of the land, who were impressed by the apparent sincerity of the secular authorities regarding the pressing need to purify the *sasana* through *sangha* reorganization.[47] The enhanced legitimacy and political stability fostered by the introduction of a constitutional basis for representative government as compared with the military junta (ruling by decree at the time of the previous attempt) probably played a part in creating a general sense of goodwill and confidence amongst the *sangha* as well as the lay polity which, in turn, was conducive to such a reform exercise. As regards the nature of the convention itself, the Hmawbi gathering was more of a discussion in which free-wheeling debates were allowed and had neither the mandate nor the intention to reach a decision on behalf of the whole *sangha* order. On the other hand, the Congregation of 1980 was conducted in an extremely systematic and orderly manner with strong imperatives for reform channelled through organs of state power.[48]

With the successful adoption of the rules for organizing the *sangha* into a national hierarchy of administrative tiers, the basic super-structure for the institutionalization of the reforms proposed and introduced by the First Congregation was essentially completed. The reorganizational phase of *sangha* reforms was successfully concluded and what followed was to be the formulation and implementation of the reform process in the spirit of purifying, perpetuating, and propagating the *sasana* as envisaged by the leading proponents of the reform movement.[49]

The implementation phase which began after the supervisory mechanism for the *sangha* as a whole had been set up in the form of Sangha Nayaka Committees turned out to be a most challenging task for the *sayadaw* concerned as they encountered a host of problems ranging from lack of communication to sheer inertia in the target group. The first and foremost task was probably identified as the need to have an accurate and up-to-date census of the members of the order. As a logical follow-up on the introduction of *sangha* membership records for legitimate and genuine members of the order, it was decided that an annual census of monks and novices be taken regularly based on the number present (at monasteries) during the Buddhist lent (*vassa* or *wazo* period) which usually falls between June and October. *Sasana* membership records (or iden-tification) were to be given to all monks and novices except those ordained temporarily for a fixed period, through the respective Sangha Nayaka Committees with assistance from the local Immigration and Manpower Department offices. This was successfully carried out within a year after the Congregation. Table 2 gives the results of the censuses of *rahan* and *samanera* from 1980 to 1988 together with the status of membership record presentation.

Various bodies at different levels of the *sangha* during the tenure mandated by the First Congregation implemented many tasks related to its objectives which included, *inter alia*, (1) setting up and convening *vinicchaya* committees to settle *vinaya* offences and conflicts; (2) forming "special state *vinayadhara* committees" to try *vada* (or doctrinal) disputes; (3) facilitating the removal of lay persons from the monastic premises with the co-operation of the organs of state power; (4) investigating, prosecuting, and disrobing bogus monks and monks who had committed serious *vinaya* offences with the assistance of local authorities; (5) scrutinizing applications from monks who wished to go abroad; (6) scrutinizing religious manuscripts before publication; (7) evaluating existing government-sponsored religious examinations and, when necessary, proposing revisions of syllabi and procedures for conducting lessons and examinations; (8) drafting a comprehensive *Pariyatti* education scheme involving a structured, modernized *sangha* educational system with provisions for different levels from the elementary introductory course to the international postgraduate level culminating in the formation of State Pariyatti Sasana Tekatho or Buddhist Universities at Yangon and Mandalay; and (9) instituting training courses and multiplier courses for *vinayadhara*, abbots or heads of monasteries, and Sangha Nayaka members.[50]

On 11 January 1985 the First Special Meeting of the State Central Working Committee of the Sangha was held to prepare the necessary arrangements and programmes leading to the Second Congregation of the Sangha of All Orders to be convened from 29 to 31 May 1985. The additions and amendments to the "Fundamental Rules of the Sangha Organization" and the principles of the election of different levels of the *sangha* organization pertaining to the Second Congregation were approved at this special meeting. Subsequently, elections for the different levels of the Sangha Organization were conducted throughout the country beginning from 21 January 1985.[51] The *sangha samutiya* representatives to the Second Congregation were elected according to *gaing* and region and according to the quota allotted to each base area (that is, township) under the supervision of the incumbent state/ divisional and central level Sangha Nayaka members.

The Second Congregation of the Sangha of All Orders of the Socialist Republic of the Union of Burma for Purification, Perpetuation, and Propagation of the Sasana (hereafter cited as the "Second Congregation") commenced on 29 May 1985 as scheduled and approved the list of the 300-member Second State Central Working Committee of the Sangha. The Working Committee convened its first meeting on 30 May and the incumbent president was re-elected. It approved the list of other office-bearers and also the list of the 47-member Second State Sangha Maha Nayaka Committee as presented by the president elect.[52] The Working Committee also approved the list of State Ovadacariya Sayadaw before concluding its first meeting. The Second Congregation then ratified these approved lists of members of the central *sangha* bodies and the report of the First State Central Working Committee. The draft proposals of amendments and appendices to the "Procedures of the Sangha Organizations" and to the "Procedures Regarding the Settlement and Decision on Vinaya Dhammakamma Adhikarana Disputes" were also approved in the plenary session of the Second Congregation as presented by the Second Working Committee. The following five resolutions were passed by the Second Congregation: the removal of lay persons residing in the precincts of monasteries and pagodas; the taking of effective action under relevant laws against undisciplined *rahan* and *samanera*; the provision of guidance to activities of Buddhist religious associations in accordance with the (rules of) *dhamma vinaya*; the use of the *sasana* flag in accordance with the promulgation of the *Sangha Nayaka Manual*; and the adoption of measures for the purification of the *sasana* and the promotion of *Pariyatti* education adopted at the First Congregation.

In the closing address delivered at the Second Congregation, the President Sayadaw stressed:

> During the first five years' tenure [of the First Congregation] ... directives and notifications and so forth were issued to different levels of the Sangha Nayakas but they were not heeded to the full and as such it has been found that success has not been achieved to the full. [Thus] during this second tenure we are determined to take action according to rules, procedures, directives and notifications.

The Three *P*s and Renewal of *Sasana*

The motto of the Buddhist *sangha* of all *gaing* in Myanmar as adopted by the First Congregation has all along been "for the purification, perpetuation, and propagation of the Buddha *sasana*", which may be abbreviated as the "Three *P*s". *Sangha* reforms have been carried out in the name of the Three *P*s and the hierarchy of *sangha* bodies subscribing to a unified Myanmar *sangha* order has been in place for nearly a decade. Their tasks entailed various executive, supervisory, and legislative functions not dissimilar to the secular centralized system of civil administration of the day. The trinity of *sangha* organs formed a sub-set within a larger system of another trinity in the form of the state, the *sangha*, and lay devotees or the public. Within the *sangha* system the *ovadacariya* and *vinayadhara sayadaw* are constituted into three tiers from the township level to the central or state level organizations whereas Sangha Nayaka Committees are formed into four tiers down to the ward/village-tract level. *Ovadacariya* are more concerned with the general principles encompassing the Buddhist ethos as well as *sangha* and *sasana*'s affairs as a whole and have a purely advisory function to the respective Sangha Nayaka Committees. The *vinayadhara sayadaw* function as standing ecclesiastical juries to arbitrate and settle the eighteen kinds of *Vivadadhiharana* disputes, four kinds of *Anuvadadhikarna* accusations, seven kinds of *Appattadhikavan* offences, and four kinds of *Kicca* actions (Department of Religious Affairs, Myanmar 1985*b*, annex tables 1 to 4). Elections of regional *vinayadhara sayadaw* according to a proportional quota system are supervised by the Township Sangha Nayaka Committees and potential candidates are selected from among the responsible senior monks (with at least ten years' *vassa*) in the monasteries (Sangha Nayaka Committee members and *ovadacariya sayadaw* are excluded).[53] Once elected, these *sayadaw* comprised a standing list from which a *vinnichaya* committee of three to five would be formed, by the corresponding Sangha Maha Nayaka Committee to consider a *vinaya dhammakamma* case as the occasion demands. Appeals against the decisions of the Township Vinnichaya Committee are considered by the State or Divisional Sangha Nayaka Committee which may convene a State or Divisional Vinnichaya Committee to retry the case. At this stage there is a further avenue for appeal to the State Sangha Nayaka Committee which, in turn, may convene a State Vinnichaya Committee with State Central

Working Committee members (excluding those from the same base area or township where the dispute occurred) to reconsider the case again.[54] On the other hand, cases of inter-*gaing* disputes and disputes involving lay persons on possession issues are to be tried only at the state/divisional level. When a case involving a dispute which requires *dhamma* or *adhamma* decisions affecting the *sasana* as a whole arises, the State Sangha Nayaka Committee is required to form the Special State Vinayadhara Committee composed of suitable numbers of State Central Working Committee members to adjudge it and there is no appeal against the decisions of such a committee.

It is apparent that the respective Sangha Nayaka Committees play a most important role in their functions as supervisory bodies on *sasana* and *sangha* affairs. Even in the *vinaya dhammakamma* procedures they play a crucial role in performing the executive functions in support of the various Vinnichaya Committees and their decisions and also have a hand in the formation of the Vinnichaya Committees themselves as well as the consideration of appeals to determine whether such appeals warrant further retrials/reconsiderations at the next level of Vinnichaya Committees. In implementing the policies of adopting by the quinquennial Sangha Congregation in pursuit of the three *P*s, different levels of Sangha Nayaka Committees have to deal with day-to-day matters relating to the execution of *sasana* and *sangha* affairs. In this process these organizations have to seek support from secular authorities and lay devotees which not only provide manpower, financial, and administrative resources but also, in the case of the former, secular authority to ensure that the decisions made by the Sangha Nayaka Committees are abided by those concerned.

To facilitate the formulation and implementation of policies and measures towards realizing the three *P*s, the central level State Sangha Maha Nayaka Committee split itself into three sub-groups of fifteen residing at a time, taking turns to take charge of the relevant matters in each session. During each session the sub-group concerned is further sub-divided into three functional sections: Vinnichaya Group; Sasana Affairs Group; and Educational Group.[55] On the other hand, the State Sangha Maha Nayaka Committees of the First and Second Congregations occasionally issued directives to its subordinate organizations regarding policy matters, specific measures, and clarifications with respect to *vinnichaya* matters, *sasana* affairs, as well as educational issues. Of the seventy-seven directives issued between

30 May 1980 and 12 July 1989, twelve were on *vinnichaya* matters, fifty-five were concerned with *sasana* affairs, and nine were on educational issues.[56]

The purification part of the three Ps falls within the purview of the Vinnichaya Group. This group deals with procedural, legislative, and executive matters on contraventions of the *vinaya* rules by the *sangha* and between members of the *sangha* and the lay polity.

Following the First Congregation's fourth resolution on removing bogus and undisciplined monks from the *sasana*, more than 300 persons were found to be guilty of serious offences within fifteen months — especially the first *parajjika* — which warranted disrobing and reversion to the lay state. The Ministry of Home and Religious Affairs through the investigative powers of the police offered considerable assistance in this effort.[57] In continuing the remedial measures to purify the *sasana* through stricter imposition of *vinaya* rules for the *sangha*, the State Sangha Maha Nayaka Committee issued Directive No. 65 on 8 August 1984, directing Township Sangha Nayaka Committees to supervise members of the *sangha* through the head abbots of monasteries concerned for observing the *vinaya* and for preventing the protection of those who broke *vinaya* (by their mentors).[58] Apparently, this was insufficient to control the small minority of undisciplined elements which continued to plague the *sangha* community. Hence on 20 June 1986, the Sangha Directive No. 72 explicitly imposing appropriate rules of conduct for head abbots (of monasteries or *kyaung*) as well as resident monks and novices was issued by the State Sangha Maha Nayaka Committee. The directive also set out the responsibilities and obligations required of the three levels of regional *sangha* organizations which must enforce the *vinaya* in co-ordination with the local people's councils concerned. The directive specified nine infringements to be prohibited which included, *inter alia*: intoxication; gambling; business transactions and black-marketeering; enjoying sports and public entertainment; unruly behaviour; soliciting valuables and cash; and soliciting dry rations and eatables after midday without specific supplication by the *dayaka* concerned. A field compaign was launched to explain the directive to regional bodies of the *sangha* throughout the country in the next few months. The Council of Ministers followed up with a notification in October 1986 asking State/Divisional and Township People's Councils to assist *sangha* organizations concerned in enforcing Sangha Directive No. 72 and to employ the full force of the law against erring monks and novices who resort to violence or those who contravene existing laws of the state. These actions apparently indicated the determination of the authorities concerned to enforce discipline among the *sangha* and also the extent and seriousness of these infringements which warranted such concerted efforts by both the relevant *sangha* authorities as well as the state.

Even these measures failed to effectively curb the infringement of *vinaya* rules in the conduct of *rahan* and *samanera*. There were many cases of guilty parties refusing to acknowledge and abide by the admonishments and decisions of the Township Sangha Nayaka Committee regarding contraventions of house rules of the respective monastery or monastery complex; violation of the rules of conduct set out in Directive No. 72; and continued occupation or construction of buildings which were deemed to be inappropriate as a monastery.[59] In response to these hindrances to the purification process, Directive No. 75 was issued on 3 July 1987 after the Third Meeting of the Second Central Working Committee in June 1987 had amended Article 47 of the "Procedures for Solution of Cases and Conflicts" (Department of Religious Affairs, Myanmar 1985*b*) on the right to appeal against the Township Vinnichaya Committee's decisions. This amendment was in the form of additional passages describing the procedures to convene a "Special Township Sangha Vinnichaya Committee" to try all cases involving the intransigents who refused to abide by the decisions of the Township Sangha Nayaka Committee on violations of house rules, Directive No. 72, and inappropriate monasteries (see above). This directive spelt out in detail the rules and procedures to be followed in exercising Article 47 in the execution of disciplinary actions according to the *vinaya*.

In mid-August a two-day meeting was held in Yangon at Kaba Aye Hill (where the office of the State Sangha Maha Nayaka Committee is situated) to explain and clarify the implications of Directive No. 75. Chairmen *sayadaw* of the State and Divisional Sangha Nayaka Committees were invited; and State Sangha Nayaka Committee members, officials from the Department of Religious Affairs, legal experts from the Central Court and the Central Law Office, and State and Divisional Religious Affairs Department heads also took part in the discussions. This kicked off a cascade of explanations in the respective states and divisions and the base areas (townships) concerned for the next six months as the renewed purification drive with support from secular authorities was conveyed to the *sangha* polity through the hierarchy of regional organizations.[60]

The Sasana Affairs Group's purview encompasses all the three *P*s and it also deals with organizational matters relating to the formation and functioning of the various tiers of regional *sangha* organizations. Some of its salient functions are given below:

1. electing and forming *sangha* organizations at different levels;
2. formulating rules, procedures, and handbooks on various organizational and operational aspects of the *sangha* organizations thus formed;
3. directing *vassa* or *wazo sangha* census-taking;
4. directing and facilitating the issuing of Sasana Membership Records;[61]
5. taking appropriate disciplinary action in *vada* disputes which requires *dhamma* or *adhamma* decisions affecting the *sasana* as a whole and have to be adjudged by a Special State Vinayadhara Committee;[62]
6. scrutinizing, supervising, and supporting meditation centres or *kammahtana* or *Patipatti Yeiktha* where meditational doctrines and practices are developed;[63]
7. scrutinizing squatter monasteries;
8. settling disputes relating to *sasana* land and general religious affairs;
9. scrutinizing applications for consecrating *sima* (ordination halls);
10. scrutinizing applications from monks who wished to go abroad;[64]
11. promoting missionary work in the (animist) hill regions of Myanmar;[65]
12. instituting training courses and multiplier courses for *vinayadhara*, abbots, and Sangha Nayaka Committee members;
13. formulating and issuing directives to regional organizations; and
14. scrutinizing sermons given by the *dhammakathika* (public lecturers who deliver sermons to lay devotees).

The Educational Group is mainly concerned with implementing the "Pariyatti Education Plan" adopted by the plenary session of the First State Central Working Committee in June 1982.[66] Endorsed also by peers of the scholastic community it was well received by the general public, who donated generously to support its implementation. Subsequently, the curricula for the Pali Pathamabyan Examinations were revised and the new system of religious education was gradually introduced starting at the Pathamange level in 1985. The "basic primary" course or Muladan was introduced in 1984 at the township level in contrast with the existing three national levels of Pathamabyan Examinations. State Sangha Universities sponsored by the State Sangha Maha Nayaka Committee were instituted with public funds in Yangon and Mandalay to accommodate advanced *sangha* aspirants who have already passed Pathamagyi course. Dhammacariya (equivalent to a Bachelor's degree) and Mahadhammacariya (equivalent to a Master's degree) courses are offered in these *sangha tekkatho,* which are run on a systematic and modern institutional basis. The Dhammacariya Examination which has been a *de facto* qualification examination for monks aspiring to a lectureship in the scholarly community was continued under the new *sangha* organizational set-up. So also were the Abhiddhama and Visuddhi Magga Examinations which have been open to lay persons as well.

The Pariyatti Education Plan was based on these four main objectives: to promote good habits and moral conduct; to be well-versed in *Pitaka* scriptures; to master the Pali language; and to excel in written Myanmar language and literature. In order to fulfil these objectives a plan was developed incorporating the abbot training scheme, the revised Pali Pathamabyan Examinations, the new Pariyatti Sasana Tekkatho or Sangha University system, and the revised Tipitakadhara Selection Examination (see Figure 2).

The Sasana Universities in this scheme play a crucial and innovative role by providing the most advanced level for scholastic achievement in Myanmar. Modern pedagogical techniques are to be incorporated and integrated with the traditional emphasis on reproduction and recall. Independent research is to be encouraged at the Master's level in thesis work. Different majors emphasizing either *vinaya* or *sutta* or *Abhidhamma* are offered and linguistic studies involving Sanskrit, Pali, and English are also planned for as electives. Studies of other religions as well as Myanmar literature are also part of the curriculum. The construction of universities situated in Yangon and Mandalay are funded by public donations.[67] The Yangon institution was opened in June 1986 followed by the Mandalay one in August of the same year.

The Abbot Training School Scheme envisaged the institution of at least one school in every state and division but so far only three have been opened: in Yangon, Mandalay, and Sagaing divisions.

FIGURE 2
The Pariyatti Education Plan

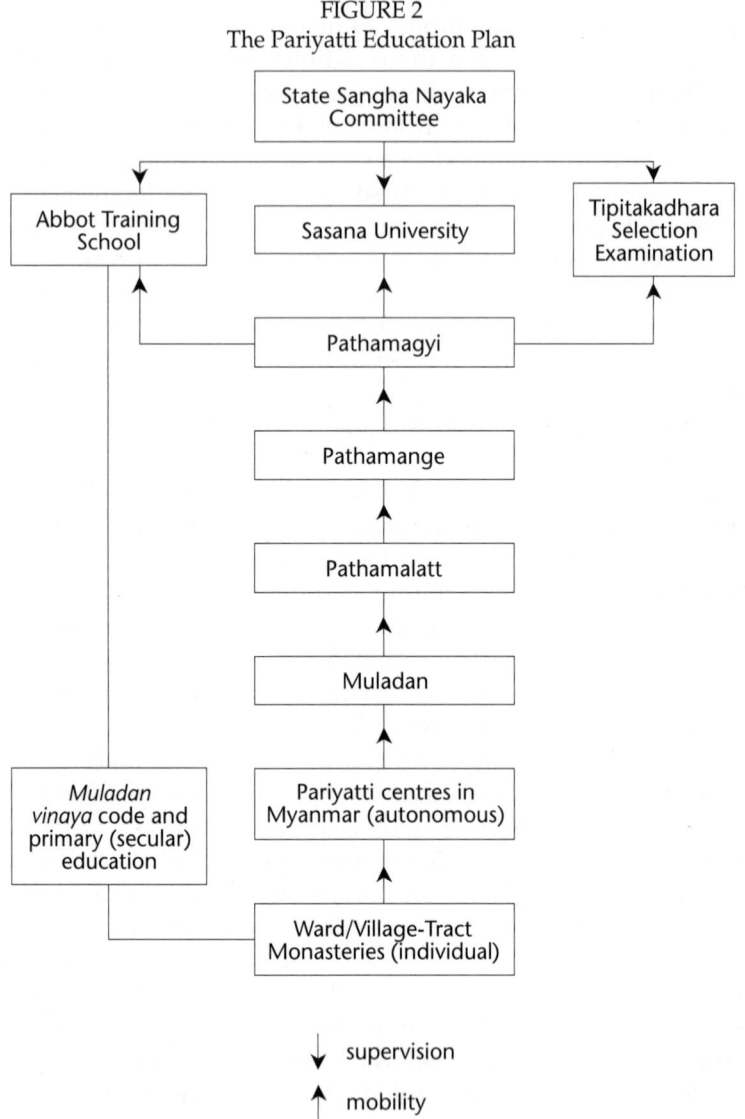

SOURCE: Adapted from Department of Religious Affairs, Myanmar, *Pariyatti Pyinyayei Simamkain* (1982, annex chart).

The Educational Group has also encouraged the propagation of interest in, and values based on, Buddhism among the Myanmar people, as well as the enhancement of the moral and ethical aspects of their educational experience, which were initiated through the holding of annual Buddhist Culture Examinations at township level. These examinations have been supervised by Township Sangha Nayaka Committees since 1984 when nearly 100,000 youths and children participated in more than one hundred towns. By 1987 the participation had increased to 227 townships, involving 129,500 youths.

The scrutinization of religious manuscripts before publication is one of the tasks of the Educational Group since the dissemination of the Buddhist religion is a sensitive and important matter of concern to the State Sangha Maha Nayaka Committee. Manuscripts are evaluated and categorized in the following ways: those that are approved; those requiring deletions prior to approval; those requiring revision prior to approval; those requiring revision and re-submission; and those that are not approved.[68]

The most significant symbolic event following the First Congregation was the construction of a *chettiya* or pagoda on a hillock across from the legendary Shwedagon Pagoda to commemorate the formation of a unified body of the *sangha* in the country. The Mahavijaya Pagoda or Maha Wizaya Zedi is the name of the pagoda being constructed, as a symbol of the unification of the *sangha* of all orders which had assembled at the congregation for the purpose of purifying, perpetuating, and propagating the *sasana*, as requested by the State Sangha Maha Nayaka Committee. Paid for by public donations (estimated at more than 50 million kyats), supervised by a central committee, chaired by the chairman of the Rangoon Division People's Council, and supported by nine working committees, it took more than five-and-a-half years before the *Hti* or Golden Umbrella could be hoisted to its pinnacle on 28 February 1986. The pagoda is intended to be a permanent symbol marking the achievement of *sangha* unity at the First Congregation.[69]

If the *sangha* and *sasana* could be said to be enjoying a renewal following *sangha* reforms, then it may also be said that the lay organizations which support them are also experiencing important changes in terms of their activities. Their roles, for example, have become more integrated with the re-established *sangha*. These organizations have benefited from the "admonishments" and guidance conveyed through the central bodies of *sangha* organizations and, apart from their traditional tasks, have been actively engaged in supporting the programmes and projects implemented by *sangha* organizations at different levels. One notable example is the extremely successful effort by the Tipitaka Nikaya Society in soliciting funds (of the order of 50 million kyats within six years) for financing the State Pariyatti Sasana Tekkatho. All in all, the *sangha* and the polity seem to be enjoying unprecedented *rapport*, basking in the revived glory of Buddha *sasana* despite the introduction of a secular constitutional state in Myanmar.

* * *

During the widespread demonstrations in August and September 1988, individual monks joined the agitations for democracy and later coalesced into a variety of organizational groupings popularly known as *thamegga*. These organizations deviating from the orthodox *sangha* hierarchy were quickly brought in line when the militant leaders either went underground or were "neutralized" by security agencies when the State Law and Order Restoration Council (SLORC) took control of the state on 18 September 1988.

Overt action has been practically impossible for the remnants of these dissident groups under the strict control exercised by the military regime which operates in a martial law setting. However, clandestine organizations such as Rahan Pyo Aphwe and Sangha Samaggi resorted to covert action exploiting allegations of human rights violations and improper conduct towards the *sangha* by security forces.[70] The most serious confrontation against the state authorities occurred in August 1990 after the alleged fatal shooting of a monk on 8 August in Mandalay while restoring order during an ostensibly pro-democracy demonstration. Although the authorities repeatedly denied any fatalities among the *sangha* in what was deemed a legitimate suppression of extralegal agitation by unruly elements, a religious boycott was organized by some monks in Mandalay, on 27 August, against members of the security apparatus and their families. This act in which monks categorically refuse to offer any religious service to the ostracized individual or group, fired by rumours and insinuations, appeared to have a snowballing effect and threatened to spread throughout the country. The highest authorities intervened rapidly to diffuse this unprecedented situation by submitting supplications to the leading monks of the unified *sangha* organization as well as influential leaders of the officially recognized sects and teaching monasteries. Meanwhile, negotiations were conducted at the local and national levels with the boycott leaders and representatives.

Finally, the ruling SLORC issued Order 6/90 on 20 October 1990 dissolving "illegal" monk organizations while reiterating the primacy of the official hierarchical *sangha* organization formed since 1980. It was followed by Order 7/90 on the next day declaring that any monk or novice who contravened regulations against non-religious activities would be dissociated from the *sangha* and would be liable for prosecution under existing laws of the land. The following day security forces raided over 130 monasteries in Mandalay and "cleaned up" the premises. Those deemed to have contravened the rule of law were arrested and unethical and illicit activities of the "robed persons" (they no longer qualify as "monks") were exposed to the public in a media blitz in the following days. In a move to further consolidate such actions against deviants in the established order of monks, SLORC Law 20/90, known as the Law Concerning Sangha Organizations, was promulgated on 31 October 1990 prescribing restrictions and penalties relating to the establishment of extra-legal *sangha* organizations other than the officially recognized hierarchy of Ovardacariya and Sangha Nayaka Organizations. Subsequently, more than 200 monks and novices were found to be guilty of contravening these rules and regulations and were stripped of their monkhood.

The SLORC government apparently spared no effort in sponsoring the pursuance of the aforementioned "Three *P*s". The numbers of distinguished *sayadaw* who were conferred the Abhidaja Maha Rattha Guru and Agga Maha Pandita titles were considerably increased from (totals of) three and eighteen, respectively, during the previous three years to nine and 109 over the fiscal years 1988/89 to 1990/91. The annual stipends for these title-holders as well as donations to monks who distinguished themselves in religious examinations were increased to four to six times the previous amounts. The most notable achievement seems to be the rapid construction, extension, and renovation of pagodas, monasteries, and associated religious infrastructure such as roads, ponds, and gardens. It was reported that nearly 440 million kyats donated by the public under the auspices of the SLORC government had been utilized in fifty-seven state-supervised major construction projects within the two-and-a-half years up to 31 March 1991 (*Myanmar Naingan Taingkyoe Pyeipyu*, 1991, pp. 387–89).[71]

APPENDIX TABLE 1

Hierarchy of Sangha Organizations: Second Congregation, 1985/86

			State/Divisional Sangha Nayaka Committees				Regional Bodies (*Gaing*-wise, Autonomous) Township Sangha Nayaka Committees			
Gaing	States and Divisions Covered	Town- Ships Covered	Valid[a]	Elected Members	Void[b]	Elected Members	Valid[a]	Elected Members	Void[b]	Elected Members
Thudhamma	14	303	14	120	—	—	286	2,576	17	20
Shwegyin	12	158	10	55	2	3	117	590	41	65
Maha Dwaya	6	68	6	34	—	—	42	199	24	24
Mula Dwaya	10	64	6	30	2	2	29	135	32	42
Hngettwin	10	60	6	27	2	2	5	22	36	46
Weiluwun	5	34	4	20	1	1	21	99	12	18
Mahayin	4	11	1	5	3	5	7	32	3	7
Gado	1	4	1	5	—	—	4	20	—	—
Anaukchaung Dwaya	2	3	1	5	—	—	2	10	—	—
Total			49	301	10	13	513	3,683	165	222

[a] Valid means a full-fledged Sangha Nayaka Committee.
[b] Void means that a committee could not be formed as the number of elected monks fell short of the stipulated quorum.

SOURCE: Department of Religious Affairs, Myanmar (1985a, annex c).

| | Ward/Village-Tract Sangha Nayaka Committees | | | | Vinaya-dhara Elected | National Level Control Bodies (Homogeneous) | | |
| | | | | | | Central Working Committee | State Sangha Maha Nayaka Committee | State Ovada-cariya Committee |
Valid[a]	Elected Members	Void[b]	Elected Members					
3,517	19,302	3,644	13,234	3,939	264	41	68
103	518	1,153	1,702	404	21	3	17
17	84	141	162	84	5	1	7
—	—	106	110	39	3	1	2
—	—	40	44	19	1	—	1
14	69	104	132	43	3	1	4
—	—	18	22	8	1	—	1
2	10	—	—	16	1	—	1
—	—	27	27	8	1	—	1
3,653	19,983	5,233	15,433	4,560	300	47	102

APPENDIX TABLE 2

Regional Distribution of *Rahan* and *Samanera*, 31 January 1988

State (S) or Division (D)	No. of Townships	No. of Townships with Sangha	No. of Samanera	No. of Rahan	Ranking Samanera	Ranking Rahan
Kachin (S)	18	13	1,688 (1,627)	1,556 (1,371)	12 (12)	12 (12)
Kayah (S)	6	6	553 (540)	347 (284)	13 (13)	13 (13)
Kayin (S)	7	7	7,279 (7,293)	5,239 (4,776)	9 (9)	9 (9)
Chin (S)	9	8	20 (21)	82 (65)	14 (14)	14 (14)
Sagaing (D)	38	38	22,526 (27,642)	15,408 (14,207)	3 (3)	3 (3)
Tanintharyi (D)	10	10	3,560 (3,290)	2,919 (2,719)	11 (11)	11 (11)
Bago (D)	28	28	10,726 (13,540)	13,873 (13,804)	5 (5)	4 (4)
Magway (D)	25	25	10,496 (17,057)	11,685 (10,346)	7 (4)	6 (8)
Mandalay (D)	29	29	31,614 (37,891)	24,558 (21,894)	2 (2)	1 (1)
Mon (S)	10	10	11,708 (11,680)	11,129 (10,822)	4 (7)	8 (6)
Rakhine (S)	17	17	5,142 (4,192)	4,190 (3,598)	10 (10)	10 (10)
Yangon (D)	39	37	9,368 (10,643)	18,147 (17,516)	8 (8)	2 (2)
Shan (S)	52	49	38,771 (40,852)	11,398 (10,611)	1 (1)	7 (7)
Ayeyarwady (D)	26	26	10,614 (12,264)	13,727 (12,306)	6 (6)	5 (5)
	314	303	164,065 (188,532)	134,258 (124,319)	—	—

NOTE: Figures within parentheses are from the *vassa* list of 1984.

SOURCE: Report of the State Sangha Maha Nayaka Committee to the Fourth Meeting of the Second State Central Working Committee, May 1988; Department of Religious Affairs, Myanmar (1985a, annex a).

NOTES

* When the State Law and Order Restoration Council (SLORC, the military junta which took over the powers of the state on 18 September 1989) enacted on 18 June 1989, the "Adaptation of Expressions Law", it stipulated that the English language expressions "Burma" or "Burman" or "Burmese" be substituted by the expression "Myanmar". The same law also stipulated changes in the names of the geographical places to conform with the Myanmar pronunciation, for example, "Rangoon" becomes "Yangon" and the racial expression for the "Burman" or "Burmese" becomes "Bamar".

1. Of course, Theravada Buddhism co-existed with various Hinduistic practices, mysticism, and locally adapted forms of animism. This admixture of orthodoxy and heresy has persisted for centuries and has become part and parcel of Myanmar culture though most Myanmar people would claim that they subscribe to a Buddhist ethos of the purest form. See, for example, Spiro (1967, 1982), Schober (1988), and Katsumi (1983).

2. However, for want of a better term, "sect" is the most widely used term for an exclusive group of monks who are bonded by behavioural affinities. The Myanmar word *gaing,* derived from the Pali term *gana* (which generally means an assemblage of any kind), is the popular as well as the "official" term in this context and will be used throughout this study. The term *nikaya,* which formally denotes the exclusivity of the *gaing,* has been used in official titles of the *sangha gaing,* such as Shwegyin, Weiluwun, and Dwaya. It may be used for a faction, set, or collection and can be defined as "an exclusive group of *bikkhu* [monks] who share a distinctive name, have a roster of officers, and collectively perform the higher ordination ceremony (*upasampada*)" (quoted in Kemper 1980, p. 31).

3. Perhaps, the most important feature among these characteristics is the adherence to an exclusive set of behavioural practices based on a certain interpretation of *vinaya* rules by the founder of the *gaing.* Thus Bechert (1980, p. 33) uses the term "*vinaya* sects" to differentiate them from doctrinal sects and philosophical schools that resulted from schisms in the fundamental doctrines and religious philosophy as a whole. He even classifies the Theravada School of Buddhism as a *vinaya* sect even though it was derived from the Hinayana School which resulted from philosophical dichotomy in Buddhism after the Buddha's passing away. For orthodox accounts of the Hinayana-Mahayana split and

subsequent cleavages, see Ray (1946), Dutt (1978), and Dhammagawtha U Maung Maung (1984). For a "revisionist" viewpoint sympathetic to Mahayana see Ikeda (1977).

4. For fuller accounts of the history of monastic sectarianism in Myanmar see Ray (1946) and Mendelson (1975). The following section is mainly based on Myanmar sources (Nwe Tharki 1989; Thaki Swe 1988*a*, 1988*b*, 1988*c*; Than Tun 1981; Maung Htin Aung, ed. and trans. 1966).

5. See Ray (1946, pp. 217–36) and Mendelson (1975, pp. 58–61, 66–67, 76–77). The controversy is also known as the dispute between *Ekamsika* (one-shoulder covered) and *Parupana* (two-shoulder covered).

6. The origins of Shwegyin Gaing as a formal entity is rather obscure and the reputed tension between the Thudhamma Assembly constituted by King Mindon in June 1862 (derived from the name of the *zayat* or hall where the assembly used to convene) to preside over *sangha* affairs and U Jagara, which allegedly led to the breakaway of Shwegyin followers is also controversial — Thudhamma and Shwegyin historiographers had offered different accounts (Mendelson 1975, pp. 96–98; Than Tun 1981, pp. 34–35; Panditta 1988, pp. 111–12). Moreover, the motivations and intentions of King Mindon, who while advocating *sangha* unity on the one hand appeared on the other hand to be partial towards *sayadaw* (literally, "royal teacher") U Jagara and apparently encouraged the *sayadaw's* exclusivity, cannot be ascertained. Another interesting point is that there was no reference in official Shwegyin history of any participation of U Jagara or Shewgyin Gaing as a group in Mindon's Fifth *Sangayana* or Synod or Grand Convocation (literally, "to compare the texts with one another and recite the same together" [Lin 1954, p. 41]) held in 1871 (Ferguson 1978, p. 75). All in all, it seems that the Shwegyin Gaing resulted from the desire of its founder to recreate the tradition of the ancestral forest-dwellers in an urban setting (Panditta 1988, p. 107) rather than from the tension between U Jagara and the Thudhamma Assembly, either as individuals in the case of Muang-Htaung Sayadaw U Nyaya or as a collective.

7. This entailed a change in the text of the time-honoured *Awkasa Shikko* (a pledge-cum-prayer dedicated to the Buddha), which generated conflict and controversy between its followers (lay people as well as monks) and the conservative orthodoxy (Maung Htin Aung, ed. and trans. 1966, pp. 22–23; Mendelson 1975, pp. 89–90).

8. Anaukchaung Dwaya was a somewhat parallel development to the original Dwaya Gaing founded by Okpo Sayadaw. It subscribed to the principles and practices of Okpo's movement but after a

controversial decision over a *vinaya* infringement of a Dwaya monk in Ngathaingchaung town, a group of monks led by six *sayadaw* formed an exclusive group. The *gaing's* name was derived from the name of the river that flows through the area in which the *gaing* flourished. This river, which branched out from the Irrawaddy river, was the westernmost among its branches, hence the name Anaukchaung, meaning "western stream". Mula Dwaya was another breakaway sub-sect which challenged monks from Henzada who dominated the Dwaya Gaing after the passing away of the Okpo Sayadaw. They refused to attend the Dwaya Convention in 1918, where Henzada monks institutionalized their faction as "Maha Dwaya". In response, the monks from Okpo (Ingapu) township formed their own "Mula Dwaya" (the "original" Dwaya).

9. Branded as unorthodox and extremist by its detractors, Hngwettwin Gaing became known by several names. The original name was derived from the local reference to caves in the Sagaing Hill which was utilized by the founder as a meditation site — Hngettwin being literally, "caves carved out by birds". It has also been known as Shwe Minwun (the range of hills where the caves are situated), Mahasatipatthana (with reference to the method of meditation advocated), Lepaw (the name of the monastery where the founder presided after moving to the south), Ajivahtammaka (based on the precepts undertaken by the *yogi*), and Catubhummika-megga (in relation to the path taken to achieve *nibbana*) (Mendelson 1975, pp. 105–11; Maung Htin Aung, ed. and trans. 1966, pp. 20–22; Dhammagawtha U Maung Maung 1981, pp. 37–38).

10. According to Weiluwun sources elements of Anaukchaung Dwaya and Pwint-Hla Theingon Nikaya of Pyi were integrated with those of Weiluwun in late 1940 under the leadership of its second supreme president, who happened to be the first Weiluwun Sayadaw U Pandhavamsa (Weiluwun 1982, p. 3; see also pp. 1–4).

11. This listing of nine *gaing* officially acknowledged as the post-independence manifestation of sectarianism in the Myanmar *sangha* is not entirely exhaustive. There could be several sub-sects of these mainstream *gaing* as well as localized *gaing* centred around leading personalities, distinguished by their doctrinal idiosyncrasies or individual *vinaya* practices or meditational methods. One example is the Palidaw Gaing established around 1900 at Sagaing Hill to emphasize the Pali core of the *vinaya* at the expense of the commentaries and which later attracted followers from the adjacent Minwun Range as well. It was subsumed under Thudhamma Gaing only in 1980 in

response to the preparation for the *sangha* unification effort. Within the Thudhamma Gaing there have been instances of dissident factions who challenged the authority of the *thathanabaing* and formed their own *gaing*; for example, the "Two and Ten Gaing" (*c.* 1895) which advocated their mentor for the *thathanabaing* position and the "Payagyi Gaing" led by the Payagyi Monastery which sought exclusivity against the authority of Taungkhwin Sayadaw (elected as *thathanabaing* in 1902) (Dhammagawtha U Maung Maung 1984, pp. 174–78).

12. Ferguson (1978, pp. 69–71) identified four sets of rivalries as bonded relationships which transcend factionalism and assume some sort of a dynamic tension allowing flexibility and resiliency in the Myanmar *sangha*. They are forest-dwellers versus urban monks; meditation practice versus scholastic learning; Upper Myanmar (Bamar) versus Lower Myanmar (Mon); and Myanmar versus Sinhalese (in terms of tradition/lineage). This concept is an interesting and useful paradigm for the analysis of sectarianism in Myanmar but such analysis is beyond the scope of this chapter.

13. Keyes' assertion that "the construal of the role of the Sangha as being a source of merit rather than being (except in very rare instances) a means to the attainment of ultimate Salvation, *Nibbana*" (Keyes 1983, p. 274) aptly puts in a nutshell the role played by the *sangha* in Theravada societies in general and Myanmar in particular. This "field of merit" concept, combined with the reinterpretation of *kammic* (from *kamma*; causal relationship governing actions and deeds) concept accommodating merit-transference, reinforces the complementarity of the ruler and the *sangha* in the political culture in Myanmar which serves as a role model for the polity as well (Keyes 1983; Woodward 1988, pp. 57–60; Ferguson 1978, pp. 66–69; Aung-Thwin 1983; Sarkisyanz 1965; Smith 1965, pp. 20–31, 307–20). On the other hand, it is also possible that sectarian differences are exploited by the ruling élite for their own ends, such as legitimacy of their leadership or their moral superiority *vis-à-vis* other contenders to power. King Mindon and Premier U Nu stand out as obvious examples of such attempts, albeit unsuccessful ones (Mendelson 1975, pp. 81–85, 112–14, 283–94).

14. The figures in Table 1 are believed to be based on official data collected over a period of several months prior to the convening of the Congregation of 1980 by the Department of Religious Affairs in a nationwide exercise with the help of the local administrative bodies (Pyithu Councils) down to the ward/village-tract level. It should be fairly accurate and, except for areas where security problems prevented

consistent and reliable communication, bound to be extensive in coverage as well. This serves, at worst, as a lower limit for the *sangha* population of Myanmar at that time.

15. The 42 per cent growth is derived from the rounded figures of 70,000 and 100,000 arrived at for the total *sangha* population in 1931 and 1973, respectively. The 1931 census noted that there were 71,365 persons under the category of "*Pongyis, Upazins*, priests, ministers, etc." which obviously included non-Buddhist religious preachers and mendicants as well (Bennison 1933). On the other hand, the 1973 census recorded 153,430 monks and novices. The figure of 100,000 was deduced from the age distribution of this total which yielded 101,600 for the cohorts of those above the age of nineteen, the minimum age to become a full-fledged monk or *rahan*. Since there could be some who though qualified for monkhood by virtue of age decided to remain a novice, a round figure of 100,000 was adopted (*Union of Burma Population Census*, 1973). It should be noted that the male population increased by 86 per cent during the same period, 1931–73.

16. This is rather speculative but given that the hierarchical organization of monks created by the Convention of 1980 has been dominated by Thudhamma and Shwegyin *sayadaw* by virtue of sheer numbers and that the two largest *gaing* have also been prominent in the *Pariyat* scene (the domain of learning and scholarship), it is not unnatural to assume that they have the critical masses to attract new disciples of the Buddha.

17. There are altogether ten definitions in the dictionary. See the *Shorter Oxford Dictionary*, third edition, revised, with addenda, volume II, published by the Oxford University Press, reprinted in 1969.

18. In this context "reform movements" within the *sangha* which led to the formation of *gaing* are excluded, as they represent attempts to withdraw exclusively from the establishment and as such confine their "reforms" within sectarian boundaries. Of course one may argue that by setting an example in the form of internalized reforms in a *gaing* they have upheld the "spirit" of reform, though in a seemingly convoluted manner.

19. There is also the possibility that once the members of the *sangha* order completely withdrew from interactions with the secular world, the order itself would practically become irrelevant to the lay polity.

20. It may also reflect the tensions existing in the triangular relationship among the *sangha*, the state (or ruler), and the polity. Aung-Thwin (1979) contended that "*sasana* reforms in Burma recurred in cycles precisely because monastic landlordism remained a persistent element of

Burmese dynastic history" (p. 685). For arguments against this emphasis
on economic dimensions, see Lieberman (1980) and Aye Chan (1988);
see also Aung-Thwin's reply to Lieberman in Aung-Thwin (1980).

21. For example, King Badon or Bodawpaya (reign: 1782–1819) instituted
sasana reforms embracing both the *sangha* and the laity, but even during
his reign he failed to achieve his aims though some of his actions
appeared to be inconsistent (Mendelson 1975, pp. 66–77; Than Tun
1988*a*, pp. vii–xvi; 1988*b*, p. x). It has been said that in carrying out
reforms two actions are involved: *niggaha*, which means condemning
those who deserved to be so and *paggaha*, which is bestowing honour
to whom honour is due. Myanmar kings almost always implemented
the latter but most failed to practise the former.

22. Dhammaceti's order contained four main points: to prohibit the
induction of undesirable persons into the order of monks and novices;
to ostracize monks who practised worldly trades and professions, those
who were corrupt, and those who gambled, womanized, stole, drank
liquor, got intoxicated, and accumulated wealth; to accept only those
who had acquired a sufficient knowledge of *vinaya* rules and codes of
conduct as *samanera* and monks; and to unify the *sangha* through
ordination according to the Sinhalese Mahavihara tradition
(Dhammagawtha U Maung Maung 1984, pp. 138–40).

23. Punishments for *alajji* acts and the more serious *parajika* acts — four
major crimes which necessitate the loss of monkhood, namely, having
sexual relations, stealing property or breach of trust, committing
homicide, and claiming *arahatship* — ranged from admonishment and
public apology to disrobement and could include physical labour and
penance as well. See Mendelson (1975, p. 73) and Dhammagawtha U
Maung Maung (1984, pp. 154–55) on the *Mahadan* office which oversaw
sangha affairs and enforced punishment on *vinaya* offenders deemed
guilty by their peers.

24. See Mendelson (1975, chap. 2) for a general exposition of the *sangha*
during the monarchy's last century when state-*sangha* relationship
intensified and complex relationships developed between the king and
leading monks. Circumstances which spawned the so-called Mindon
sects also undermined the power and prestige of the office of the
thathanabaing and perhaps led to erosion in the traditional authority of
abbots (monks in charge of a monastery) and other local *sangha* leaders
who would have been directly responsible for enforcing *vinaya* rules
of conduct among their wards.

25. See Mendelson (1975, pp. 203–4) for an account of the formation of the

GCSS. Dhammagawtha U Maung Maung (1984, p. 192) referred to the formation of the first chapter of the GCSS in Yangon around 1919 but it is most likely that it assumed a national character only after the political activist monk U Ottama was released from jail in 1922.

26. For accounts of the radicalization and politicization of the *sangha* in the nationalist struggle for independence, see Smith (1965, chap. 3) and Mendelson (1975, chap. 4).

27. For a report on the Sixth Synod, see Ohn Gaing (1954). Accounts of the *sangha's* political activities in post-independence Myanmar can be found in Smith (1965, chap. 6) and Mendelson (1975, chap. 5); see also Tharki Swe (1988*b*). For a summary of the government's attempts to institutionalize Buddhism, see Tinker (1967, pp. 165–77) and Smith (1965, chaps. 5, 7).

28. After a four-day preliminary meeting (11 to 14 March 1965) at Yangon of twenty-one leading monks and seventy-seven representatives from thirty-eight districts, a national congregation of the *sangha* was convened at Hmawbi (a small town about 30 km. northwest of the capital) under the chairmanship of the Pakoku Sayadaw. About 2,000 monks attended the government-sponsored "All-Burma All-Sect Sangha Convention", where representatives from forty-two districts (about 90 per cent of the country's administrative provinces) deliberated (from 17 to 19 March) on formulating a draft law for organizing the *sangha* which included, *inter alia*: supervision through a hierarchy of *sangha* administration; instituting identification records for members of the *sangha*; and drawing up procedures to settle disputes in accordance with the *vinaya*. Following protests from dissident monks in Yangon and other major cities the draft proposal was never implemented. See *Far Eastern Economic Review*, 10 June 1965, p. 499, and various issues of the *Working People's Daily* in March 1965.

29. The former exploited the escapist tendencies of its clients who had all along retained the affinity to supernaturalism and chiliastic elements of their pre-Buddhist forefathers. At the more mundane level the mystic *gaing* served as mediating structures for power brokers and their clientele. See Schober (1988) for a succinct account of mysticism in contemporary Myanmar. The latter was facilitated by the resurgence of interest for meditation leading to insight knowledge. The advent of the cheap cassette-tape player/recorder apparently facilitated the spread of religious teachings, orthodox or otherwise.

30. The production of calendars depicting famous pagodas, images of the Buddha and related Buddhist symbols became a very profitable

industry. Similarly, the use of such religious images and symbols in postcards and writing materials and the publication of books and pamphlets on religious themes, some of which were of a questionable nature in terms of authenticity and textual conformity (with the *Tipitaka* and the orthodox commentaries), also flourished. The emergence of an admixture of charismatic monks, ascetics, magical *bodaw*, and mendicants as potential power brokers and cult figures of considerable influence was also noticed with apprehension by the authorities as well as the orthodox *sayadaw* who strictly followed the *vinaya* (Aung Kin 1981).

31. The title of Agga Maha Pandita (the Supremely Learned One) was established by the British in 1915 and was re-instituted by the parliamentary government after independence. The title of Abhidaja Maha Rattha Guru (Noble Banner and Great Preceptor of the State) was created in 1953 as a higher honorific reserved for the most revered patrons of the *sangha* (Mendelson 1975, pp. 284 ff.). In reintroducing these religious titles after an absence of more than fifteen years, the state opted for continuity by following the same set of rules and regulations pertaining to the choice of recipients prescribed in the *Ovada Katha Report* of 1953. These rules stressed the *Pariyatti* achievements of the prospective recipients amongst other desirable qualities such as age and *vassa* (seniority). This symbolic gesture of continuity emulating the time-honoured state sponsorship of the *sangha* probably struck a most sympathetic chord amongst many lay devotees of the older generation and in all likelihood created empathy for "positive" or "constructive" intervention by the state which professed to support the wishes of the *thera* (elders) to purify the *sasana*.

32. The nation's President and the Chairman of the Council of State U Ne Win in leading the discussion at the Council of State meeting on 4 August 1979 with regard to the need for ecclesiastical courts to settle *sangha* disputes, directed the Council of Ministers (Cabinet) to consider and implement the matter not as state intervention without the *sangha*'s consent but as *sangha* affairs which should be handled by the *sangha* for the sake of the *sasana*. The two points to be implemented by the Cabinet were: to facilitate the *sangha* to live and act according to the *vinaya dhamma*, and to arbitrate and settle disputes and monastic cases among members of the *sangha* by forming ecclesiastical juries composed of *sangha* duly elected by the *sangha* polity (Kelasa 1980, p. 5).

33. The People's Councils from the basic ward and village-tract level to the state and divisional bodies consisted of elected people's rep-

resentatives. They are defined as local organs of state power with jurisdiction to run the day-to-day affairs of the state within their respective locale and responsible to the Council at the next higher level with the Council of State at the apex of the hierarchy.

34. Based on a preliminary survey carried out by the Department of Religious Affairs in the last quarter of 1979, nine *gaing* or orders were officially recognized by the state. Of these nine, four of the largest *gaing* were represented in the Working Committee. There were fifty-eight from Thudhamma Gaing, five from Shwegyin Nikaya, two from Mahadwaya Gaing, and one from Muladwaya Gaing.

35. The Tipitakadhara Dhamma Bandagarika is the highest honour that may be bestowed in recognition of *Pariyatti* achievements. It is accorded only to those who can satisfactorily reproduce the entire *Tipitaka* curriculum in the annual Tipitakadhara Selection Examinations. This includes oral recitation and (theory) written examinations. The oral examination covers the entire *Tipitaka*, consisting of twenty books of standard textual material amounting to 8,032 pages. The theory part includes not only these twenty books but also an additional set of commentaries comprising some thirty books (*Encyclopaedia Burmanica Yearbook, 1987*, p. 54). In its forty-one (consecutive) years of history there have been only five successful aspirants with the first successful candidate being U Vicittasarabivamsa whose 1953 record is still unsurpassed and who is the most revered *Pariyatti* scholar throughout the nation.

36. Regarding the other five *gaing* not represented in the Working Committee, senior *sayadaw* from such *gaing* were invited and their services were solicited for explaining the proposals and channelling feedback from their respective constituencies. In the course of the field trips the members of the Working Committee held audience with more than 84,000 members of the *sangha* while having solicited written consent from another 19,000 monks who were absent from such meetings, a coverage of some 95 per cent of the total *sangha* population at that time.

37. The word *samutiya* comes from *sammuti*, which means a generally accepted choice. The computational basis for *gaing*-wise representation was not revealed but the quotas realized closely corresponded to the numerical strength of the constituents of each *gaing* as enumerated by the Department of Religious Affairs' survey depicted in Table 1. They were Shwegyin Nikaya, 90; Maha Dwaya Nikaya, 21; Weiluwun Nikaya, 12; Mula Dwaya Nikaya, 10; Mahayin, 3; Hngettwin, 3; Gado, 3;

and Anaukchaung Dwaya, 1 (Dhammagawtha U Maung Maung 1984, pp. 312–13).

38. Although the draft list of candidates had provisions for 300 members, the actual number elected for the State Central Working Committee of the Sangha turned out to be 299. The six office-bearers on the State Central Working Committee of the Sangha were also *de jure* executives holding identical positions on the standing committee called the State Sangha Maha Nayaka Committee, which would be divided into three groups of eleven *sayadaw*, each group residing in Yangon at Zabudipa Hall (in the Kaba Aye Pagoda complex) for four months in rotation to conduct office all the year round. The president elect was no other than the chairman of the Working Committee (of sixty-six *sayadaw*) which was formed earlier to undertake preliminary work leading to the Congregation and a patron of the Thudhamma sect. Later the State Sangha Maha Nayaka Committee was expanded to forty-five members and the executive positions increased by three more vice-presidents as well as three more joint-secretaries. These new positions were filled by election from within the original thirty-three members while the twelve . additional members to the Committee were drawn from the State Central Working Committee of the Sangha at its First Extraordinary Emergency Meeting on 17 June 1981.

39. References to these central level state *sangha* organizations were sometimes preceded by the word "First" in relation to the "First Congregation", whose mandate would last five years.

40. Council of State Order No. 2/80 (28 May 1980); Amnesty Order. See Aung Kin (1981, pp. 106 ff.) for reactions to this order. This is reminiscent of the traditional practice of *dhammaraja* pardoning convicted criminals on auspicious occasions.

41. Except for the Thudhamma Gaing, the other eight *gaing* elected their respective organizations under the central supervision and co-ordination of their own sectarian central administrative bodies. One or more of the three tiers sanctioned were formed *gaing*-wise, depending upon the numerical strength of the membership in the locality concerned. The Thudhamma Gaing was able to hold election at all three levels throughout the nation by universal suffrage.

42. After the coup of 18 September 1988, when the SLORC became the supreme executive and legislative body, the People's Councils at all levels were replaced by respective "Law and Order Restoration Councils" composed mainly of military commanders and civil servants. This does not produce any significant change in the schema of Figure 1

except for the substitution of appropriate local or regional Law and Order Restoration Councils in place of People's Council at the same tier.

43. They are (1) title or name; (2) residence (monastery, town, state or division); (3) birthplace (village/ward, town, state or division); (4) date of birth (Myanmar calendar); (5) citizenship; (6) national registration or foreigner's registration card serial number; (7) place of noviciation or ordination; (8) date of noviciation or ordination (in both the *sasana* and Myanmar calendar); (9) title and residence of noviciation or ordination preceptor (*upajjhaya*); (10) father's name; (11) father's national or foreigner's registration card serial number; (12) mother's name; (13) mother's national or foreigner's registration card serial number; (14) parents' address; (15) noviciation or ordination *dayaka*'s (male donor/ sponsor) name; (16) noviciation or ordination *dayikama*'s (female donor/ sponsor) name; and (17) address of the donor/sponsor.

44. This consists of seven columns on the following: serial number; residential address including the name of the monastery; date of arrival; presiding abbot's signature; the record holder's *Pariyat* and *Patipat* actions/achievements; date of transfer; and the presiding abbot's signature (presumably on departure).

45. Those who are noviciated/ordained as a *dhonlaba* on a temporary basis are not required to have such a record. However, they do have the traditional *yet-choke* or summary record of noviciation/ordination which is usually a one-page note containing information on the time, date, and place of noviciation/ordination, the name of the novice/ monk, the name(s) of the preceptor(s), and the time and date of leaving the *sasana* on reversion to layman status.

46. *Vinayadhara sayadaw* were to be elected under the auspices of Township Sangha Maha Committees by a majority vote of eligible members of the *sangha* in the same locality. Thus the elections may involve members of the same *gaing* where elected *vinayadhara* hold jurisdiction within their respective *gaing*. For cases transcending sectarian boundaries or involving laymen, State/Divisional Vinnicchaya Committees may be formed by the State Sangha Maha Nayaka Committee from the standing list of *vinayadhara* in the same state/division irrespective of their affiliation to any *gaing* (Department of Religious Affairs, Myanmar 1985*b*). The First Extraordinary session of the "Second Pyithu Hluttaw" was convened on 25 June 1980, when the Vinaya Dhammakamma Bill was passed as the Pyithu Hluttaw Law No. 3 1980, confirming the procedures for settling disputes according to the *vinaya* as envisaged

in the document adopted by the Congregation and prescribing the rules for the enforcement of decisions made by the Sangha Vinnichaya Committees. According to this Law, the state or divisional or township People's Council Executive Committee concerned shall carry out administrative matters relating to the "Procedures for Solution of Cases in Conflicts in Accordance with the Rules of the Order" (*Working People's Daily*, 4 July 1980).

47. For an interesting background on the organized political monks' reaction to the military junta's policies and actions, see Smith (1965, chap. 8). For an account of the elaborate preparations made by the secular authorities leading to the 1980 Congregation, see Kelasa (1980, pp. 5–71) and Sao Htun Hmat Win (1981, pp. 31–37).

48. It might occur to students of socialist systems that the process is reminiscent of electoral proceedings at party congresses where "democratic centralism" was exercised in any orderly manner where lobbying as a rule was forbidden. However, it could also be argued that in such a hierarchical organization with different sectarian allegiances there is no viable alternative to such conduct in order to ensure consensus and to avoid long and acrimonious debates.

49. The leading proponents are ostensibly the *thera*, who were patrons of the Congregation, the active members of the *sangha* executive, and the secular authorities backing them. Intellectual and technical inputs for such a reform seemed to have emanated from the Ministry of Home and Religious Affairs where lay specialists — many of them ex-monks — in the Department of Religious Affairs have accumulated a wealth of ideas and experiences on *vinaya*, educational, and general *sasana* affairs. They formed the core support staff to the resident State Sangha Maha Nayaka Committee and together with a small but influential coterie of independent scholars and advisers have been responsible for the conceptualization and formulation of the various schemes for *sangha* reforms and the renewal of *sasana*.

50. The Pyithu Hluttaw in September 1983 passed the law known as "The Law Safeguarding the Settlement and Decisions of Vinaya Dhammakamma" as Pyithu Hluttaw Law No. 9 of 1983. This was in response to the request by the First State Central Working Committee which had unanimously agreed that the force of law is needed to enforce the decisions of *vinayadhara* in ecclesiastical case and doctrinal disputes. In the past there had been no specific penalties for convictions against the transgressors of the decisions made by the *sangha* courts whereby the accused though convicted might continue the status quo with

impunity, giving rise to serious threats against the solidarity, tranquillity, and dignity of the monastic order. The law prescribed punishment in terms of jail sentences ranging from six months to five years for offences related to those who, having fallen from monkhood by committing the *parajika appati*, try to don the robes again; to those disguising as monks or novices; to those disseminating doctrines already deemed *adhamma vada* (theses or views contrary to the teachings of the Buddha).

51. This was different from the First Congregation where the various regional and sectarian *sangha* organizations were formed only after the conclusion of the Congregation. From the Second Congregation onwards such elections would precede the convening of the Congregation since the mechanism in the form of the Procedure for the Sangha Organization was already in place.

52. The State Sangha Maha Nayaka Committee was expanded to forty-seven members, thereby exempting the President Sayadaw and the Secretary Sayadaw (who were both re-elected incumbents) from the three groups of fifteen members formed to hold office (for four months each) in rotation at Zabudipa Hall in the Kaba Aye Pagoda complex about 12 km. from the centre of Yangon. Two vice-presidents and two join-secretaries acted as executives for each group.

53. The numbers of *vinayadhara sayadaw* to be selected are based on the total number of monks present during the Buddhist lent: five for a population of between fifty and one hundred monks; ten for 101 to 200 monks; fifteen for 201 to 300 monks; twenty for 301 to 500 monks; and twenty-five for a population of 501 monks or more (Department of Religious Affairs, Myanmar 1985*b*, p. 16).

54. Even at this final stage there is a further check against abuse of judicial power. There is a provision for a final retrial if the State Sangha Nayaka Committee felt that the decision has either contravened the letter or spirit of the *vinaya* or the procedural handbook of *vinnichaya* matters. By a 75 per cent majority in a secret voting the State Sangha Maha Nayaka Committee may form a "Special State Vinayadhara Committee" composed of State Central Working Committee members. If and when a state level working committee or an *ovadacariya* member stand accused of *parajjika appatti*, the State Sangha Maha Nayaka Committee is required to institute the "Special Sangha Vinnichaya Committee" with five State Central Working Committee members to hear the case. In the event of an appeal the State Sangha Nayaka Committee may decide to form the "Special State Sangha Vinnichaya

Committee" with five to seven members drawn from the standing list of the State Central Working Committee members excluding those from the same base area pertaining to the parties involved in the dispute (Department of Religious Affairs, Myanmar 1985*b*, pp. 50–52).

55. Similarly, the central level State Sangha Vinnichaya Committee of fifteen members also formed into three groups which take turns to reside in Yangon for four-month sessions in order to facilitate hearing appeal cases brought up to the state level.

56. Directive No. 67 was not available to the present writer. It is believed to be under revision for unknown reasons.

57. However, after the promulgation of Directive No. 28 on 22 August 1981, which sanctioned Township Sangha Nayaka Committees to take full charge of the investigation on cases of *rahan* accused of contravening the first *parajjika* (illicit sexual relationship), the number of disrobing fell to only twenty-one in the next three-and-a-half years. According to a submission placed at the Second Congregation for a speedier implementation of the first *parajjika*, it was due to the hesitation on the part of the township organizations who were confronted with various measures taken by the guilty parties who resorted to all available means — including extra-legal measures — to confuse and hinder the investigative process.

58. Directive No. 65 was issued by the Sasana Affairs Groups presumably because it concerned the behaviour of the *sangha* which in turn had serious ramifications on the state of the *sasana* and involved executive action by the township level committees.

59. To ensure concordance with *vinaya* rules regarding the construction and consecration of monasteries, scrutinization bodies were formed at the state/divisional level and during the five-year tenure of the First Congregation decided upon 878 cases, of which 560 of them secured official recognition on a temporary basis. It is interesting to note that the *wazo* list in mid-1984 recorded 47,983 monasteries in the country.

60. The results of such an elaborate exercise could not be ascertained because of the uncertainties associated with the upheavals of August/ September 1988 which had their antecedents in the disturbances of March and June of the same year. Apparently this did not prevent some young monks and novices from joining the demonstrators during the upheavals. There had been reports of formations of *thamegga* (or unions) which called for the dismantling of the organizational hierarchy and some violence committed by persons wearing robes during the period the administration broke down as well as cases where the *sangha* took

charge of many cities and towns (through activism or by default). Apparently with the military takeover on 18 September 1988, calm and order were restored in the *sangha* as the organizational set-up was quickly reinstated.

61. The proportion of monks who received these records as a percentage of the total population was 85 per cent in 1981/82 (the year after the institution of records), which rose to 93 per cent in the following year and remained at a high level of more than 95 per cent thereafter. For 1988/89 the proportion was over 98 per cent. For *samanera* the proportion was much smaller and more unstable due to the (lower) age limit of twelve years as well as the fact that a large number of them were noviciates for a very short period (as part of the Myanmar Buddhist ethos of having sons live as noviciates at least a few days in a symbolic gesture).

62. Up to January 1988 nine *vada* (doctrines) were adjudged as *adhamma vada* (wrong or deviant doctrine) by the Special State Vinayadhara Committees formed to hear their cases by the State Sangha Nayaka Committee, namely, Lu-they Lu-Phyit Shin Okkahta Vada, Sammadithti Thutaythana Vada, and Shwe Abhidhamma Vada (of the same school of thought); Kyaukthinbaw Vada; Kyaukpon Tawya Vada; Kyaunpan Tawya Vada; Dhamma Niti Vada; Moe Nyo (North Okkalapa) Vada; Malarwara (Yetarshay) Vada; Htundon Letkyan U Htin Vada; and Theinthamoathmu (consecration of Ordination Hall) Vada of U Puunyacara. Three other *vada* which persevered after being adjudged as *adhamma* well before the time of the First Congregation were also promulgated as *adhamma vada* by the State Sangha Nayaka Committee in lieu of the formation of and trial by the Special State Vinayadhara Committee. All twelve *vada* were banned in Myanmar and the *sangha* and lay proponents of such *vada* reportedly signed pledges renouncing their *vada*. All references to these *vada* in print or on audio tapes were confiscated and destroyed. All organizations related to the perpetuation and propagation of these views were also disbanded.

63. According to the approved list of *patipatti htana* or *yeiktha* in July 1980 there were 326 *kammahtana* which were recognized by the government. Apparently there could be hundreds of *kammahtana* operating on their own or as part of the network of prominent *kammahtana* such as Mahasi Vipanana, Mogok Vipessana, Soonlun Vipanana, and so forth. The State Sangha Nayaka Committee has yet to formulate a scheme to deal with the proliferation of meditation centres in the country (Tin Maung

Maung Than 1988, pp. 32, 53, n. 15). Scrutinization and supervision has been taken up only on an *ad hoc* basis whenever there is evidence that the practice involves *adhamma vada*.

64. Buddhist monks wishing to go abroad are divided into three categories as to the reason for such a visit: social visit on supplication by relatives and devotees; educational purpose to enhance scholarly knowledge; *sasana-pyu* or to propagate the teachings of the Buddha. The State Sangha Nayaka Committee accordingly scrutinizes these applications and decides upon them. In early 1983 it issued Directive No. 52, which prescribed the minimum requirements and qualifications for the *sangha* applying for permission to go abroad. During the tenure of the First Congregation forty-two monks were allowed to go abroad and two were refused permission; twenty on social visits; four on educational trips; and eighteen on *sasana-pyu* trips. The foreign exchange allowance for such trips was only US$65 per individual before 1988. Later the SLORC government increased it to between US$300 and US$500, depending on the status and seniority of the monk concerned.

65. Concerning the missionary work in the hill regions of Myanmar, the central direction which apparently lapsed after the abolishment of the Buddha Sasana Council was reaffirmed with the formation of the Hill Region Central Sangha Committee under the supervision of the State Sangha Maha Nayaka Committee. This missionary effort which involved seventy-seven monks and thirty-four lay preachers covering six states and divisions in 1980 grew to ninety-nine monks and thirty-seven lay preachers in 1988. It was further enhanced by the opening of the Hill Region Buddhist Missionary Central Training School in May 1987. The endowment fund instituted after the adoption of the "Rules and Procedures for the Hill Region Buddhist Propagation Central Body" in June 1982 stood at about 0.6 million kyats in early 1988.

66. Prior to the adoption of the proposed plan a draft was presented to *sangha* gatherings at fifty-eight places in the whole country over a period of several months. Written replies to questionnaires were solicited and 98 per cent of the nearly 19,200 replies agreed to the proposal. It is interesting to note that the dissent vote in Mandalay division — reportedly steeped in scholastic tradition — at nearly 5 per cent is more than double the national average of around 2 per cent.

67. Donations amounted to over 64 million kyats up to 1988 out of which over 38 million kyats had been spent on the construction of buildings and infrastructure. Anecdotal evidence seems to suggest that the teething troubles in the Sasana Universities have not been eradicated.

There has been a substantial loss of teaching staff and the attrition rate has been remarkably high among them. The Sasana University Project Plan and the Fundamental Rules of Organization were still in draft form up to early 1989 while the composition of the advisory council and academic board have not stabilized as such.

68. During the five-year term of the First Congregation, 646 manuscripts were considered, out of which seventy-two were disapproved and twenty-two were required to be re-submitted after revision.

69. Donations solicited up to the end of May 1989 were reported as amounting to over 35 million kyats, of which nearly 34 million kyats were spent on construction and embellishment work.

70. Spokesmen for the ruling SLORC have divulged information in several press conferences that the now-defunct Burma Communist Party's (BCP) underground elements had infiltrated the so-called pro-democracy movement since its inception and were in control of the clandestine *sangha* organizations through their "moles" as well as by active support for militant and radical elements in these bodies. See, for example, Press Conference No. 107 of 7 December 1990 reported in *Working People's Daily* (8 December 1990). The state deemed the actions of the dissident monks an attempt to divide and destroy the officially sanctioned *sangha* organization.

71. The amount of donations should be seen in the context of an economy in which private sector construction work averaged only 653 million kyats for the fiscal years 1988/89 and 1989/90.

REFERENCES

Aung Kin. "Burma in 1980: Pouring Balm on Sore Spots". In *Southeast Asian Affairs 1981*. Singapore: Institute of Southeast Asian Studies, 1981.

Aung-Thwin, Michael. "The Role of Sasana Reform in Burmese History: Economic Dimensions of a Religious Purification". *Journal of Asian Studies* 38, no. 4 (1979): 671–88.

_____. "A Reply to Lieberman". *Journal of Asian Studies* 40, no. 1 (1980): 87–90.

_____. "Divinity, Spirit, and Human: Conceptions of Classical Burmese Kingship". In *Centers, Symbols, and Hierarchies: Essays on the Classical States of Southeast Asia*, edited by Lorraine Gesick. Yale University

Southeast Asia Studies Monograph Series no. 26. New Haven: Yale University Press, 1983.

———. *Pagan: The Origins of Modern Burma*. Honolulu: University of Hawaii Press, 1985*a*.

———. "The British 'Pacification' of Burma: Order Without Meaning". *Journal of Southeast Asia Studies* 16, no. 2 (1985*b*): 245–61.

Aye Chan. "The Nature of Land and Labour Endowments to Sasana in Medieval Burmese History: Review of the Theory of 'Merit-Path-to-Salvation'" (Review article). *Southeast Asian Studies 26*, no. 1 (1988): 86–95.

Bechert, H. "Buddhism in the Modern States of Southeast Asia". In *Southeast Asia in the Modern World*, edited by B. Grossman. Proceedings of a seminar in April 1970. Wiesbaden: Otto Harrassowitz, 1972.

———. "The Structure of the Sangha in Burma: A Comparative View". In *Studies in History of Buddhism*, edited by A.K. Narain. Papers presented at the International Conference on the History of Buddhism, Madison, Wisconsin, 19–21 August 1976. New Delhi: B.R. Publishing, 1980.

Bernison, J.J. *Census of India, 1931. Vol XI: Burma, Part 1 Report*. Rangoon: Superintendent, Government Printing and Stationery, 1933.

Department of Religious Affairs, Myanmar. *Pariyatti Pyinyayei Simamkain*. Yangon, 1982.

———. *Fundamental Rules for the Sangha Organization and Procedures: Revised and Updated* (in Myanmar). Yangon, 1985*a*.

———. *Procedures for Solution of Cases and Conflicts in Accordance with the Rules of the Order: Revised and Updated* (in Myanmar). Yangon, 1985*b*.

Dhammagawtha U Maung Maung. *Sangha Gaing Gyi Koe Gaing Akyaung*. Yangon: Pyithu Alin Sarpay, 1981.

———. *Sangha Ah Phaya Yon Gei Thee*. 2nd ed. Yangon: Shay Pyay Sar Pay Taik, 1984.

Dutt, N. *Buddhist Sects in India*. New Delhi: Motilal Banarsidass, 1978.

Encyclopaedia Burmanica Yearbook, 1982 (in Myanmar). Yangon: Sarpay Beikman, 1982.

Encyclopaedia Burmanica Yearbook, 1987 (in Myanmar). Yangon: Sarpay Beikman, 1987.

Ferguson, John P. "The Quest for Legitimation by Burmese Monks and Kings: The Case of the Shwegyin Sect (19th–20th Centuries)". In *Religion and Legitimation of Power in Thailand, Laos and Burma*, edited by Bardwell L. Smith. Chambersburg, PA: Anima Books, 1978.

Ikeda, Daisaku. *Buddhism, the First Millennium*, translated by Burton Watson. Tokyo and New York: Kodansha International, 1977.

Ikumo, Zenno. "Nine Sects (Gaings) of Theravada Buddhism in Burma". In *Burma and Japan: Basic Studies on Their Cultural and Social Structure*, edited by the Burma Research Group, Tokyo University of Foreign Studies. Tokyo: Tokyo University of Foreign Studies, 1987.

Katsumi, Tamura. "Ritual and Society: Intimate Relationships in Burma". *East Asia Cultural Studies* 22 (1983): 11–36.

Kelasa, Ashin. *Pahtamma Akyein Gaing Baungsoan Sangha Asiaway Gyi Thamaing* [The history of the First Congregation of the Sangha of All Orders] (in Myanmar). Rangoon: Department of Religious Affairs, 1980.

Kemper, Steven. "Reform and Segmentation in Monastic Fraternities in Low Country Sri Lanka". *Journal of Asian Studies* 40, no. 1 (1980): 27–41.

Keyes, Charles F. "Merit-Transference in the Kammic Theory of Popular Theravada Buddhism". In *Karma: An Anthropological Inquiry*, edited by Charles F. Keyes and E. Valentine Daniel. Berkeley, CA: University of California Press, 1983.

Lieberman, Victor B. "The Political Significance of Religious Wealth in Burmese History: Some Further Thoughts". *Journal of Asian Studies* 40, no. 4 (1980): 753–69.

Lin, Dr U. "Sangayanas and the Sasanas". *Light of the Dhamma* 2, no. 4 (1954): 41–44.

Ling, Trevor. "Divided Buddhists and Non-Buddhists in Burma". Mimeographed. 1989.

Maung Htin Aung. *A History of Burma*. New York: Columbia University Press, 1967.

————. *Burmese History Before 1287: A Defence of the Chronicles*. Oxford: Asoka Society, 1970.

Maung Htin Aung, ed. and trans. *Burmese Monk's Tales*. New York and

London: Columbia University Press, 1966.

Mendelson, E. Michael. *Sangha and State in Burma*, edited by J.P. Ferguson. Cornell: Cornell University Press, 1975.

Myanmar Naingan Taingkyoe Pyeipyu: Naingandaw Nyeinwut Pipya Mhu Teehsautyei Aphwe Ei Hsaungywet Chet Thamaing Win Hmattan, 1988 Hku Hnit Hma 1991 Khu Hnit. Yangon: Sub-Committee for Publication of "Historical Account of SLORC's Endeavours, 1988 to 1991", 1991.

Nwe Tharki. "Gaing Baungsoan Sangha Nyinyut Yei". *Loketha Pyithu Neizin* (daily), 17–19, 21, 26 April 1989.

Ohn Gaing, U. "Report on the Chatta Sangayana". *Light of the Dhamma* 2, no. 3 (1954): 32–37.

Panditta, Ashin (Shwehintha Sayadaw). *Shwegyin Nikaya Tharthanarwin Akyin*. 2nd ed. Yangon, privately published, 1988.

Ray, Nihar Ranjan. *An Introduction to the Study of Theravada Buddhism in Burma*. Calcutta: University of Calcutta, 1946.

Sao Htun Hmat Win. "The Unique Solidarity of the Sangha Order". *Light of the Dhamma* 1, no. 2 (1981): 28–37.

Sarkisyanz, E. *Buddhist Backgrounds of the Burmese Revolution*. The Hague: Martinus Nijhoff, 1965.

Schober, J. "The Path to Buddhahood: The Spiritual Mission and Social Organization of Mysticism in Contemporary Burma". *Crossroads* 4, no. 1 (1988): 13–30.

Smith, Donald E. *Religion and Politics in Burma*. Princeton: Princeton University Press, 1965.

Spiro, Melford E. *Burmese Supernaturalism*. Englewood Cliffs, NJ: Prentice-Hall, 1967.

————. *Buddhism and Society: A Great Tradition and Its Burmese Vicissitudes*. 2nd ed. Berkeley and Los Angeles: University of California Press, 1982.

Thaki Swe. "For Perpetuation of Sangha Nayaka Committees — (1)". *Working People's Daily*, 16 December 1988a.

————. "For Perpetuation of Sangha Nayaka Committees — (4)". *Working People's Daily*, 16 December 1988b.

————. "For Perpetuation of Sangha Nayaka Committees — (5)". *Working People's Daily*, 16 December 1988c.

Than Tun. *Khit Haung Myanmar Yarzawin*. Yangon: Maha Dagon Press, 1964.

————. "History of Shwegyin Nikaya (Shwegyin Sect in the Order of Buddhist Monks) in Burma (1)–(5)". *Shiroku* (Kagoshima University), nos. 14–18 (1981–85).

————. *The Royal Orders of Burma, A.D. 1598–1885: Part Seven, A.D. 1811–1819*. Kyoto: Center for Southeast Asian Studies, Kyoto University, 1988*a*.

————. *The Royal Orders of Burma, A.D. 1598–1885: Part Eight, A.D. 1819–1853*. Kyoto: Center for Southeast Asian Studies, Kyoto University, 1988*b*.

Tin Hla Thaw. "The Age of the Shwe Dagon Pagoda". *Shiroku* (Kagoshima University), no. 2 (1969), pp. 33–39.

Tin Maung Maung Than. "The *Sangha* and *Sasana* in Socialist Burma". *SOJOURN: Social Issues in Southeast Asia* 3, no. 1 (1988): 26–61.

Tinker, Hugh. *Union of Burma: A Study of the First Years of Independence*. 4th ed. London: Oxford University Press, for Royal Institute of International Affairs, 1967.

Union of Burma Population Census. Union Volume. Rangoon: Immigration and Manpower Department, Ministry of Home and Religious Affairs, 1973.

Von der Mehden, F.R. "The Changing Pattern of Religion and Politics in Burma". In *Studies on Asia*, edited by R.K. Sabai. Lincoln: University of Nebraska, 1961.

Weiluwun Nikaya Gaing. "Sadhtamma Akyein Myauk Weiluwun Nikaya Mahanayaka Dhipitti Samutti Sartan". Mimeographed. Yangon: Weiluwun Nikaya Gaing, 1982.

Woodward Mark R. "When One Wheel Stops: Theravada Buddhism and the British Raj in Upper Burma". *Crossroads* 4, no. 1 (1988): 57–90.

CHAPTER THREE

Re-Interpreting the Traiphuum Phra Ruang: Political Functions of Buddhist Symbolism in Contemporary Thailand

PETER A. JACKSON

Introduction

The important political functions performed by Buddhist teachings and the Buddhist *sangha* in the histories of Thailand and the other Theravada polities of Southeast Asia have been described in a number of studies (for example, see F. Reynolds [1975a, p. 175] and Ling [1976, pp. 284–86]). In the case of Thailand the historical continuity of the institution of the *sangha* and its relationship to the Thai state up to the present day has meant that Buddhist doctrines and practices in that country have retained an especially high degree of symbolic significance and relevance to political activities and debates. Fundamental to the ongoing significance of Buddhist teachings, in particular, in Thailand has been their interpretative plasticity, that is, their capacity to continue to be used to confer symbolic legitimation upon the exercise of political authority and the structures of political power, whether those structures have been founded upon absolute monarchical rule, military rule, or upon a popularly elected government.

However, the changing forms of government in Thailand in this century have created tensions and dissonances within the traditional structures of Thai Buddhist thought. In their analyses of the relations between Theravada Buddhism and the state in Thailand, Keyes and Tambiah, among others, have described what they regard to be a "crisis of legitimacy" (Keyes 1975, pp. 160–61; Tambiah 1984, p. 344) which has afflicted the Thai state since the overthrow of the absolute monarchy in 1932. By this Keyes and Tambiah mean that the overthrow of the absolute monarchy created a disjuncture between the state and the traditional interpretations of Buddhist doctrine and practice which had historically been referred to in justifying the monarchical political order of the pre-modern Thai kingdoms.

These scholars have also noted the ongoing quest among both *bhikkhu* and lay Buddhists in Thailand in this century to develop more appropriate forms of religious doctrine and practice capable of lending legitimacy to contemporary political processes (for example, see Butt [1975, p. 49]). However, previous analyses of the ongoing efforts to re-legitimize the Thai political order in Buddhist terms have tended to view the modern Thai state as a single, monolithic political unit and have not acknowledged the complex patterns of conflict between the various factional groupings of the élite which now vie for political and economic dominance in Thailand. The Thai state in the final decades of the twentieth century is no longer the unitary political structure which existed under the absolute monarchy in the nineteenth century or under totalitarian military regimes in previous decades during this century. Rather, recent Thai politics has been dominated by factional conflicts between, on the one hand, the traditional holders of power — the aristocracy and the civilian and military bureaucracies — and, on the other hand, the increasingly influential groups of business interests and reformist-minded middle-class professionals and intellectuals.

The present writer has argued elsewhere that the intellectual and organizational history of Thai Buddhism in the past century should, by and large, be understood in terms of the political and economic history of Thailand during this period (Jackson 1989). In particular, the ultimate provenance of the major disputes about Buddhist doctrine and the administration of the *sangha* in the past one hundred years in Thailand has lain in the conflicts between the various competing factions of the Thai political and economic élite. The relationships between the Buddhist *sangha* and the secular organs of state power in Thailand are so intimate and numerous that Thai Buddhism could not avoid being shaken by the waves of political agitation and struggle which have emanated from Bangkok in this century. Conflicts within Thai Buddhism do not mirror all the minutiae of Thai political life. However, the dominant debates about Buddhist practice, organization, and doctrine, both within the *sangha* and among the laity, do demonstrate a responsiveness to, and a keen awareness of, the major political issues of the day by the participants in these debates. Indeed, political issues have provided the driving force for changes within the *sangha* in the past century, for there is a markedly consistent relationship between the political positions of Thai political actors and the interpretations of Buddhist teaching and practice that such actors support, to the extent that one can speak of a nexus between political and religious beliefs in Thailand (ibid., pp. 40–61).

As the patterns of political conflict have altered over the decades, so too have the dominant doctrinal debates and arguments about the proper role of the *sangha* in contemporary Thailand. In the years following the overthrow of the absolute monarchy in 1932, conflicts between royalist and anti-royalist factions had their parallel within the *sangha* organization in conflicts between the Thammayut and Mahanikay orders of monks. However, since the mid-1970s debates about Thai politics have been dominated by liberal critiques of military authoritarianism, and the response of political conservatives to these critiques. Here the terms *traditionalist* and *reformist* are used to refer to the generally integrated systems of political and religious beliefs professed by these competing conservative and liberal political factions.

In broad terms the traditionalists support centralized political structures which are often patterned after the historical model of the absolute monarchy. In the religious domain these political conservatives tend to support more traditional, metaphysical formulations of Buddhist doctrine which emphasize the determinative influence of *kamma* and religious merit and demerit on human well-being and socio-economic status. In previous centuries such formulations of Buddhism were used to lend legitimacy to the absolute monarchy.[1] In contrast, liberal reformists tend to be drawn from the middle class and from professional groupings, and support more participative or democratic political structures. In terms of religious doctrine, political reformists support more rationalist or demythologized interpretations of Buddhist teachings which de-emphasize the significance of the doctrine of *kamma* and instead emphasize the capacity of individuals to attain their own religious and, by implication, political liberation.[2]

The rationalist formulations of Buddhism supported by reformist Thai also emphasize the importance of the individual attainment of *nibbana*. There is a close theoretical relationship between the two aspects of the reformists' dual emphasis on the attainment of personal salvation and the development of participatory political forms, for both place individuals in an active role, able, at least in theory, to determine their spiritual condition as well as their social and political environment. This view of human existence as the active determination of one's own destiny in accord with Buddhist ethical guidelines contrasts sharply with the traditional, conservative interpretation of human existence. In conservative interpretations of Buddhist teachings the individual members of the Thai polity are regarded as passive subjects or observers of their spiritual and political fates, accepting personal suffering and political disenfranchisement as the *kammic*-ly determined consequences of their immoral actions in previous existences.

The fundamental nature of the political and religious disagreements between traditionalist and reformist factions of the Thai political and economic élite in recent decades has meant that no single legitimatory structure, that is, no single formulation of Thai Buddhist doctrine and practice, has been capable of resolving the crisis of political legitimation faced in contemporary Thailand. The differing political visions and objectives of the competing traditionalist and reformist factions within the élite are so distinct as to require markedly different legitimatory religious systems. Indeed, in the 1980s political conflicts between these two main factions of the Thai political and economic élite manifested themselves, among other ways, in a competition for theoretical control over the interpretation of certain key religious symbols of political legitimacy.

Here is documented the continuing ideological significance of one particularly influential medieval Thai Buddhist text, the *Traiphuum Phra Ruang*, to contemporary Thai political debates and factional conflicts. The primary objective is to analyse the alternative interpretations which competing traditionalist and reformist political factions of the Thai political élite have attributed to this historically important Thai Buddhist text in this century. However, this analysis is also intended to counter the view that the *Traiphuum Phra Ruang* had no political or legitimatory significance in Thailand after the mid-nineteenth century, when Prince Mongkut, the future King Rama IV, initiated a rationalist re-evaluation of traditional Thai Buddhist teachings. Craig Reynolds has analysed the critical demythologization of metaphysical interpretations of Buddhist cosmography, such as traditionally ascribed to the *Traiphuum*, which was undertaken by Mongkut and other rationalist-inclined members of the Thai political and intellectual élite in the nineteenth century (C. Reynolds 1976, pp. 203–20). In concluding his analysis, Reynolds describes the *Traiphuum* as now being "a kind of relic" with only "a residual hold on the Siamese imagination" (ibid., p. 220). While Mongkut's rationalist critique of the *Traiphuum Phra Ruang* marked the end of the text's pre-eminent place in Thai intellectual life, this chapter aims to show that the *Traiphuum* has nevertheless continued to be referred to throughout the twentieth century in order to support a wide range of often conflicting political positions.

Despite the rationalist demythologization of the text in the nineteenth century, the symbolic associations of the *Traiphuum Phra Ruang* with the legitimate exercise of political authority in Thailand were never completely severed, and for this reason the *Traiphuum* has not faded from the Thai intellectual scene in this century. The lasting symbolic power of the *Traiphuum* has been such that conservative sections of the Thai élite have effectively ignored Mongkut's rationalist critique of the text in order to re-assert the primacy of the traditional Buddhist cosmography that it describes. In contrast, reformist sections of the Thai élite have attempted to evade the subversive impact of rationalist critiques on the legitimatory power of the *Traiphuum* by claiming that the true symbolic meaning of the text is in fact consistent with the rationalist view of Buddhism that they support. By arguing for a metaphorical interpretation of the *Traiphuum*, reformists attempt to draw on the rich symbolic legacy of the text to lend legitimacy to their democratic and socialist visions of Thailand's social and political future. These respective conservative and rationalist approaches to the *Traiphuum* in the twentieth century have represented much more than a mere scholarly debate about approaches to textual exegesis. The competing interpretations of the *Traiphuum* put forward by various ideologues in this century have all reflected fundamental political conflicts within the élite groups of Thai society and have demonstrated the continuing political significance of Buddhist symbology in general, and of the *Traiphuum Phra Ruang* in particular, in contemporary Thailand. However, before tracing the various politically influenced interpretations ascribed to the text in this century, the history of the

Traiphuum Phra Ruang is briefly recounted and its political significance in pre-modern Thailand is described.

History of the *Traiphuum Phra Ruang*

The text which is now called the *Traiphuum (Traibhumi) Phra Ruang* (The three worlds cosmography of Phra Ruang) is generally regarded by Thai scholars as having been composed in AD 1345[3] by Lithai,[4] then *uparaja* ("second king") of Srisatchanalai, the second most important urban centre of the early Thai kingdom of Sukhothai.[5] According to popular Thai history, Lithai succeeded his father, Lelithai, as the fourth king of the Phra Ruang dynasty of Sukhothai in *c*. AD 1346, ruling until his death in *c*. AD 1374.[6]

In the *Traiphuum* Lithai describes the conditions and characteristics of those beings which inhabit the various realms of the Buddhist universe. This universe consists of eleven realms in the world of desire (*kamabhumi*), sixteen celestial realms in the world with only a remnant of material qualities (*rupabhumi*), and four higher celestial realms in the world without material qualities (*arupabhumi*). A being's birth in one or other of the thirty-one realms of the three worlds (*traibhumi*) is interpreted as being determined by its store of *kammic* merit (*bun*) or demerit (*paap*). Lithai's text concludes with a description of the Buddhist method of attaining salvation from the unsatisfactoriness of the cycle of birth, death, and rebirth, which involves liberation from the three worlds of phenomenal existence and the attainment of *nibbana*.

The major proportion of the contents of the *Traiphuum* can be described as metaphysical, dealing in considerable detail with the features of the thirty-one cosmic realms of rebirth and the types of actions which ordain humans to be born in one or other of these realms. However, the text also contains a large central portion dealing with the world of ordinary men and women and includes descriptions of the characteristics of a cosmic ruler, a *mahacakkavattiraja* ("The Great Wheel-Turning Monarch"), and his relations with his subjects. Furthermore, the final section of the *Traiphuum* deals with the attainment of final salvation or *nibbana*, which is a condition totally distinct from any of the thirty-one realms. Thai rationalists emphasize the sociological and soteriological sections of the text and attempt to distil meanings with contemporary relevance from these sections while effectively ignoring the long descriptions of the thirty-one cosmic realms. By contrast, religious conservatives maintain that the *Traiphuum*'s long discourses on the thirty-one realms demonstrate the importance of *kamma* and of merit and demerit in determining individual and collective human well-being.

The oldest surviving version of the *Traiphuum* was inscribed by a monk, Phra Maha Chuay, in a ten-volume palm leaf manuscript in AD 1778 during the reign of King Taksin. The source or sources from which the Phra Maha Chuay version was compiled are not known as no complete copy of the text is believed to have survived the Myanmar sacking of the former Thai capital of Ayutthaya in 1767. The Thai historian Somphong Chaulaem states that the Phra Maha Chuay version was apparently lost or hidden after the death of Taksin, for in 1783 King Rama I directed a group of monks to compile yet another version of the *Traiphuum* (Somphong 1985, p. 1). This subsequent text is known as the Phra Maha Jan version, after the principal compiler. However, when he reviewed the resulting text some nineteen years later in 1802, King Rama I found it to be inconsistent and stylistically uneven, and ordered that it be rewritten. The resulting revised text is now known by the title of the *Traiphuumlokawinnitchai* (Pali: *Traibhumilokavinicchaya*). This text appears to have been the only version of the *Traiphuum* known to Thai scholars such as Mongkut throughout the nineteenth century.

The older Phra Maha Chuay version of the *Traiphuum* was brought to light early this century when Prince Damrong directed that large numbers of old manuscripts be collected from provincial monastery libraries and stored for safe keeping in the then newly established National Library. The Phra Maha Chuay version is now regarded as the most authoritative version of the text and it was this version that Prince Damrong chose to publish in 1912, when the first printed version of the *Traiphuum Phra Ruang* was published in Thailand.[7]

Political Function of the *Traiphuum* in Pre-Modern Thailand

The political function of the *Traiphuum Phra Ruang* in modern Thailand is based on a long political history for the text and, indeed, a number of analysts regard the motivation underlying the original composition of the *Traiphuum* to have been fundamentally political. Frank Reynolds suggests that Lithai wrote the *Traiphuum* in order to assist in attaining a number of immediate political objectives related to his succession to the throne of Sukhothai and the re-establishment of central Sukhothai authority over nearby principalities (Reynolds and Reynolds 1982, p. 10).

The political intention underlying the composition of the *Traiphuum* is indicated by a number of explicit references as well as by the general structure and tenor of the text. For example, Lithai gives a central place to the notion of the *mahacakkavattiraja* or universal monarch in the *Traiphuum*, and suggests that the teachings of a universal monarch are equivalent to the teachings of a fully realized Buddha. In a review of the history of Thai political thought, Sombat Jantharawong and Chai-anan Samudavanija note that Lithai portrays the *mahacakkavattiraja*, with whom he compares himself,[8]

> as being like a representative of the Lord Buddha in this world when a Buddha is not present, "If in any *kalpa* [cosmic epoch] there is no self-enlightened Buddha [*sammasambuddha*] or *paccekabuddha* then there is a Phraya Mahajakraphat [*mahacakkavattiraja*] instead".
> (Sombat and Chai-anan 1980, p. 100)

Sombat and Chai-anan maintain that by this association of the monarch with the Buddha, Lithai attempted to lend religious authority and legitimacy to his rule. They note that the socio-political aspects of the *Traiphuum* indicate "the close relationship between being a person who knows the *dhamma* and being a [political] administrator in the traditional Thai political order" (ibid., p. 93). On this point the literary analyst Somphorn Mantasuut has commented that

> Lithai's true intention was to instruct the people of Sukhothai in ethics so that they would abide by the *dhamma* and make the state peaceful and prosperous . . . and this was for the political benefit of the government of that time, because if the people were well-established in ethics, fearful of sinning and not daring to do wrong, problems such as robbery, assault and other problems of crime would be lessened or may not even arise. This would have the result of permitting the government of the country to proceed smoothly.
> (Somphorn 1981, pp. 29–30)

The *Traiphuum* continued to be an important text for Thai rulers long after Lithai's particular political concerns had been forgotten. The enduring significance of the *Traiphuum* to the Thai state flowed from its capacity to be interpreted to reflect the political interests of the rulers of the day. Buddhist cosmological conceptions, which constitute a major part of the contents of the *Traiphuum*, played a central role in the political organization of pre-modern Thai kingdoms. The socio-political orders of the Thai kingdoms of the Sukhothai, Ayutthaya, Thonburi, and early Bangkok periods were self-consciously modelled on the cosmic Buddhist order described in the *Traiphuum*. In these kingdoms the structure of the Buddhist cosmos, in particular, its hierarchical, merit-determined order, was reproduced at the level of human social and political organization. Even the physical layouts of the capitals of the pre-modern Thai kingdoms were grounded in religious beliefs manifested in the *Traiphuum* (Kirsch 1975, p. 55).

The continuing socio-political importance of the *Traiphuum* in Thailand up until the early Bangkok period is shown by the fact that King Rama I gave priority to the compilation of a new version of the text when consolidating his power after the turmoil and disarray surrounding the destruction of Ayutthaya in 1767 and the overthrow and execution of King Taksin in 1782. However, C. Reynolds notes that no Thai king after Rama I commissioned a new recension of the *Traiphuum*. He attributes this to the fact that in the middle of the nineteenth century the metaphysical cosmography described in the text came under increasing attack (C. Reynolds 1976, p. 203). From the 1830s the influence of Western ideas on science and cosmology and the establishment of the reformist Thammayut monastic movement by Prince Mongkut combined to force a new awareness of Thailand's cultural and intellectual traditions on many educated Thai. Many educated Thai in the second half of the nineteenth century came to regard supernaturalism and traditional Buddhist metaphysics, including the cosmography described in the *Traiphuum*, as representing obstacles in coming to terms with the empirically derived and naturalistic systems of knowledge introduced by Westerners. In 1851 one Western observer in Bangkok, John Taylor Jones, noted that the *Traiphuum*'s cosmographical descriptions were "frequently denied by many of the shrewder Buddhists in Siam" (ibid., p. 214).

But while in certain Thai circles, belief in the metaphysical aspects of the *Traiphuum* was shaken by the impact of Western ideas, there nevertheless were attempts to retain and re-assert the value of the ethical teachings contained in the text. For example, in his instructional text *Nangsyy Sadaeng Kitjaanukit* (A book explaining various things) King Mongkut's foreign minister, Jau Phraya Thiphakorawong (Kham Bunnak), criticized non-empirical explanations of natural phenomena, such as presented in the *Traiphuum*, as being unsustainable.[9]

Thiphakorawong nevertheless concluded that the *Traiphuum*'s teachings on the ethical aspects of Buddhism, that is, on matters such as *kamma*, merit, and rebirth remained valid and true. By this Thiphakorawong acted to retain the symbolic value of the *Traiphuum* by dissociating its socio-political significance from what by then were the increasingly discredited metaphysical aspects of the text, emphasizing instead Lithai's ethical teachings. By this he was able to retain some semblance of the text's original symbolic significance by focusing on the purely ethical justification for the socio-political order centred on the institution of the absolute monarchy.

The emphasis on a rational and ethical, as opposed to metaphysical, interpretation of Buddhism which was initiated by Mongkut and his followers represented an important shift in the political and theoretical function of Buddhist doctrine in Thailand. In Mongkut's view of Buddhism political legitimacy no longer flowed from the possession of sacred objects such as relics of the Buddha or spiritually empowered Buddha images, nor did it flow from the construction of an earthly parallel of the supposed structure of the cosmos. Instead, political legitimation flowed from the personal morality of individual monarchs and political leaders and from the spiritual status that they attained through ethical and/or meditative practice. Mongkut's ethical and rationalist interpretation of Buddhism created a divide between the traditional metaphysical interpretations of the religion's teachings and those views which were more influenced by scientific thinking. In the twentieth century reformist Thai thinkers have used the theoretical divide created by Mongkut to criticize religious conservatives, whom they describe as clinging to "superficial" and "external" shows of religiosity.

In the twentieth century movements across the political spectrum from pro-monarchists to radical socialists have acknowledged the continuing symbolic importance of the *Traiphuum* in lending legitimacy to political goals, activities, and systems in Thailand. All of these diverse groups have found the text too valuable to let questions of the literal validity or invalidity of its cosmographical contents override its long-established function of lending theoretical legitimacy to political structures and political aspirations. As a consequence, new interpretative strategies have been applied to the *Traiphuum* which aim to retain the political and symbolic potency of the text in spite of the debunking of the traditional Buddhist cosmography by rationalists and reformists. The two main interpretative strategies used in this century have been the development of selective and discriminating interpretations of certain parts of the text, which attempt to avoid the currently less acceptable metaphysical sections, and attempts to reinterpret the entire text in allegorical terms, rather than as a literal description of the actual structure of the cosmos.

While often employing similar interpretative strategies, competing political groups have nevertheless sought to ascribe their own interpretations to the text in order to support their particular political objectives. As already noted above, the *Traiphuum Phra Ruang* is a complex text, and by the selective emphasis and the careful management of interpretations of its contents it has been able to be used for a range of quite different and sometimes conflicting purposes in different periods during this century. There have been two main political strands to the analysis and interpretation of the *Traiphuum* in the twentieth century. The first has focused on the Utopian symbolism of the section of the text describing the fantastic land of Uttarakuru. The second and more important analytical emphasis in Thai studies of the *Traiphuum* has been concerned with revealing the underlying symbolic meaning of the text as a whole. This second analytical strand has also been associated with attempts to relate the symbolic meaning of the text purportedly revealed by such studies to an idealized interpretation of the historical significance of the political and cultural legacy of the early Thai kingdom of Sukhothai. These two analytical emphases are considered in turn below.

Uttarakuru: The Buddhist Utopia

Uttarakuru is the name of the northern continent (Uttarakurudvipa) in the *Traiphuum*'s mythological geography of Manussabhumi, the human realm. Lithai portrays the inhabitants of Uttarakuru as being the most moral, and their society as being the least degenerate and the least subject to corruption, of the four continents of the human realm.[10] According to Lithai:

> The Uttarakuru people are neither too short nor too tall, neither too fat nor too thin. They are beautiful and everything about them is suitable. . . . These Uttarakuru people have no worries, because they do not ever have to till the soil or exert themselves in commerce in order to earn their living. (Ibid., p. 127)

In this century the *Traiphuum*'s account of Uttarakuru has been interpreted by a number of Thai commentators as presenting a model of a Thai Buddhist Utopia. Comparison of Uttarakuru with Thomas More's *Utopia* dates at least from an article written in English by King Rama VI, Wachirawut, in 1912 entitled "Uttarakuru — An Asiatic Wonderland". This article opens with an explicit comparison of Lithai's account of Uttarakuru and More's description of Utopia. However, the purpose of this comparison was to ridicule the Thai socialist thought of the early years of this century by maintaining that it was as unrealistically idealistic as was More's mythical land of Utopia. The objective of this mockery of socialist ideas was to support the political status quo and the absolute monarchy. Commenting on Lithai's description of the people of Uttarakuru as not needing to work, Wachirawut wrote:

> What! The manual labourers should like that because we always hear that manual labourers wish to do the least possible work, but at the same time maintain that they are not a despised capitalist who has never known work. . . . We should realise that this world [Uttarakuru] is nothing new. (Somkiat 1983, p. 89)

Wachirawut's basic argument was that socialist ideas are neither new nor progressive, but rather had already been thought of in ancient times, as evidenced by the discussion of Uttarakuru contained in the *Traiphuum Phra Ruang*. However, Wachirawut maintains that just as the idea of Uttarakuru was idealistic nonsense at the time of the composition of the *Traiphuum*, and never existed in this human world of Jambudvipa, so too the socialist ideas of his day were equally impractical and of no value for this world. Somkiat Wanthana, a reformist academic, summarizes Wachirawut's use of the *Traiphuum* in order to support the monarchical political structure as follows:

> This piece severely attacked the democrats and socialists of the time and made derogatory insinuations about them throughout. . . . When ideas of democracy, republicanism and socialism fanned across Siam in the time of King Rama VI the *Traiphuum Phra Ruang* was used to revive the past and was given new life in the context of the new society. (Ibid., pp. 89–91)

Sulak Sivaraksa concurs, saying that the jingoistic nationalism of Rama VI's reign "in one sense was a return to the *Traiphuum Phra Ruang*" (Sulak 1989, p. 31) in terms of the traditional ideology of state control that he promoted.

The *Traiphuum*'s account of Uttarakuru was also called upon by a later generation of Thai political conservatives in the 1960s in order to bolster anti-socialist and anti-communist policies in Thailand. No original Thai language version of Wachirawut's article on Uttarakuru survives[11] and in 1965 Krommamyyn Bidhyalabh translated the original English language article into Thai. In the introduction to this translation Bidhyalabh, then head of the Privy Council and a staunch supporter of the anti-communist policies of Thai military governments in the 1960s, wrote:

> The article which His Majesty composed at that time, containing decisive and refreshing language, in fact criticised leftist ideology as a whole, because at that time [Thai] socialism had not yet split off clearly from the ideology which bred Communist thought. Now we can see clearly that the points which are criticised in this article refer directly to communism, and it is appropriate to re-print it now in order to show [His Majesty's] far sighted wisdom. (Krommamyyn Bidyalabh 1974, pp. 345–46)

This statement by Krommamyyn Bidyalabh explicitly relates his translation of Wachirawut's article on Uttarakuru to the anti-communist policies of Prime Minister Sarit Thanarat and his successor, Thanom Kittikachorn. That is, the imagery of the *Traiphuum Phra Ruang* retained sufficient currency and emotive force in the mid-1960s to be called upon to lend support to the anti-communist policies of the military governments of the time.

However, while conservative Thai have read Lithai's account of Uttarakuru as debunking socialist ideas, Thai supportive of socialism have interpreted the comparison of Uttarakuru to More's *Utopia* in radically different terms. Some Thai socialists have attached importance to the socialist ideals which they regard as having been expressed in the section of the *Traiphuum* dealing with Uttarakuru. These Thai socialists have valued Lithai's account of Uttarakuru because of what they read as its presentation of the possibility of an alternative social order. Sittha Phinitphuwadon comments on the symbolic significance of Uttarakuru for Thai socialists as follows:

> Socialists in Thailand since the time of King Rama VI have regarded the land of Uttarakuru as a land of socialism, because the described characteristics of Uttarakuru emphasised the point that wealth was

centrally owned. No one accumulated wealth, cultivated the land or engaged in trade for their personal benefit. This centralised method of allocating wealth was based on the *kapparukkha* [Sanskrit: *kalpavrks'a*, or wish-giving] tree. Whoever wanted any kind of wealth came and took it from the *kapparukkha* tree, including jewels, silver, gold rings and precious stones to decorate their bodies. Every person had the right to collectively use the *kapparukkha* tree. The *kapparukkha* tree can be compared to the central national organisation of a socialist state which allocates the necessities of life to the people, who do not need to engage in buying or selling. (Sittha 1982, p. 143)

In another article Sittha has compared the notions of an ideal society found in the *Traiphuum*, in Thomas More's *Utopia*, and in the *Tao Te Ching* in order to express his views on the continuing social and political value in Thailand of Utopian ideas, such as are expressed in the *Traiphuum* (Sittha 1984, p. 95).

Contemporary Conservative Interpretations of the *Traiphuum*

Krommamyyn Bidyalabh's translation of Wachirawut's article on Uttarakuru in 1965 marked a resurgence of interest in the *Traiphuum* among Thai conservatives. This resurgence occurred after several decades of relative neglect of the text following the publication of Wachirawut's article in 1912 and Damrong's printing of the Phra Maha Chuay version of the *Traiphuum* in the same year. C. Reynolds has commented that the demythologization of the *Traiphuum* by sections of the ruling Thai élite in the second half of the nineteenth century divorced "the cosmography from contemporary monarchical symbolism" (C. Reynolds 1976, p. 218). However, since the late 1950s there have been a number of concerted attempts by political conservatives to re-establish the symbolic link between the *Traiphuum* and the exercise of political authority. Sarit Thanarat's rehabilitation of the Thai monarchy as a symbolic focus of his authoritarian military regime was also associated with a renewed emphasis on the traditional legitimatory symbols associated with the monarchy. As Tambiah has remarked:

> The soldiers who captured and exercised power simply replaced the authoritarian and hierarchical system of monarchical times with a structure that manifested the same or similar authoritarianism.

There is thus a continuity of political power, although continuity
of political legitimacy is problematic. (Tambiah 1975, p. 128)

Sarit and his immediate successors sought in part to resolve this
"crisis of legitimacy" by re-emphasizing the traditional political
integrative role of the monarchy and by symbolically associating their
regimes with the re-imputed legitimacy of the monarchy. A more
general emphasis on the achievements and ascribed significance of
Thailand's past and present monarchs has also become an important
part of the promotion of conservative definitions of Thai "identity"
(*eekalak*) and conservative political structures in the 1970s and 1980s. In
recent years there has been a concerted official effort to establish symbols
traditionally associated with the absolute monarchy and the élite culture
of pre-modern Thailand as an integral part of the definition of modern
Thailand's cultural and political "identity". The importance attached
to establishing this conservative definition of Thai identity is evidenced
by the setting up in the early 1980s of the Thai National Identity Office
(Samnak-ngaan Serm-saang Eekalak Khorng Chaat) within the Office
of the Prime Minister. The primary function of the Thai National Identity
Office appears to be to popularize traditional élite culture among the
general Thai populace and to present that élite culture as a national
treasure to be valued by all Thai of all social strata. Notwithstanding
the artistic, literary, and intellectual value of the traditional élite culture
of Thailand, its official promotion in the contemporary political context
simultaneously functions as a medium for reviving and sustaining
traditional patterns of respect for political authority. In recent decades
Thai military regimes and political parties aligned with or sympathetic
with the military have found the manipulation of the symbolism which
historically surrounded and supported the absolute monarchy to
provide a convenient legitimatory basis for the autocratic and
centralized exercise of political power.

The *Traiphuum*, one of the most important textual symbols of
legitimate political authority in pre-modern Thailand, has received
growing attention and interest from Thai conservatives in parallel with
the rehabilitation of the monarchy and the official promotion of
traditional élite culture. The recent resurgence of interest in the
Traiphuum in Thailand is shown by the fact that a revised version of the
text was commissioned in 1974 by the Director-General of the
Department of Fine Arts. This 1974 revision of the *Traiphuum* was the

first new recension of the text to have been prepared since King Rama I ordered the compilation of the *Traiphuumlokawinnitchai* in 1787.[12] The renewed interest in the *Traiphuum Phra Ruang* in recent decades reflects an effort to revive and re-establish the symbolic significance of the text so that it can continue to fulfil its legitimatory function in the contemporary political context. As a cultural product of the early Thai kingdom of Sukhothai, and as reputedly the oldest book written in the Thai language, the *Traiphuum* is ascribed the double authority of being associated with the historical sources of both the political identity and the Buddhist cultural identity of modern Thailand.

Recent conservative discussions of the *Traiphuum* have been characterized by a form of intellectual atavism in which the rationalist debunking of the text's metaphysical contents is all but ignored and the traditional ethical teachings founded on the doctrine of *kamma* are brought to the fore. Such conservative discussions tend to ignore the implications of the rationalist critique of the traditional Buddhist cosmography and involve selective readings of the *Traiphuum* which draw out sections and chapters of the text that appear to support the institution of the monarchy and traditional patterns of respect for authority. The approach of contemporary Thai conservatives to the *Traiphuum* was clearly expressed at a conference on the text organized by the Department of Fine Arts in December 1983 as part of the government-sponsored celebrations of the 700th anniversary of the development of the Thai script by King Ramkhamhaeng, the grandfather of Lithai. The primary emphasis of the papers given at this conference was on the continued relevance of the ethical teachings of the *Traiphuum Phra Ruang* to contemporary Thai life and institutions — including politics, government administration, religion, philosophy, and art. The interpretations of the *Traiphuum* presented at this conference emphasized the importance of the text to the officially sanctioned interpretation of Thai identity, to efforts to support traditional institutional arrangements and to "national security".

The conservative tenor of the interpretations of the *Traiphuum Phra Ruang* presented at this conference is typified by the comments of one speaker, Associate Professor Sangiam Sawatdikaan, who presented the contents of the *Traiphuum* in their traditional metaphysical formulation, which, as already noted, emphasizes the role of *kamma* in determining the place of individuals in the Thai social order. Sangiam states that the *Traiphuum Phra Ruang* shows us what will result from doing good and doing bad, as well as the results which can be achieved by cleansing the mind [of evil]. . . . Lithai divides the realms of existence according to the good and bad actions and the *vipaka* [*kammic* consequences] which lead one to be born in one realm or another. . . . In summary, Lithai shows that [the meaning of the *Traiphuum*] is the law of *kamma*, which cannot be evaded because it is the law of reason — when there is a cause there will be a result. (Krom Silpakorn, *Sarup Phon Kaan-samanaa Ryang Traiphuum Phra Ruang*, 1984, p. 205)

Sangiam interprets the *Traiphuum* at face value. He presents the traditional metaphysical view of the teaching of *kamma* and implies belief in the literal reality of the various realms of suffering and pleasure described in the *Traiphuum*. Sangiam's presentation demonstrates the extent to which the *Traiphuum* continues to be interpreted by members of the political establishment and their ideological supporters in ways which re-inforce traditional Thai ethical and political patterns.

Contemporary Reformist Interpretations of the *Traiphuum*

However, the re-attribution of traditional metaphysical interpretations to the *Traiphuum* by conservatives has not gone unchallenged. Since the mid-1970s, and particularly since the beginning of the 1980s, reformist Thai have developed their own rationalist interpretations of the text as part of a broader effort to counter conservative, officially supported images of Thai identity and to subvert conservative uses of Buddhist symbolism. In contrast to conservatives, Thai reformists have sought to redefine the traditional religious and political symbolism of the *Traiphuum* in ways that purge it of authoritarian associations, and re-orient this symbolism towards the nurturing of a progressive approach to socio-economic development and the revelation of an indigenous political basis for democracy in Thailand. This resurgence of interest in the *Traiphuum* by reformist thinkers is historically quite recent and reflects the greater self-confidence of oppositional thinkers in Thailand since 1973, when a broad popular movement forced the dictatorial clique of Prime Minister Thanom Kittikachorn to flee the country.

In considering the recent resurgence of interest in the *Traiphuum* it is important to distinguish attempts by political conservatives to resuscitate the text because of its assumed support for the institution of the monarchy from reformist attempts to re-interpret the *Traiphuum*'s symbolism in order to develop a justification for a reformed social and political order. Particular care must be exercised because both conservative and reformist analysts of the *Traiphuum* claim to find teachings of lasting value and guidelines for the present in the pages of the text. That is, the two groups of politically opposed analysts differ not so much in their general attitudes on the contemporary relevance of the text but rather in the social values and political objectives which they ascribe to Lithai's writings.

F. Reynolds has argued that the traditional Buddhist conception of hierarchical cosmic and social orders in which religious merit (*bun*) determines the socio-religious position of the individual still provides the implicit ideological framework upon which Thai society and Thai politics function (F. Reynolds 1975a, p. 105). I would qualify Reynolds' position by specifying that the traditional Buddhist metaphysic provides the implicit ideological framework upon which conservative Thai politics still functions. Reformist political theorists explicitly reject both the metaphysical formulations of Buddhism and the politically centralized and hierarchical social order which those formulations have historically been used to legitimate.[13]

In sharp contrast with the conservative idealization of the monarchy, reformist Thai regard the symbolism of the absolute monarchy as having unacceptable associations with political authoritarianism and military dictatorship. They maintain that the introduction of more participative and democratic political structures is essential for Thailand's further social, economic, and political development. Throughout the 1980s a number of reformist Thai theorists, through their re-interpretation of Thailand's political and cultural history and the symbolic significance of key Buddhist texts, have attempted to subvert the conservative manipulation of the symbolism of the Thai monarchy. They have attempted to transfer the *baramii* or charisma of legitimate power traditionally ascribed to the king to a democratically elected government. Reformists have attempted to effect this transfer of charisma by emphasizing references in the canonical Buddhist scriptures to kingship as an institution founded upon the election of a wise and capable leader by the populace at large.[14] Underlying such analyses of accounts of elected kingship is an unstated argument that the modern Thai constitutional monarchy retains associations with the legitimate exercise of political authority only to the extent that it now becomes a symbol of the practical realization of the canonical Buddhist notion of a popularly elected leadership.

Reformist Buddhists reject literalist interpretations of the metaphysical aspects of the *Traiphuum*, which, at least to a superficial reading, appear to be the dominant theme of the text. This is because, given their commitment to alternative, democratic political structures, they seek to undermine the historical use of the *Traiphuum*'s cosmographical symbolism to support the traditional hierarchical Thai social order. Current discussions about the *Traiphuum* among reformist Thai intellectuals instead focus on the social and political context of the text and the assumed creative intention of its author, Lithai, which, it is claimed, was to present a Buddhist model for a just social order.

In addition to a general rationalist stance, reformist critiques of conservative interpretations of the *Traiphuum Phra Ruang* have two other important features. Firstly, in their analyses reformists idealize the political institutions and cultural products of Sukhothai as providing a true Buddhist model of a participative, liberal form of government. In contrast, reformists associate the conservative idealization of centralized forms of government modelled on the absolute monarchy with the purportedly corrupting impact of Khmer Brahmanism on the society, religion, and politics of the Ayutthaya and early Bangkok periods. Secondly, reformist critiques of conservative interpretations of the *Traiphuum* tend to maintain that the core scriptures of Thai Buddhism, in which some include the *Traiphuum*, were composed in symbolic language which requires careful exegesis to be correctly understood. This methodological approach is linked with the eulogization of Sukhothai and the denigration of Ayutthaya to construct an argument that literal interpretations of accounts of heaven, hell, and other metaphysical notions described in the *Traiphuum Phra Ruang* are the product of Brahmanical misconceptions dating from the Ayutthaya period. Reformists maintain that those influenced by such Brahmanical notions will fail to appreciate the true intention that Lithai had in writing the text, namely, to lead the individual reader towards the Buddhist salvation of *nibbana* and lead Thai society as a whole towards a state of justice and general welfare.

The origins of the modern idealization of Sukhothai society and culture and the rationalist symbolic interpretation of Thai Buddhist scriptures can both be traced to Mongkut and his reforms of the Thai *sangha* in the nineteenth century. F. Reynolds has commented on the value that Mongkut attached to symbols and relics of Sukhothai, noting that Mongkut established

> in the royal compound in Bangkok a stele on which the greatest ruler of the ancient and powerful Thai kingdom of Sukhothai [that is, Ramkhamhaeng] had set out a kind of charter for an ideal Thai state. (F. Reynolds 1975a, p. 103)

However, contemporary reformists have adapted this emphasis on the ideal characteristics of Sukhothai to support democratic institutions rather than the institution of the absolute monarchy, which underpinned Mongkut's interest in associating his reign with Sukhothai. It is interresting that in recent decades the rationalist and scripturalist religious trend initiated by Mongkut in the nineteenth century has been adapted by reformists to support their political demands for more democratic and liberal approaches to government, and that efforts to achieve religious reform and political reform are now closely related in modern Thailand.

Reformists regard the Sukhothai period as a golden age of Thai history which has fundamental ethical and political lessons for the present. Reformists also maintain that they uphold the true essence of "Thainess", an essence whose first historical manifestation they find recorded in that literature of the Sukhothai period which has survived. The reformist idealization of Sukhothai represents an attempt to develop an indigenous basis for Thai political and religious thought and Thai values which support democracy and social justice. Sulak summarizes the reformist view of Sukhothai as a model of a liberal, just Thai society as follows:

> The profound roots of Thai thought are clearly manifested in the first stone inscription of King Ramkhamhaeng of Sukhothai. . . . This inscription is like pure gold which expresses "Buddhist-ness" and "Thai-ness". . . . I consider it to be a proclamation of the political, economic and cultural trends which were associated with [Sukhothai] . . . and which emphasised liberty, equality and fraternity [seeriiphaap, samoephaak, phraadaraphaap]. (Sulak 1989, p. 26)

While reformists present Sukhothai as a model of religious purity and political justice, Ayutthaya is in contrast associated with the "erroneous" religious beliefs introduced by Khmer Brahmanism and with the autocratic and tyrannical forms of government that reformists regard as having been epitomized by the institution of the absolute monarchy. For example, the reformist monk Phra Phaisaan Wisaalai claims that the political authoritarianism of Thai governments after the Sukhothai period

> resulted from the establishment of Khmer Brahmanism in the [Thai] Royal Palace from the beginning of the Ayutthayan period and the acceptance of the belief that absolute authority based on harsh and strong punishments was necessary for government. . . .
>
> It can be said that the Sukhothai form of government (which was influenced by the [Buddhist] *dhammaraja* theory) was a government for the benefit and well-being of the people, but the Ayutthayan form of government (which accepted the [Brahmanical] *devaraja* theory) was a government for the power of the state. (Phra Phaisaan Wisaalai 1986, pp. 119–21)

Reformists have attempted to counter the conservative manipulation of the symbols of Buddhism and the monarchy to lend support to centralized and authoritarian political structures by maintaining that conservative political and religious thought has been infected by the Brahmanically influenced notion that the institution of the monarchy has divine origins or associations. For example, the reformist critic Krajaang Nanthapho has said:

> Buddhism is in contradiction with the principles of feudal or dictatorial and tyrannical government. However, in Thailand the feudal groups have long used Buddhism as a tool in governing and in protecting the power of their own group. . . . The feudal groups have at all times relied upon ritualistic expressions, which are but the outer coating of religion, to build up the people's belief in the feudal system of government of the group of the supposed *devaraja* [Brahmanical god-king]. (Krajaang 1985, pp. 254–55)

Reformist Thai Buddhists maintain that steadfast abidance by the true principles of Buddhism by political leaders is important for the maintenance of a just social and political order. It is a corollary of this belief that the Thai society which loses its way religiously will also lose its way politically. This argument underlies reformist attempts to discredit Ayutthayan and Ayutthayan-modelled religious and political forms as being polluted by Brahmanical influences. Buddhist reformists also use this same argument — that a just Thai society can only be constructed upon a pure Buddhist base — to explain the occurrence of "non-Buddhist" political authoritarianism in certain periods of Thai history. In particular, reformists maintain that Thai religion during the period of the absolute monarchy in Ayutthaya and Bangkok and during the military dictatorships in the twentieth century was polluted by Brahmanism. Those conservative sections of the Thai political and intellectual élite who today interpret the *Traiphuum* in literalist or "Ayutthayan" terms, and who support political notions and practices rooted in the authoritarian "Ayutthayan" tradition, are regarded as being "non-Buddhist" and so effectively "non-Thai" by the reformists.

Reformist criticisms of authoritarian Ayutthayan political structures and the Brahmanical beliefs regarded as underpinning them have a direct relevance to the present political situation in Thailand. This is because all the monarchs of the ruling Chakri dynasty from King Rama I to the present king have regarded the continuation of the traditions of Ayutthaya as an important basis of the modern Thai kingdom centred on Bangkok. The symbolic associations between Ayutthaya and the present dynasty have been apparent since the establishment of Bangkok as the new capital. For example, John Butt observes that the first monarch of the Bangkok dynasty, Rama I, was

> concerned throughout his reign to identify himself and his kingdom with the heritage of Ayutthia and to restore that kingdom's traditions to the Thai nation. It is significant that one of the royal titles bestowed on the new ruler at his first coronation in 1782 was Rama Tibodi, an appellation also given to the first king of Ayutthia. (Butt 1975, p. 41)

Butt also notes that the layout of Bangkok was modelled as far as possible after the former capital of Ayutthaya in order to impress visibly upon the populace the similarity between the two kingdoms (ibid., p. 42). Kirsch concurs on this point saying that in reconstructing the Thai socio-political order after the Myanmar destruction of Ayutthaya both Taksin and Rama I

> chose to precisely emulate the pattern of the traditional Ayutthayan social order, including the model of the Buddhist macrocosm provided by the *Traiphum*. (Kirsch 1975, p. 56)

In the contemporary Thai politico-legal context, in which the crime of *lèse-majesté* attracts severe penalties, it is not possible to openly criticize the monarchy, or for that matter the symbolic manipulation of the monarchy by political conservatives. In this context reformist criticisms of the supposedly negative characteristics of the Ayutthaya period in fact represent an attack upon the present Thai political establishment, which supports an Ayutthayan-modelled monarchy in order to legitimate its political position. The contemporary interpretation of symbols linked with Sukhothai and Ayutthaya therefore should not be read simply as scholarly attempts to construct or reconstruct Thai history. These interpretations also represent attempts to construct a symbolic legitimation of present political structures. At the level of theory the contemporary political and ideological conflict between reformist and traditionalist factions of the Thai élite is being waged in the form of a symbolic battle between the two extinct kingdoms of Sukhothai and Ayutthaya. The spirits of the long-dead kings of these two kingdoms are being invoked to engage in a battle whose modern combatants seek the right to determine the future form of the religious and political soul of the Thai nation in line with their respective competing political visions.

Reformist Re-Interpretations of the *Traiphuum*

Not all reformists, however, agree on the symbolic value of the *Traiphuum Phra Ruang*. Sulak, for example, maintains that the *Traiphuum*, despite being a literary product of the Sukhothai period, has closer associations with the political authoritarianism of the Ayutthaya period and so should be rejected by reformist Thai. Sulak has said:

> Afterwards [in the Ayutthaya period] the *Traiphuum Phra Ruang* almost completely obscured this fundamental current of [Sukhothai] thought [expressed in the Ramkhamhaeng inscription]. Even though the *Traiphuum* quotes the words of the Buddha and relates these to the ending of suffering in accord with Buddhist teachings, it nevertheless overemphasises *pubbekatapunnata* [reaping the benefits of meritorious deeds performed in a previous life]. It speaks too much about heaven and hell and places too much stress on teachings which encourage the people to be subordinate to the ruling class. Furthermore, it introduces supernatural [*saiyaasaat*] cosmological beliefs as if they were scientific.
>
> The impact of the thought expressed in the *Traiphuum* of Sukhothai was compounded by the fact that Ayutthaya accepted supernatural beliefs from Cambodia when we [Thai] repeatedly attacked the Cambodian capital. This led to a decline in the "Thainess" of our thought, a reduction in liberty and equality. (Sulak 1989, pp. 26–27)

However, other reformists, such as the prominent intellectual monk Phra Thepwethi,[15] disagree with those who repudiate the text because of its imputed Khmer Brahmanical influences and its associations with political authoritarianism, and have developed an alternative political analysis of the *Traiphuum*. Rather than simply rejecting the *Traiphuum*, Thepwethi attempts to interpret the text in symbolic terms as in fact presenting reformist ideals in a covert form. He criticizes not the *Traiphuum* itself but the methods of interpretation which have traditionally been applied to it and, by implication, those conservatives who have used these methodological approaches. This methodological critique achieves a similar political objective to the outright rejection of the *Traiphuum*, namely, the criticism of the use of Buddhist teachings and symbology to support authoritarian political structures. In other words, by applying a symbolic interpretation of the text, Thepwethi attempts to wrest theoretical control of the *Traiphuum*, and its rich symbolic associations with the supposed roots of Thai Buddhist identity, from those conservative groups which have historically used the text to support their own socio-political positions. He attempts to redirect the legitimatory power ascribed to the *Traiphuum* from bolstering authoritarianism and monarchism to supporting democratic political structures.

In his study of the *Traiphuum Phra Ruang*, Thepwethi emphasizes the individual soteriological and ethical aspects of the text rather than its cosmographical descriptions. He re-interprets the *Traiphuum* in terms of the activist outlook of contemporary Buddhist reformists and maintains that the text does not, as conservatives maintain, teach that *kamma* determines all of human existence. Rather, he argues that the text in fact teaches about the need to transcend worldly fetters and to attain the ultimate spiritual salvation or *nibbana*. Thepwethi says that even though the text is called the *Traiphuum* (The three worlds), its true objective is in fact a fourth realm, *lokuttara* or the transcendence of the three worlds of phenomenal existence. Thepwethi claims that Lithai's intention in writing the *Traiphuum* was to show a way out of the suffering of phenomenal or worldly existence in the three *lokiyabhumi*:

> I wish to emphasise the significant point that the fact that Lithai speaks of *lokuttarabhumi* shows that the objective of his text, the *Traiphuum*, was to lead the reader or the person who listened to its teachings to see . . . the harm [*dosa*] of the three [worldly] *bhumi* in

order to liberate them from those three *bhumi* and so attain the fourth
bhumi, namely, *lokuttarabhumi*. (Ratchaworamuni 1984, p. 8)

Indeed, Thepwethi says that he regards the proper name of the
Traiphuum Phra Ruang to be "The Traibhumi and Liberation from the
Traibhumi (into Lokuttarabhumi)" (ibid., p. 52). Thepwethi maintains
that the Buddhist notion of *kamma* denotes the possibility of liberative
action which leads one out of the strictures of social classes and castes.
He says that Buddhism does not emphasize the enslaving aspect of
action but rather the liberative potential of understanding the relations
between cause and effect mediated by intentional action (ibid., pp. 11–
12). Thepwethi contends that

> the line of explanation [in the *Traiphuum*] leads us to see that Lithai
> intended people to consider their good and bad actions which will
> lead them to meeting with good and bad consequences in the future.
> He did not intend pointing out evil actions in the past so that people
> accept either their own or others' present situation. (Ibid., p. 37)

Thepwethi says that traditionalists interpret the *Traiphuum* statically,
as a description of how things came to be the way they are, while he
interprets it dynamically, as indicating a process of liberation from the
present order of things. He also criticizes the version of the *Traiphuum*
which was commissioned by the first monarch of the Bangkok dynasty,
implying that this version was infected by Brahmanical beliefs. He
maintains that the *Traiphuumlokawinnitchai* compiled in the reign of King
Rama I does not have the same emphasis on individual salvation and
the attainment of *nibbana* as the older Phra Maha Chuay text compiled
in the reign of Taksin. Thepwethi praises the *Traiphuum* of Phra Maha
Chuay as being a more truly Buddhist document. In contrast, he asks
of the *Traiphuumlokawinnitchai*, "Could it be that at that time [of the
composition of the *Traiphuumlokawinnitchai*] thought of this goal [that
is, *nibbana*] had already become dim?" (ibid., p. 23). Rather than
reflecting the truths of Buddhism, Thepwethi maintains that the
Traiphuumlokawinnitchai commissioned by King Rama I "is a reflection
of thought and belief about the *Traiphuum* which had been in a static
condition . . . for a long time" (ibid., p. 24). That is, Thepwethi criticizes
the Ayutthaya-influenced political élite of the early Bangkok period,
and those contemporary conservatives who model their political ideals
on the élite on that period, for having become distracted from the true
goal of Buddhism.

While Thepwethi maintains that the objective of the *Traiphuum* is to lead the reader or listener towards *nibbana*, he says that Lithai's line of approach in the text was to begin by speaking of the more immediately comprehensible matters of *kamma* and the fruits of actions (*vipaka*). He is critical of those who concentrate on these superficial aspects of the text and who fail to appreciate what he regards to be the original spiritual intention underlying its composition. Thepwethi says:

> We have now forgotten that [original intention]. People nowadays have become narrower [in their understanding of Buddhism] than in the past [era of Lithai]. Now we speak only of heaven, but people in the past also spoke of *nibbana*, and this point should be noted well. (Ibid., p. 22)

Another analyst, the academic Suthiwong Phongphaibun, has also ascribed a reformist interpretation to the *Traiphuum*. Like Thepwethi, Suthiwong claims that the *Traiphuum* was written in a symbolic form which, when deciphered, reveals the true intention of the author as being to lead the reader to ultimate salvation:

> The *Traiphuum Phra Ruang* was written in a style which used symbols. . . . That is, it used a method of taking one thing to stand for a line of thought, which enables an intelligent and capable person to interpret it very broadly. . . . This style of writing can be regarded as having been very far ahead of its time. (Suthiwong 1983, p. 123)

Suthiwong attempts to appropriate the *Traiphuum* for the reformist Buddhist movement by claiming that, contrary to traditional literalist readings of the text which interpret it as referring to metaphysical phenomena, it is in fact a text which supports a modernist and rationalist Buddhist world-view.

In their criticisms of traditional metaphysical readings of the *Traiphuum*, Suthiwong and Thepwethi also attempt to counter conservative interpretations of the *Traiphuum* which are used to sanction a monarchically modelled social order and political authoritarianism. Thepwethi, in particular, extracts elements of what he interprets as a compassionate, Buddhist social policy from the *Traiphuum*. One section of the text dealing with the virtues of the *cakkavattiraja* or universal Buddhist monarch describes the ideal ruler as teaching that no living being should be killed pointlessly, and that no matter how evil a person's deeds he should be instructed in the *dhamma* and should not be executed for his crimes. Thepwethi comments that "this point shows that King

Lithai did not support execution as a form of punishment" (Ratcha-woramuni 1984, p. 32). However, he adds that

> afterwards in the Ayutthaya period this principle [of compassion and leniency in the punishment of wrongdoers] was changed because of the influence of Brahmanism, which has a system of meting out severe and violent punishments. . . . We can see that in subsequent periods in Thailand [that is, the Ayutthaya and Bangkok periods] the ruling circles also resorted to increasingly severe punishments. Could it be that this principle came from Hinduism, especially given that that religion developed [its influence] in the Ayutthaya period? (Ibid., p. 44)

According to Thepwethi's reformist analysis of Thai political and religious history, Brahmanical influences on Thai society and government have led to tyranny. Furthermore, according to this view of Thai history, if a just form of government is to be realized in Thailand, true Buddhism, that is, a radically doctrinal or rationalist interpretation of Buddhist teachings, must be supported and promoted.

Thepwethi reveals the political motivation underlying his analysis of the *Traiphuum Phra Ruang* when he expands on Lithai's text by noting Jataka stories which maintain that if a monarch causes difficulties for his subjects and fails to uphold the *dasarajadhamma*, the ethical principles appropriate for a king, the people should rise up and protest, forcing the monarch to reconsider his actions and edicts. Thepwethi maintains that this scriptural reference can be regarded as

> an origin of the contemporary idea of demonstrating. This comes from the period of the Jatakas, and the Jatakas cite a large number of instances of [the people] demonstrating in this way. This is the Buddhist system of government. (Ibid., p. 45)

In other words, Thepwethi maintains that Buddhism condones popular unrest against an unjust ruler. He also observes that the primary political emphasis of the *Traiphuum Phra Ruang* is on the responsibility of the state to the people, rather than of the people to the state, which has been the predominant ideological emphasis in Thailand's recent political history:

> Apart from the severe consequences of doing wrong to one's parents, to a *samanabrahmacariya* and to a monk upholding the moral precepts, and to old people, which have already been mentioned many times [above], the *Traiphuum Phra Ruang* also emphasises

the severe consequences of the evil actions of rulers, or of public officials who oppress and exploit the people or govern unjustly. (No mention is made of the responsibility of the ruled to their rulers.) (Ibid., p. 37)

Reformist Criticisms of the *Traiphuum*

Nevertheless, despite the not insignificant theoretical and re-interpretative efforts of reformist thinkers such as Thepwethi, there are limits to the extent to which the *Traiphuum* can be interpreted as lending support to modernist views of Buddhist doctrine and to a liberal, democratic political order. Even those involved in efforts to revive and sustain the ancient symbolic power of the text admit that their interpretative strategies may ultimately fail. Reformist analysts of the *Traiphuum*, such as Thepwethi and Suthiwong, do countenance the possibility of a not-too-distant end to the centuries-long legitimatory function of the text, and they also refer to the consequent need to find a religious text which can replace the *Traiphuum* and provide a Buddhist basis for contemporary Thai society and government.

It is noteworthy that in developing his interpretation of the teachings of the *Traiphuum* Thepwethi emphasizes the comparatively shorter section of the text dealing with the attainment of *nibbana* rather than the much longer sections dealing with the suffering experienced by those beings living in the various Buddhist hells and the joys experienced by those beings inhabiting the various heavens. Thepwethi's is thus a selective reading arrived at by emphasizing specific aspects of the text. However, given the large amount of space that Lithai devoted to descriptions of the retributions of hell and the rewards of heaven in the original text, it would appear difficult not to regard such matters as having been prominent in the author's mind at the time he compiled the text. This is particularly so given the almost incalculable aeons over which Lithai maintains that heaven is enjoyed and over which hell is suffered. Suthiwong makes just such a criticism of the *Traiphuum* in his concluding remarks on the text. Suthiwong agrees that the *Traiphuum Phra Ruang* contains true Buddhist teachings about salvation and *nibbana*. However, he criticizes the presentation of materials in the *Traiphuum*, saying that Lithai's attempt to convey Buddhist teachings in symbolic form was not successful because the symbols became so complicated and involved as to obscure the original underlying ideas:

> The final result was that the core [of spiritual ideas] was swamped and disappeared under the superficial coating [of material symbols]. For example, when Lithai refers to *narakabhumi* [hell] he explains it thoroughly and in detail . . . complete with numerals and examples piled upon examples. In the end the reader or listener becomes lost, remembering only the numbers and the examples and unable to return to the core [idea of *nibbana*]. Lithai explains in great detail that beings which are born in Sanghatanaraka [hell] remain there for 2,000 years. In Sanghatanaraka one day and one night is equivalent to 145,000,000 human years. . . . When he explains in such detail the unthinking reader will believe it all and his thought will remain stuck at the level of the numbers and names of the hells. He will forget to translate and interpret the symbols in terms of *dhamma* [that is, symbolic] language.[16] Thus Lithai conveyed only the numbers and the belief in hell as a legacy for his descendants. This indicates the failure of the *Traiphuum Phra Ruang* to lead Buddhists to the higher *dhamma*. (Suthiwong 1983, p. 124)

Suthiwong concludes that "this book can consequently be regarded as an obstacle to propagating the *dhamma* in a form which can lead people to the highest truth" (ibid., p. 125). Suthiwong maintains that the *Traiphuum* does indeed contain Buddhist truths about salvation hidden within its complex symbolism, truths which are acceptable to contemporary reformist Buddhists. However, he criticizes Lithai for failing to successfully convey these truths. It should be noted, however, that this is not a criticism of the meaning or literary intention underlying the *Traiphuum* but rather of Lithai's literary method. It is a criticism of the failure of the text to achieve what is interpreted to be the author's true goal of attempting to convey Buddhist truths. Thus, Suthiwong's criticism does not represent a debunking of the ascribed literary intention of the author, which is lauded and retained, but rather of Lithai's symbolic literary style, which is rejected.

Despite his broad support for the teachings of the *Traiphuum Phra Ruang*, as he has interpreted them, Thepwethi also criticizes Lithai for having placed too much emphasis on the severe consequences of evil actions instead of the positive consequences of good actions. He maintains that if Lithai had given greater emphasis to analysing good actions, such as showing

> the good consequences of assisting people, being established in justice and fairness, etc., then [the *Traiphuum*] may have been able to become a forerunner or prototype for the wider development of more constructive and positive thought and action in the succeeding centuries. (Ratchaworamuni 1984, p. 38)

Because of this inadequacy in the *Traiphuum*, Thepwethi concludes his analysis by suggesting that the text may need to be replaced by a Buddhist analysis which is more appropriate for contemporary Thai society:

> Even if society is changing markedly the principle of salvation [taught in] the *Traiphuum* . . . can still be an appropriate ideal and ideology for Thai society. [The *Traiphuum*] can be used as a trail blazer in correctly developing Thai society in accord with *dhamma*. But it may have to be revised and the obscuring factors may have to be removed so that it can be clearly understood. If for one or other reason the old version of the *Traiphuum*, which has been prepared from commentaries and post-canonical texts, proves inappropriate for the contemporary situation we may also have to consider the possibility of developing a book similar to the *Traiphuum* as a new text which is able to lead the thought of contemporary people today. (Ibid., p. 57)

In this statement Thepwethi gives further insight into the reasons for the resurgent interest in the *Traiphuum* in Thailand today, namely, the need to develop new sources of legitimating Buddhist authority in the contemporary Thai social order. This need has led traditionalists and reformists alike to return to traditional sources of religio-political authority in an attempt to adapt them to contemporary purposes. However, Thepwethi points out that such ancient texts as the *Traiphuum* may not be able to be successfully adapted to meet contemporary needs and he raises the possibility of developing the equivalent of a new Thai Buddhist gospel capable of meeting the need for new sources of religious and political legitimacy in Thailand today. Thepwethi proposes that the *Traiphuum* may have to be superseded by a more amenable contemporary medium for the original intention that he regards as having underlain the foundation of the Thai state. Significantly, Thepwethi's own definitive study of Buddhist doctrine, the thousand-plus page *opus Phutthatham* (Phra Ratchaworamuni 1984*a*), is in the process of becoming a new Buddhist gospel for many progressive Buddhists. *Phutthatham* is a scholarly work with the potential of becoming a modern *Visuddhimagga*,[17] a new standard text on Buddhist doctrine among Thai intellectuals. In his above statement Thepwethi perhaps reveals the motivation which underlay the writing of his great scholarly effort.

Concluding Comments

C. Reynolds' description of the *Traiphuum* as a relic is apt, for the text can be compared to a revered religious relic whose antiquity only enhances its contemporary value and significance. The *Traiphuum* is certainly not merely an antiquity empty of meaning for modern Thai. The rationalist debunkings of the metaphysical contents of the text in the nineteenth century did not mark the end of the political history of the *Traiphuum*. Ideologues aligned with the conservative political establishment in Thailand, by their evasion of the rationalist critiques and their support for traditional readings of the text, demonstrate that in Thailand political might is still capable of overriding considerations of mere logic or reason. In contrast, the metaphysical contents of the *Traiphuum* are now largely irrelevant to the message being attributed to the text by religious and political reformists. For these groups the *Traiphuum* now exists primarily as a symbol, however imperfect, of the purported formative intention of the founders of the first Thai kingdom to create a just Buddhist state. The contemporary symbolic value of the *Traiphuum* for reformists lies not so much in its contents but rather in its simple existence as a reminder of the hope that Lithai purportedly had for a perfect Buddhist social order. The *Traiphuum* is taken as revealing the hidden and long-lost political essence and the true meaning of being Thai, which reformists maintain was distorted and lost in the Ayutthaya and early Bangkok periods. This is the truth that the historical roots and the true nature of being Thai is to be democratic, and that political authoritarianism, whether of an absolute monarch in past periods or of a military dictator in recent decades, represents a perversion of the true essence of being Thai.

NOTES

* A shorter version of this paper was presented at a Conference entitled "Thailand: Aspects of Identity, 1939–89" held at the Centre of South East Asian Studies at Monash University, Melbourne, on 8–9 September 1989. That shorter version was published in the papers of that conference under the heading "Thai Buddhist Identity: Debates on the *Traiphuum Phra Ruang*", in C. Reynolds, ed. (1991).

1. Contemporary metaphysical formulations of Thai Buddhist doctrine are revealed clearly in the teachings of such conservative monks as Phra Kittiwuttho and such conservative Buddhist movements as the Wat Phra Thammakaay sect. See, for example, Phra Udornkhanaphirak (Kittiwuttho) Bhikkhu (1986) and Phra Thattachiwo Bhikkhu (1987).

2. Two of the most prominent reformist Thai Buddhist thinkers are Phra Phutthathat (Buddhadasa) Bhikkhu, and Phra Thepwethi Bhikkhu, formerly, Phra Ratchaworamuni. See Phutthathat (1978), Phutthathat (1981), and Phra Ratchaworamuni (1984).

3. The Thai historian Wannau Yuuden maintains that, given the limited archaeological and literary information currently available, the composition of the text cannot be precisely dated. Wannau suggests that the *Traiphuum* was composed some time between AD 1347 and AD 1376 (Wannau 1984, p. 30).

4. In contrast with popular Thai historiography, Michael Vickery has attributed the *Traiphuum* to Lithai's successor and grandson, Sai Lithai (Vickery 1974, pp. 275–84).

5. In this article the Thai term *Traiphuum* is used to refer to the text ascribed to Lithai, and the Sanskrit term *traibhumi* is used to refer to the notion of the three worlds which constitute the Buddhist universe, namely, *kamabhumi* (the realm of sensual desire), *rupabhumi* (the realm with a remnant of material factors), and *arupabhumi* (the realm without material factors).

6. Wannau dates Lithai's reign as AD 1354–76 (Wannau 1984, p. 30).

7. The *Traiphuum Phra Ruang* was first printed in Thailand as a cremation volume for the funerals of Phra Ong Jau Prasansrisai and Phra Ong Jau Praphaisrisa-at in 1912.

8. Note that Lithai's formal title upon coronation was Mahadhammaraja, Great King of the Dhamma.

9. (Jau Phraya) Thiphakorawong Mahakosathibodi (1971). Note that *Nangsyy Sadaeng Kitjaanukit* was first published in 1867.

10. The other three continents of the human realm are Jambudvipa, the present world inhabited by men and women, Pubbavidehadvipa, the eastern continent, and Aparagoyanadvipa, the southern continent (Reynolds and Reynolds, trans. 1982, p. 10).

11. Wachirawut's article was originally published in 1912 in English in the *Siam Observer* (Somkiat 1983, p. 87).

12. Phithun Maliwan, head of the editorial committee, prepared the revised and emended version of the *Traiphuum* by comparing three versions of the text, the Phra Maha Chuay version written in 1778, the Phra Maha Jan version written in 1787 at the direction of King Rama I, and another incomplete manuscript thought to date from the late Ayutthaya period (*Traiphuumikatha Ryy Traiphuum Phra Ruang*, 1983, introduction).

13. See Jackson (1988, pp. 96–102). Nevertheless, there are certain fundamental religious conceptions shared by both traditionalists and reformists and which inform the political conceptions of both factions. As Tambiah has observed, "There is a deeply entrenched Buddhist conception of political sovereignty and righteousness as the ordinating principle in society, a conception of political ethics and morality which acts as an enduring yardstick by which to measure political performance and as an inspiring but not wrought-in-detail ideal to which political aspirations of different complexions can equally refer themselves" (Tambiah 1975, p. 123). It is this notion of righteous sovereignty, variously interpreted by conservative and reformist political theorists, which constitutes the common ideological basis of all Buddhist participants in the Thai political system.

14. Somboon Suksamran, a political scientist, traces the origins of the Buddhist theory of popularly elected leadership to the *Aganna Sutta* in the canonical Theravada scriptures (Somboon 1984, p. 19).

15. Phra Thepwethi (Prayut Payuttho) formerly held the clerical title of Ratchaworamuni, and this is the name that appears on most of his earlier publications, including that referred to in this chapter.

16. Suthiwong adopts the symbolic method of interpreting the Buddhist scriptures in terms of *"dhamma* language" developed by the reformist monk Phutthathat (Buddhadasa) (Buddhadasa 1974).

17. The *Visuddhimagga*, written by Buddhaghosacariya in the fifth century of the Christian era, has been the most influential summative interpretation of Buddhist doctrine in Theravada countries for many centuries.

REFERENCES

Buddhadasa. *Two Kinds of Language*. Translated by Ariyananda Bhikkhu. Bangkok: n.p., 1974.

Butt, John W. "Thai Kingship and Religious Reform (18th–19th Centuries)". In *Religion and Legitimation of Power in Thailand, Laos and Burma*, edited by Bardwell L. Smith. Chambersburg, PA: Anima Books, 1975.

Jackson, Peter A. *Buddhadasa: A Buddhist Thinker for the Modern World*. Bangkok: Siam Society, 1988.

_____. *Buddhism, Legitimation and Conflict: The Political Functions of Urban Thai Buddhism*. Singapore: Institute of Southeast Asian Studies, 1989.

_____. "Thai Buddhist Identity: Debates on the *Traiphuum Phra Ruang*". In *National Identity and Its Defenders in Thailand, 1939–1989*, edited by Craig Reynolds. Monash Papers on Southeast Asia no. 25. Melbourne: Centre of Southeast Asian Studies, Monash University, 1991.

Keyes, Charles F. "Political Crisis and Militant Buddhism in Contemporary Thailand". In *Religion and Legitimation of Power in Thailand, Laos and Burma*, edited by Bardwell L. Smith. Chambersburg, PA: Anima Books, 1975.

Kirsch, Thomas. "Modernising Implications of Nineteenth Century Reforms of the Thai Sangha". In *Religion and Legitimation of Power in Thailand, Laos and Burma*, edited by Bardwell L. Smith. Chambersburg, PA: Anima Books, 1975.

Krajaang Nanthapho. *Mahanikay — Thammayut: Khwaam-khat-yaeng Phaay-nai Khorng Khana Song Thai* [Mahanikay — Thammayut: the internal contradictions of the Thai *sangha*]. Nonthaburi: Samnak-phim Santitham, 2528 [1985].

Krom Silpakorn. *Sarup Phon Kaan-samanaa Ryang Traiphuum Phra Ruang* [Summary of the proceedings of a conference on the *Traiphuum Phra Ruang*]. Bangkok: Department of Fine Arts, 2527 [1984].

Krommamyyn Bidhyalabh. *Chum-num Phra Niphon Khorng Phra Worawongthoe Krommamyyn Phitthayalap Phrytiyakorn* [Collected writings of Krommamyyn Bidhyalabh]. Cremation volume distributed at the funeral of Krommamyyn Bidhyalabh at Wat Thepsirin, Bangkok, 15 December 2517 [1974].

Ling, Trevor. *The Buddha — Buddhist Civilisation in India and Ceylon*. Harmondsworth, England: Penguin Books, 1976.

(Phra) Phaisaan Wisaalai. *Phutthasaasanaa Kap Khun-khaa Ruam Samay* [Buddhism and contemporary values]. Bangkok: Muunnithi Koomon Khiimthorng, 2529 [1986].

Phutthathat. *Thamma Nai Thaana Latthi Kaan-myang* [*Dhamma* as a political ideology]. Bangkok: Samnak Nangsyy Thammabuuchaa, 2521 [1978].

————. *Nipphaan* [*Nibbana*]. Bangkok: Samnak Nangsyy Thamma-buuchaa, 2524 [1981].

(Phra) Ratchaworamuni. *Phutthatham — Chabap Prap-prung Lae Khayaay-khwaam* [Buddhadhamma — emended and expanded version]. Bangkok: Thammasathaan Chulalongkorn University, 2525 [1984*a*].

————. *Khaa-niyom Baep Phut* [Buddhist values]. Bangkok: Samnak-phim Thianwan, 2527 [1984*b*].

Reynolds, Craig. "Buddhist Cosmography in Thai History — With Special Reference to Nineteenth Century Culture Change". *Journal of Asian Studies* 35, no. 2 (February 1976): 203-20.

Reynolds, Craig, ed. *National Identity and Its Defenders in Thailand, 1939–1989*. Monash Papers on Southeast Asia no. 25. Melbourne: Centre of Southeast Asian Studies, Monash University, 1991.

Reynolds, Frank E. "Sacral Kingship and National Development in the Case of Thailand". In *Religion and Legitimation of Power in Thailand, Laos and Burma*, edited by Bardwell L. Smith. Chambersburg, PA: Anima Books, 1975*a*.

————. "The Holy Emerald Jewel: Some Aspects of Buddhist Symbolism and Political Legitimation in Thailand and Laos". In *Religion and Legitimation of Power in Thailand, Laos and Burma*, edited by Bardwell L. Smith. Chambersburg, PA: Anima Books, 1975*b*.

Reynolds, Frank and Mani Reynolds, trans. *The Three Worlds According to King Ruang — A Buddhist Cosmology*. Berkeley Buddhist Series no. 4. Berkeley: University of California, Berkeley, 1982.

Sittha Phinitphuwadon. *Wannakam Sukhothai* [Sukhothai literature]. Bangkok: Thai Watthana Phanit, 2525 [1982].

————. "Kaan-syksaa Priap-thiap Naew-khit Kiaw-kap Sangkhom Udomkhati Nai Wannakhadi Ryang Traiphuum Phra Ruang Yuutopia Lae Tau Tek Keng" [A comparative study of the thought about an ideal society in the *Traiphuum Phra Ruang, Utopia,* and the *Tao Te Ching*]. *Kasetsart Journal of Social Sciences* 5, no. 2 (July–December 2527 [1984]).

Sombat Jantharawong and Chai-anan Samudavanija. *Khwaam-khit Thaang Kaan-myang Lae Sangkhom Thai* [Thai political and social thought]. Thammasaat University, Research Document no. 6. Bangkok: Thai Khadi Institute, 2523 [1980].

Somboon Suksamran. *Phutthasaasanaa Kap Kaan-pliang-plaeng Thaang Kaan-myang Lae Sangkhom* [Buddhism and political and social change]. Bangkok: Chulalongkorn University Press, 2527 [1984].

Somkiat Wanthana. "Traiphuum Phra Ruang — Din Korn Diaw Nai Din-daen" [The *Traiphuum Phra Ruang* — A single piece of earth in the land]. In *Traiphuum Phra Ruang — Itthiphon Tor Sangkhom Thai* [The *Traiphuum Phra Ruang* — its influence on Thai society], edited by Phra Ratchaworamuni. Reprint. Bangkok: Chum-num Syksaa Phutthasaat Lae Prapheenii Mahawitthayalay Thammasaat, 2526 [1983].

Somphong Chaulaem. *Traiphuumikatha — Chabap Khooy Yang Chua* [Traibhumikatha — improved version]. Bangkok: Suan Aksorn Sakhaburi, n.d. (*c.* 1985).

Somphorn Mantasuut. *Wannakam Sangkhom Lae Kaan-myang* [Social and political literature]. Bangkok: Samnak-phim Odeon Store, 2524 [1981].

Sulak Sivaraksa. *Naew-khit Thaang Pratyaa Thai* [Thai philosophical thought]. Bangkok: Khana-kammakaan Saasanaa Phya Kaan-phatthanaa, 2532 [1989].

Suthiwong Phongphaibun. "Traiphuum Phra Ruang Kap Khwaam-chya Lae Prapheenii Thaang Phutthasaasanaa" [The *Traiphuum Phra Ruang* and Buddhist beliefs and customs]. In *Phutthasaat* [Buddhist teachings]. Bangkok: Thai Watthana Phanit, 2526 [1983].

Tambiah, Stanley J. "*Sangha* and Polity in Modern Thailand: An Overview". In *Religion and Legitimation of Power in Thailand, Laos and Burma*, edited by Bardwell L. Smith. Chambersburg, PA: Anima Books, 1975.

_____. *The Buddhist Saints of the Forest and the Cult of Amulets: A Study in Charisma, Hagiography, Sectarianism and Millenial Buddhism*. Cambridge: Cambridge University Press, 1984.

(Phra) Thattachiwo Bhikkhu. *Luang Phor Torp Panhaa* [Luang Phor responds to problems]. Pathumthani: Muunnithi Thammakaay, 2530 [1987].

(Jau Phraya) Thiphakorawong Mahakosathibodi. *Nangsyy Sadaeng Kitjaanukit* [A book explaining various things]. Bangkok: Ongkaan Khaa Khorng Khurusaphaa, 2514 [1971].

Traiphuumikatha Ryy Traiphuum Phra Ruang — *Phra Raatchaniphon Phra Mahathammaratcha Thii 1 Phraya Lithai, Chabap Truat Sorp Chamra Mai* [The *Traibhumikatha* or *Traiphuum Phra Ruang* — a royal composition of Phra Mahadhammaraja the First, Phraya Lithai, revised and emended version]. Bangkok: Krom Silpakorn, 2526 [1983].

(Phra) Udornkhanaphirak (Kittiwuttho) Bhikkhu. *Ryang Phra Sayamthewathirat* [About Phra Sayamthewathirat]. Bangkok: Saphaa Sangkhom Songkhror Haeng Pratheet Thai, 2529 [1986].

Vickery, Michael. "Note on the Date of the Traibhumikatha". *Journal of the Siam Society* 62, no. 2 (July 1974): 275–84.

Wannau Yuuden. *Prawat Wannakhadii Samay Sukhothai Lae Ayutthaya* [The history of the literature of Sukhothai and Ayutthaya periods]. Bangkok: Thai Watthana Phanit, 2527 [1984].

Buddhism, Political Authority, and Legitimacy in Thailand and Cambodia

SOMBOON SUKSAMRAN

Introduction

In Southeast Asia, Buddhism and Islam and the values associated with (moulded by) these religious traditions both influence and are influenced by the political processes and socio-political changes in the region. It is also evident that the interaction between religion (the processes of) and socio-political change has both negative and positive aspects. On the one hand, socio-political changes may tend to weaken religious values and practices. This has been the case particularly in those countries where socio-political changes have taken place so abruptly that the traditional socio-economic and political structures were destroyed and replaced by structures which were ideologically hostile to religion. On the other hand, where socio-political change does not involve revolutionary change and the old structures and religious values remain intact, religious values and norms can illuminate and clarify the objectives of planned social change.

In the Buddhist countries of Southeast Asia, Buddhism and its associated values constitute the core of traditional culture. For centuries,

Buddhism has acted as an integrative force in assuring the survival of Buddhist societies in Southeast Asia (for the functions of religion as integrative and social forces, see Durkheim [1971], Malinowski [1954], and Weber [1985]). It has also permeated the life of the nations of Buddhist countries in Southeast Asia, leaving its distinctive mark on social, cultural, and individual activity.

It can be said, therefore, that Buddhism has long served as one of the main socializing, acculturating, and unifying forces in certain Southeast Asian societies. It has profoundly influenced the cultural, economic, and political development of Buddhist nations, and continues to mould the social and political values of a great majority of the people. In other words, Buddhism may be seen in many cases as the root from which national identity and the political and social heritage grow (Mendelson 1975, 1963; Smith 1965; Von der Mehden 1963; Phadnis 1976; Somboon 1977, 1982).

Buddhist Ethics and the Buddhist Community

Buddhism as an ethic consists of two components: the *dhamma* and the *vinaya*. Both *dhamma* and *vinaya* constitute, in fact, the main body of the teachings of the Buddha, which deal with the well-being of the Buddhist community, including both spiritual and material welfare. The *dhamma* deals with ideas, doctrines, and principles which apply to both monks and lay people while the *vinaya* consists mainly of the rules of life for the monks. These two components of Buddhist teachings signify the concern of the Buddha for the improvement of the conditions of human life, both spiritual and material. It would be a grave mistake to view Buddhism as being concerned only with personal salvation, the spiritual life, and as lacking doctrinal guidelines dealing with worldly life. Buddhism is far from a form of escapism, and in fact has significant ties and involvement with almost every kind of social movement (Phra Rajavaramuni 1983).

The Buddhist community consists of the four assemblies of monks, nuns, lay male devotees, and lay female devotees. While there are general rules and regulations laid down by the Buddha and intended to be guidelines of thought and conduct for the Buddhist community, the Buddha also recognized that there would be differences in the structure, function, responsibilities, and the nature of each component of the Buddhist community, and therefore he prescribed specific *dhamma* and *vinaya* for each group. For example, the community of monks, the *sangha*, is expected to follow 227 rules of conduct, while the laity is expected to follow a minimum of five precepts. There are different forms of teachings and different ethical prescriptions to be followed by lay people of different social status and levels of understanding. For example, the ruler and the ruling class are expected to keep steadfast to the Ten Royal Virtues (*dasarajadhamma*) and other elements of the *dhamma* for righteous rule, while the ruled are encouraged to follow certain *dhamma*, or rules of personal and interpersonal conduct.

Despite these structural and functional differences, the different parts of the Buddhist community are interdependent. This inter-dependence has assumed the form of reciprocal and interlocking relationships within the state: that is, the king, the *sangha*, and the people. The state, represented by the ruler, upholds Buddhism by providing support and protection for the *sangha* and, in effect acts as a law enforcement officer with regard to the monastic code of discipline, the *vinaya*. The *sangha*, in co-operation with the ruler and sometimes advising him, provides a symbol of morality, integrity, and legitimacy for the state. In their relationship with the people, *sangha* members act as teachers, religious guides, and mentors, and provide the model of moral conduct which the people regard as an ideal to be striven for, even though they themselves might not always attain it. For their part, the people give material support in the form of daily offerings of food, material for housing, clothing, and medicine. The ruler's role *vis-à-vis* his subjects is that of law maker and administrator and also of defender against external attacks; the people in return observe the laws of the realm and contribute to defraying the expenses of the state (Ling 1973).

Thus, the teachings of the Buddha were intended to achieve harmony within the Buddhist society. Such harmony would be realized when the members of the society kept steadfast to the principal teachings of the Buddha, both the *dhamma* and the *vinaya*. The *dhamma* focuses on the domain of legislation, regulation, and social organization. The *dhamma* is regarded as "natural" law in the sense that it acts directly on the development process and the perfection of the individual. The *vinaya*, on the other hand, is man-made law, laid down for the good of a Buddhist society. The rules and regulations are based on the general ideas and principles enunciated by the Buddha (Phra Rajvaramuni 1983). What follows here is intended to illustrate and illuminate the political and social ideal of the Buddhist society.

The Buddhist Concept of Political Authority

In Buddhist scripture, political authority is viewed as having been established because of the imperfections of man and the need for social order. This view of things is best understood if one examines the myths of creation. In the beginning, the world evolved as a part of the universe. From fire came solids, liquids, and gases, which became the earth, the moon and sun, the planetary system, and stellar constellations. Plant and animal life evolved, and over time became increasingly differentiated. Eventually, human beings became differentiated from other animals, and fed on rice. They then became stronger, and differences in physical type appeared. At this stage, fragrant and clear-grained rice in unlimited supply was available in open spaces and became communal property. Every human being enjoyed as much of it as his body required. Some males and females became interested in sexual intercourse beyond the natural level required for reproduction; they developed in themselves passion and lust, which were considered unnatural and immoral. These immoral persons were expelled from the existing settlements; they lived in separate huts to conceal their immorality, but were allowed to share in communal property. Then there appeared another type of greedy persons: those who collected and hoarded rice. As passion, lust, immorality, and greed increased, rice ceased to grow spontaneously, and this situation gradually degenerated. Men then divided rice fields among themselves as private property, and created boundaries. Disputes over property arose; men proceeded to steal each other's plots, and there was censure, lying, and punishment.

As men became increasingly immoral and greedy for private possessions, conflict, violence, and disorder grew. This led men to gather to discuss how their lives should be regulated in order to ensure survival. They then agreed that they needed a "certain being" who would give order to society, who would censure that which should be censured, and who would banish those who deserved to be banished. They also agreed to select the most handsome, best favoured, most attractive, and most capable from among them; and they invited him to be their ruler and to regulate their society. In return, the ruler was given a share of the rice produced by the people.

The ruler was called Mahasammata (the Great Elect) because he was chosen by the majority, of high birth (Pali: *Khattiya*), and the Lord of the Field because he protected the people's fields; and Raja (ruler) because he was righteous and guided by the *dhamma*.[1] The political ruler since then was generally embodied in kingship.

In this manner, the Buddhist concept of political authority suggests that kingship was established because of the imperfections of man and the need for social order. In Buddhist scripture the need for a king is emphasized to maintain order. The relationship between the king and his subjects is described as follows: the king has reached his exalted position because he accumulated a great deal of merit during his former lives, and this entitled him to the kingship. "Otherwise he could not have been born a king" (*Samyutta Nikaya*, vol. 1, p. 93). He governed the kingdom and reigned over the people and was endowed by them with authority to reprove, rebuke, punish, or destroy anyone who transgressed a royal command (*Milindapanha*, p. 226). He was the receiver and enjoyer of taxes submitted by the people (*Anguttara Nikaya*, vol. III, p. 45). He was their source of happiness and paternal protector (*Digha Nikaya*, vol. 3, pp. 93, 97). He was the upholder of the *dhamma* through which he watched over and protected his subjects (*Anguttara Nikaya*, vol. I, p. 109; vol. III, p. 149). The king was also endowed with five qualities: physical strength, material strength, the strength of officials, the strength of nobility, and the strength of wisdom (*Jataka*, vol. IV, p. 120).

With regard to the subjects, it was held that they needed the king for protection and that they went to the king for honour and security and esteemed him and obeyed him without challenge (ibid., vol. IV, p. 269). It followed that a person who cared for his life should refrain from despising the king, and should conduct himself properly towards him (*Samyutta Nikaya*, vol. I, p. 96).

Thus, Buddhist kingship was based on the concept of righteousness. To maintain his political authority and to regulate state affairs for the benefit of the kingdom and hence to reaffirm and enhance his authority, the king had to be a righteous ruler, the *dhamma raja*. Thus, the *dhamma* is of universal relevance, applicable as much to individual conduct as to the principles of government (Woodward 1933, pp. 114–15).

Since the *raison d'être* of the king was to uphold order, he should not act arbitrarily; he also had to be circumspect in his judgement and decisions, and be wary of favouritism, malice, delusion, or fear (*chanda, dosa, moha, bhaya*). He should also constantly observe the Ten Royal Virtues (*Dasarajadhamma*) (Phra Rajavaramuni 1975, pp.

206–8, 216–18; Siddhi 1973, pp. 149–50).

Thus, the morality and righteousness of the ruler (*dhamma raja*) were closely related to the prosperity of his kingdom and the physical and mental well-being of his subjects. The king's conduct and his action had far-reaching consequences since they affected not only his own kingship but also the fortunes of the subjects who were almost entirely dependent on him. We are told that

> when the kings are not righteous, neither are princes, brahmins, and householders, townsfolk and villagers. This being so, the moon and the sun deviate from their courses, as to constellations and stars day and night . . . months, seasons and years; the winds blow wrongly . . . the god (of rain) does not pour down showers of rain, the crops ripen in the wrong season; thus men who live on such crops have short lives and look weak and sickly. Conversely, when the kings, the rulers, are righteous, the reverse consequences follow. (*Anguttara*, vol. II, p. 74, cited in Siddhi 1973)

This conception of Buddhist kingship appears to suggest that the king is not only the ruler but also the mediator and regulator of social order. So if he acted unrighteously, he would bring disaster on his subjects; a king who did not adhere to the *dhamma* and who failed to observe the Ten Royal Virtues would lead his kingdom to ruin. He would no longer be a worthy king and the people would dethrone or kill him (*Majihima Nikaya*, vol. II, p. 88, cited in Siddhi 1973).

Rulers of Buddhist kingdoms in South Asia absorbed the concept of the ideal ruler, the *dhamma raja*, as part of their own traditions. They accepted that the maintenance of their power rested on adherence to the *dhamma raja*, and that the maintenance of their power rested on adherence to the *dhamma*, and that it was necessary for them to keep the *dhamma* alive by supporting the *sangha*, which perpetuated and disseminated the *dhamma*. By patronizing and supervising the *sangha*, the ruler preserved the *dhamma*, and ensured that his duty as a righteous king would be fulfilled. Knowledge of the teachings of the Buddha should not be allowed to die, for with it would die the norms against which the ruler's conduct could be judged.

It would require a lengthy discussion to explain why Theravada Buddhism had such great appeal to the rulers of the newly emerging kingdoms of Southeast Asia, where it was adopted as their national religion. However, Trevor Ling suggests that Theravada Buddhism was attractive to the rulers of these kingdoms because it possessed a number of valuable features:

> First, it has what seemed to them a sophisticated system of psychology and ethics — sophisticated, that is to say, by comparison with the indigenous spirit-cults and debased Indian priestcraft which had until then constituted the spiritual powers of the religion. Secondly, the professional carriers of this form of Buddhism were non-priestly. They did not claim to command supernatural forces nor were they likely to invoke supernatural sanctions. They relied on the good-will of people, the attractiveness of their philosophy and the uprightness of their philosophy and the uprightness of their own conduct. What they did seek, beyond these advantages, was the protection and support, which the kings could afford them and their way of life. For their part, kings were by no means unwilling to guarantee such support, once they came to see the potential value of this cult of the Buddha. (Ling 1977, pp. x–xi)

Ling further points out that from the point of view of the ruler, Theravada Buddhism was attractive as a socio-political system which provided the people with a perspective within which each human existence could be seen as the working out of moral gain and loss in previous existences, a scale of moral values in which equanimity, peacefulness, and generosity rated low. It also embodied an organization of voluntary teachers and moral preceptors (the *sangha*) whose main concerns were strictly non-political and who would be economically supported by the people, but were also prepared to co-operate with the ruler and advise him on religious and social matters in return for his guaranteeing them a virtual monopoly as the spiritual and religious professionals of the kingdom (ibid.). The relationship between the kings and the *sangha* was reciprocal. The king desired the co-operation of the *sangha* because he saw that this would provide his kingdom with moral legitimation and considerably assist in matters of social control. At the same time, the *sangha* sought to secure the king's adherence to Buddhist values, for this would guarantee his support. Thus, it is possible that these two interests more or less coincided: an ideology which needed a supportive political power met a political ruler looking for a legitimizing ideology.

Religion and Political Legitimacy

One of the foremost concerns of the ruling élite in a political system is the acquisition of political legitimacy. Political legitimacy refers to particular combinations of rights which are embodied in authority and political institutions, and which enable the ruler and the political regime to be acceptable to the ruled. Legitimacy is related to a set of conceptions held by significant members of the polity about the rightness of a political pattern, which, in turn, provides the pattern with a set of properties. Legitimacy is thus often determined by the goal of the polity (Apter 1969, pp. 42–43; for more variations of legitimacy, see Beer [1962, pp. 21–22]). Failure to achieve such a goal is thus prejudicial to authority. When legitimacy is withdrawn, government is weakened. A political system or a regime acquires legitimacy when the belief becomes widespread that its political institutions and procedures are right and proper for the society and that its decisions should be accepted and rules obeyed as a matter of moral obligation. It is therefore imperative for a political élite in power to strive to maximize legitimacy since it permits the élite to achieve their goal and maintain their power without resort to *coercive* power, so that such power can be reserved for possible major crises in the future.

Legitimacy, according to David E. Apter, may be derived from two possible sources, that is, consummatory and instrumental values. Consummatory values are based on a particular set of moral principles. The traditions and religions of given societies are the sources from which moral principles grow. These may be expressed in the form of a political ideology, an integrated set of cultural norms that are widely dispersed in the population, or contradictory sets held by mutually antagonistic groups. Instrumental values refer to the capacity of a government or political system to deal effectively with political, economic, and social problems, and to make provisions for the future well-being of society (Apter 1969, pp. 236–340).

While instrumental values indicate the efficiency of the government in responding to and fostering the material well-being of the people, consummatory values signify group solidarity and identity. Group solidarity provides the members of the group with shared feelings that give them a sense of mutual responsibility. Identity means the defined sense of worth of individuals and insight into the character of their relations with one another. In this sense, groups will regard a political system as legitimate or illegitimate according to the way in which its values fit in with their primary values (Lipset 1959, pp. 86–87). Throughout Southeast Asia religious values rank high, possibly highest, among the primary values of the masses. In a Buddhist country the close association of Buddhism with the political system would therefore appear to constitute an invaluable means of maximizing legitimacy. This had been the case in traditional governments in Thailand, Laos, and Cambodia.

Before the intrusion of Western ideas and Western power in the nineteenth century, absolute monarchy was a traditional form of government in these Buddhist countries. The ideal ruler was either an agent of a god or a *dhamma raja*, and the ideological basis of the state was provided by religious ideas. Buddhism and its *sangha* were strongly supported and regulated by royal authority. The relationship between kingship and Buddhism in the early Buddhist kingdoms may be largely deduced from myth. According to the *Tamnan*, the Buddhist kings of India, Myanmar, Sri Lanka, Cambodia, and Thailand are linked together as if they were in the same dynasty, that is, the dynasty of Buddhist kings. They succeeded one another as the upholders of Buddhism, their ties going back to the Buddha himself, the creator of a common tradition to which all the kings belonged. All these kings appear to have been religious men ascending to the throne as a result of merit derived from their acts as supporters and protectors of the faith. Their kingdoms were prosperous and progressive, and their positions were secure as long as they were religious and righteous (Charnvit 1977, pp. 8–11, 52–60; Jaywickrama 1968; Phraya Prachakitkornchak 1964; *Taman Munlasasana*, n.d.; *Tamnan Prakat Muang Nakhonsithammarat*, 1962).

Buddhism and the Legitimation of Power: The Historical Perspective in Thailand

It has been suggested in the preceding discussion that Buddhism not only provided the state with the ideological basis and political legitimacy but it could also be used to facilitate government and to maximize the legitimacy of traditional government. Thailand has provided the best example of a political nexus between Buddhism and traditional political rulers. The interaction between Buddhism and political rulers in Thailand is taken as a case of reference because first, since the formation of the Thai state in Sukhothai, Theravada Buddhism has uninterruptedly been the dominant religion of a great majority of its people. Second, unlike Laos and Cambodia, Thailand has not experienced the impact of colonial rule on its religion; thus its traditional mode of government has continued for many centuries. Third, it has been indicated that in the history of Cambodia it was not until the fourteenth century that Theravada Buddhism became a prominent religion of the country. Prior to this period Hinduism and local cults provided the dominant types of belief and the cultural system upon which ideology of state and mode of government were based (Coedes 1968, part II, chaps. 2, 3; part III, chap. 2). Buddhism was from time to time introduced to the society but was not recognized as having significantly influenced the form of Khmer government. Finally, Laos, throughout its history has been remarkably close to northeastern Thailand politically, ethnically, and culturally. Lao nationalism was not known before the colonization of the French, although Laos had for many centuries been politically and administratively a part of Thailand (Cady 1964, chap. 1), and the political mobilization of Buddhism for political ends can be recognized and observed only from the 1940s.

Buddhism and Kingship at Sukhothai

The Sukhothai polity has been described as paternalist. The king was regarded as the father of the people to whom respect was paid and in whom the people had faith (for the character of the Sukhothai polity, see Damrong [1959] and Griswold and Prasert [1968, 1971, 1972, 1973]).

The paternalism of Sukhothai found reinforcement in certain Buddhist values. For example, the Buddhist principle, regulating the social relationship between parents and children delineates the rights and duties of the two parties. Here, respect, gratitude, obedience, and love towards parents are strongly emphasized. Parents are advised to care for their children by expressing their parental love for them, by restraining them from doing evil deeds and exhorting them to do good (Siddhi 1973, pp. 95–100). The notion that the *dhamma* was the supreme code for regulating the entire social order, and therefore a moral guide for government also was espoused by King Ramkhamhaeng (and his successor). King Ramkhamhaeng, for example, was said to have believed that

> if society is morally sound and the people have a high spirit by keeping steadfast to Buddhism and adhering to Dhamma, the kingdom will be tranquil and prosperous. (Kriangsak 1969, p. 152)

To demonstrate their righteous rule and to provide a norm for the whole society, the kings of Sukhothai took a leading role in religious activities, promoting, and protecting Buddhism, and in patronizing the *sangha*. King Ramkhamhaeng, for instance, not only showed his subjects his own dedication to Buddhism but also taught the *dhamma* to the people. On each *ubosot* day (regular Buddhist "holy" day) he invited a learned monk to teach the *dhamma* at his palace. He personally led the people to observe Buddhist precepts strictly during the season of *vassa* retreat. At the end of *vassa* he presented *Kathina* robes and presents to the monks. He gave donations to monks who were proficient in the *dhamma* and in propagating Buddhism. He built monasteries and religious places and encouraged his subjects to follow his example. Buddhism in his reign was said to have prospered because of the king's devotion (Griswold and Prasert 1975, p. 44).

His successor, King Lithai (or Lodaiya), followed King Ramkhamhaeng's mode of government and continued to support Buddhism. This king is also said to have been a patron of Hindu cults and as a consequence the Brahmanical tradition seems to have been strengthened during his reign by influences from south India (ibid., pp. 48–49).

According to Griswold and Pasert, King Lithai, while following King Ramkhamhaeng's method of government, might have made more use of the Hindu tradition of government than had his grandfather. He is believed to have been familiar with the *Dharmasastra* (the Hindu treatise on the science of kingship) and to have made use of it. For example, at his coronation the Brahmanical ritual (*Abhiseka*) was performed to complete the ceremony. As a Buddhist king, he proclaimed himself Maha Dhammaraja (King of Righteous Kings), and is said to have studied the three *Pitaka* thoroughly. During his reign, Buddhism appears to have prospered because of his devotion. He is recorded to have been the first Thai king who donated land and slaves, probably prisoners of war, to the monasteries (ibid., pp. 56–60), a practice followed up to the early Bangkok period.

The most important religious act of Lithai was probably his ordination. He was the first Thai king who temporarily left his throne to become a monk, an act which, in Thai view, gains the highest merit. Besides being the action of a religious man, the king's ordination should be seen in the light of the political conditions of Sukhothai during this period.

When Lithai came to the throne he was confronted with at least two heavy responsibilities: first, to ward off an invasion from the newly emergent and expansive state of Ayutthaya; second, to recover his father's lost territories and to pacify rebellious vassals. In both cases he needed alliances with independent neighbouring rulers. By promoting Buddhism, and establishing himself as a righteous king, exemplified by his ordination, the state of Sukhothai became a regional centre of Buddhism. At his ordination, it was recorded, the rulers of Lanna and Nan came to participate in merit-making. They and some other rulers in the north sent diplomatic missions to Sukhothai with a view to bringing Sinhalese Theravada Buddhism to their homelands (Satuan 1962, pp. 65–69; Andaya 1971, pp. 61–83). In this fashion Lithai succeeded in cementing strong alliances against Ayutthaya or, at the least in ensuring the neutrality of his neighbours. His devotion to Buddhism assured his vassals that they would be treated with kindness and compassion, the essential virtues of a righteous Buddhist king. We are told that Lithai's policy of pacification of his vassals involved a military campaign followed by a generous peace. When he succeeded in subduing the vassals, he assured them that they could rely on his justice and mercy. He taught them to be good Buddhists (Griswold and Prasert 1975, p. 57).

Lithai's use of religion as an ideology to support the status quo and for purposes of social control is well exhibited in his own book, *Traiphuum Phra Ruang* or *Traibhumikatha* (the three worlds of Phra Ruang). The text describes the structure of the universe, the *traiphuum* cosmography, the relationship between merit and power, the destination of each category of beings and deities as determined by their *kamma*. All beings were ranked, from demons to gods in a hierarchy of the merit which had accrued to them according to their *kamma*. The text also describes the cyclic processes of birth, death, and rebirth of *deva*, human beings, and animals of various forms. Their three worlds were divided into thirty-one levels. The highest world contained four levels inhabited by high-grade *brahma* (Thai: *phrom*) deities. The middle world contained sixteen levels inhabited by lower grades of *phrom* deities. The lowest world consisted of eleven levels with human beings dwelling in the fifth level from the bottom. The six levels above the "world of mankind" were inhabited by beings of higher status than humans. Below it were creatures of less merit. The text describes the nature of each level, the conditions of existence for its inhabitants, how they came to be there, and how they might change their status.

The central emphasis of the *Traiphuum* is on the effects of good and bad *kamma*. It emphasizes that the people who have good *kamma* are rewarded, in contrast with those who acquire bad *kamma*, after death. Rewards and punishments for certain kinds of good and bad *kamma* are described. For example, when a person who has accumulated great merit dies, he goes to a higher level in the three worlds, depending on the amount of merit he had acquired while he was alive. He may even go straight to a *phrom* level, if he has sufficient merit.

This statement of the king's view of the entire world was intended for propagation throughout the kingdom. Some of its major points are of direct relevance to our study.

In the first place the notions of good and bad *kamma* and merit and demerit served to justify the social and economic position of individuals in the hierarchy of the society. In this way religious sanctions were employed to reinforce social sanctions and thus exercised an additional coercive power on the population. And the fact that the prescription of punishment for acts of demerit varies according to the status of the person concerned serves to regulate the social relationship between people of different statuses. For example, the punishment for people of high status is more severe than that for people of lower status who commit the same act of demerit. The *Traiphuum* also prescribes the appropriate relationships between people of different statuses. For example, it delineates the proper conduct between family members, the relationship between the clergy and the laity, and that between superiors and subordinates.

Apart from using the Buddhist values expressed in the *Traiphuum* as an instrument for social control, Lithai appears to have used the concept of merit to justify his right to rule. This is succinctly expressed in the following excerpt:

> One who had made and accumulated merit in previous lives by paying homage, honouring and revering the Triple Gems (the Buddha, *dhamma*, and the *sangha*) as well as having gratitude to them, adhering to *dhamma*, observing moral precepts (*sila*), practising *phuwuna* (concentration of mind on the Buddha and his *dhamma*), when he dies, goes to heaven. When he is reborn, he is born a ruler or in a higher caste with power, wealth and subordinates . . . with greater merit that others. He becomes *Chakraphat* (*Chakranvartin* — king of kings). . . . For those who

are born in the ruling class, or king, should be aware that it is so because they had good *kamma* and had accumulated merit in previous lives. It is not so because of natural causes. . . . It is merit that determines one's destination; [that is why] some people are born with wealth, wisdom, beauty, power, and have long lives as against the ones who are born with poverty, suffering, ugliness, idiocy, and have a short life. Merit and demerit determine who will be the ruler and who will be the slave or servant or governed. (King Lithai, *Traiphuum Phra Ruang*, 1966, pp. 94–98, 111, 143, 201)

Associated with his righteousness and the right to rule is his authority. His subjects have the duty to obey and to serve the ruler. The text states:

Whenever the *Chakraphat* emerges people all over the realm come to revere, pay respect and obey him. Whatever the king commands, it is legitimate because he is righteous. . . . The lesser lords come to pay him homage and offer themselves as his subordinates and render their territories to him.

From these characteristic extracts it will be seen that the *Traiphuum* can be considered as a political as well as religious treatise. It shows how religion can be used to help the ruler stabilize social order and maintain political power. By inculcating the fear of hell in the minds of the people, it discourages social and political protest. It also encourages either meek acceptance of suffering and of present status or withdrawal from the tribulations of human society.

After the death of King Lithai, which occurred some time between 1370 and 1374, Sukhothai gradually declined and fell under the control of Ayutthaya.

Buddhism and the Ayutthaya Kingship

The religio-political ideology, the concept of kingship, the administration, and political institutions of Ayutthaya were influenced by the interwoven traditions of Khmer and Mon, of Hinduism and Buddhism working in combination. From Khmer-Hindu tradition, Ayutthaya inherited its concept of divine kingship (*devaraja*). The king was considered as a receptacle of divine essence. He was Lord of Life and Lord of the Land. As the sovereign of the kingdom, his absolute power and authority were beyond challenge.

The king was described thus:

> Only the king is the highest in the land, because he is godlike. He can make the superior person (*phu yai*) be the subordinate person (*phu noi*) and vice-versa. When the king gives an order, it is the axe of heaven. If it strikes trees and mountains, the latter cannot withstand it, and will be destroyed. (Akin 1969, p. 44)

Hindu tradition manifested itself in the form of royal ceremonies such as rituals associated with the oath of allegiance and the coronation. The kings of Ayutthaya introduced and adapted from the Khmers many features of their political institutions and administration, their arts, their honorific court language, and much of their system of honorific titles and social ranking.

The influence of the Buddhist concept of the righteous king manifested itself in Pali *Dhammasattha*, the Theravada legal code for guidance in government. However, it must be emphasized that although the *Dhammasattha* was of Hindu origin, it was the Mon version that guided Thai kings. The Mon-Pali *Dhammasattha* claimed legitimacy not from Hinduism but mainly from Buddhist genesis myth contained in the *Aganna Sutta*. Lingat makes clear the Buddhist content:

> In composing this literature, Mon writers took for their model Hindu *Dharmasastras*, and this is why many provisions of the new code may be found in the Indian *Manu* code or other similar works. But (Buddhist) *Dhammasatthas* are quite different from Sanskrit *Dharmasastras*. First of all their authors left aside every matter which in Hindu codes was connected with Brahmanical religion or traditions. They were Buddhist people, and their codes were first to be applied to Buddhist people. ... The substance of law was not entirely taken from Hindu codes. They introduced, as was natural, a few customary rules prevalent among the indigenous population. (Lingat 1950, p. 14)

Prince Dhani Nivat also quotes the *Dhammasattha* as suggesting that the kings of Ayutthaya had to follow the principles of Buddhist righteous kingship:

> [The ideal monarch] abides steadfast in the ten kingly virtues minimum, constantly upholding five common precepts and on holy days the set of eight precepts, living in kindness and goodwill to all beings. He takes pains to study the Thammasat and to keep the four principles of justice, namely: to assess the right or wrong of all

service or disservice rendered to him, to uphold the righteous and truthful, and to maintain the prosperity of his state through none but just means. (Prince Dhani 1947, p. 163)

The king was also thought of as a potential Bodhisattva, that is, he was seen as one who temporarily had given up striving to achieve *nibbana*, so that he might serve his fellow men in their quest for religious and material satisfaction in this worldly life. Thus it is recorded that when King Ramadhipati and his successors died, they entered *nibbana*. This concept is probably of Mahayanist origin (Griswold and Prasert 1975, p. 69).

The political uses of Buddhism by Ayutthaya kings were manifold. The examples that follow are intended to illustrate this. At the oath of allegiance ritual which was of Hindu origin and performed by Brahmins, the Buddha, the *dhamma*, and the *sangha* were invoked to complete the ritual. From the Ayutthaya period to the early Bangkok period this ritual was performed in Buddhist monasteries, the monks taking an equal part with the Brahmins in the performance of the ritual (Chitt 1974, pp. 113–20).

Another aspect of the political exploitation of religion is manifested in the unification of Ayutthaya and Sukhothai in the reign of King Trailok of Ayutthaya (1448–88). Previous to Trailok's reign, though Ayutthaya kings had ruled over Sukhothai, they had failed to absorb it. It has been suggested that King Trailok succeeded in integrating the kingdom because he understood the importance of the Buddhist religion and recognized that military dominance alone was fruitless (Charnvit 1974, p. 446). He sought, therefore, to build a religio-political base in order to secure support from the *sangha*, and thus to reach the peasants, through the *sangha* and religion. In order to win "the hearts and minds" of the people of Sukhothai, he made great efforts to restore and build monasteries in the north. One of these activities in particular gave him the reputation of being a good Buddhist king and greatly impressed the Sukhothai population. This was the restoration of Wat Buddha Jinarat, once the spiritual centre of the kingdom, where the image of Buddha Jinnasi was housed. Following the example of King Lithai of Sukhothai, King Trailok temporarily left the throne to become a monk in the north. Politically, his ordination and his stay in the north must have pleased the Sukhothai folk, for the action followed the good example of that great Sukhothai king (ibid., pp. 448–49). On his ordination, the kings of Chiang Mai, Pegu, and Luang Prabang sent him gifts. Charnvit suggests that the king's ordination might have been planned so that he could penetrate and take command of the Sukhothai *sangha*. The idea was that the 2,348 men who were ordained with him would remain in Sukhothai and become a crucial link between the political authority and the rural population of the north (ibid., p. 449).

Another religious act which suggests that the king sought legitimacy from Buddhist tradition was manifested in his composition of the royal version of *Jakata*, a story concerning one of the Buddha's earlier lives. The political significance of this was that it emphasized the *religious* acts of the king as a prime qualification for a righteous ruler. It was also intended to follow the local tradition of King Lithai, who composed the *Traiphuum* (ibid., p. 450).

It is interesting to note that Buddhism was sometimes also used to legitimize the usurpation of the throne. For example, when King Songtham of Ayutthaya seized power from a rightful heir and established himself as king (1610–28), he sought legitimacy through his religious acts. The supreme patriarch of the sixth reign described it thus:

> The king realized that he had illegitimately seized power, and he had to beware of his unpopularity among the masses. Although at that time there was no one who dared to challenge his power, he sought support from the masses. Being accomplished in Buddhism and knowing that it was held in esteem by the people, he sought popularity and legitimacy through the religion. He encouraged ecclesiastical education and devoted his efforts to promote Buddhism. The king revised the *Jataka*, and ordered the compilation of the *Tipitaka*. He encouraged the people in the court to adhere to Dhamma. He himself regularly attended the sermons. (Somdet Phra Maha Samanachao Kromphraya Wachirayan Warorot 1971, p. 273)

The interaction of politics with religion in the Ayutthaya period may therefore be summarized as follows. Khmer-Hindu and Buddhist influences had converged in Ayutthaya and achieved a complex reworking. Each gave its own legitimation to the polity. Buddhism affirmed the role of *kingship as the expression of the* dhamma *and righteousness*, and as the fountain of justice, as well as the ordering principle of society. Its moral principles ensured that the king should be measured against the law. The *Hindu-Khmer notion of divine kingship*, in its modified form, *conceptualized the king as the embodiment of the law* and provided him with a majestic aura of mystery and a place in the cosmic order. Both traditions buttressed the *political* authority of kingship.

It should also be noted that the religious concerns of the kings of Sukhothai and Ayutthaya were examples for their successors. Their interest for us is not only that some of them were good Buddhist kings but also that they realized that Buddhism could accord them legitimacy. In this respect there is a continuity of the political uses of religion for various purposes up to the present day.

Buddhism and Kingship at Thonburi

Ayutthaya finally fell through the Myanmar invasion of 1767. The capital was looted and burnt, and many of its population, both monks and laymen, fled. Eventually, General Taksin forced back the enemies and restored Thai freedom. He became king and moved the capital to Thonburi.

In the early years of his rule, King Taksin shouldered the task of pacifying the dissidents and unifying the kingdom. Among the rebels was a group of dissident monks led by a high-ranking monk, Phra Fang. These monks organized themselves in army style and, as if they were laymen, observed no *vinaya*, and managed to seize power in the northern capital of Pitsanulok. However, they were soon attacked by Taksin. Phra Fang escaped but many of his followers were executed. In the south, Taksin also succeeded in pacifying another group of dissidents led by the ruler of Nakhon Sitthammarat.

In his efforts to unify the kingdom, Taksin sent high-ranking monks from the capital to assume important supervisory positions in the northern *sangha*. After pacifying the southern rebels, he invited the leading southern monks to receive gifts. He built new monasteries and restored ruined ones. Since Nakhon Sitthammarat was the centre of Buddhism in the south, religious acts there could be seen as an attempt by the king to utilize religion to justify his political intervention and to acquire support from the southern people (Satuan 1962, pp. 148–52).

As a king seeking legitimacy through religious values, Taksin devoted his efforts to restoring the prosperity of Buddhism, which had suffered from the Myanmar invasion. Following King Lithai's example and that of Songtham, he ordered the revision of the *Traiphuum* and commanded the compilation of a new edition of the *Tipitaka*. He also built and restored many monasteries in the country.

Taksin lived in an age when Buddhism assumed aberrant forms due in part to the lack of proper support and supervision which resulted from the perennial war with Myanmar. In consequence, the behaviour of the monks had deviated far from conventional norms of Buddhism. The king set out to purify the *sangha*, and unworthy monks were ruthlessly purged. For example, in order to distinguish virtuous monks from the unworthy, some northern monks were tried by ordeal. Taksin himself seriously took up the study of meditation and claimed to have acquired supernatural powers. Moreover, he saw himself as a *sodaban* (Pali: *sotapanna*) or stream-winner, a type of being so elevated as to have embarked on one of the stages on the road to enlightenment (Iaming and Phitsanaakha 1956, p. 299). Because of this illusion, he claimed superiority over the monks and ordered them to bow to him. Those who refused to recognize his claims were flogged and sentenced to menial labour. The supreme patriarch and two other senior monks who would not yield to his demands or recognize his claims were demoted. It was Taksin's assumption of *sodaban*, and his unorthodox treatment of the *sangha* that partly contributed to his downfall. Because of his unorthodox behaviour, he was regarded as insane and as a potential threat to the unity of the Thai nation. He was forced to abdicate and was later sentenced to death by his successor, Rama (ibid.; C. Reynolds 1973, pp. 29–34). As far as the belief that the king was the one who possessed the greatest merit is concerned, the downfall of Taksin was described thus: "When the king (Taksin) ran out of his *bun* (merit), he died at the age of 48" (Akin 1969, p. 12).

Buddhism and Kingship in Bangkok

King Rama I assumed the throne in 1782 and began the Chakri dynasty. He moved the capital of Thailand to Bangkok. During his reign, the Hindu tradition began to decline in importance: for example, in a royal decree of 1782, the king ordered that *linga*, a central feature of Hindu worship, be destroyed. In many state ceremonies, Buddhist rituals were superimposed on Brahmanical ones: for instance, in the oath of allegiance ceremony, the initial ritual became the worship of the Triple Gems instead of the former Brahmanical ceremony. Except for some adaptations, Rama I largely followed the model of Ayutthaya: for example, the Buddhist *Dhammasattha* was still his guide in the administration of justice and government, and his approach was paternalistic (Prince Dhani 1959, p. 241).

When Rama I succeeded Taksin he set himself to restore the moral tone of the kingdom, the acts that established him as a righteous Buddhist king. As a strong king who sought legitimacy and stability for his rule in the orthodoxy of Buddhism he declared that one of his main priorities was to restore the prosperity of Buddhism and the purity of the *sangha*, both of which had suffered from the Myanmar invasion and the unorthodox acts of King Taksin (Chaophraya 1962, p. 6).

One major act was the revision of the *Tipitaka* in 1788. For this task, the king appointed a council of 218, together with thirty-two Buddhist scholars. They took five months to complete the revision, the ninth since the Buddha's enlightenment. The *Tipitaka* was then considered to be correct (C. Reynolds 1973, pp. 50–53; Wenk 1968).

The revision of the *Tipitaka* had manifold implications. Symbolically, it was merit-making on a grand scale, the greatest merit accruing to the king as sponsor. Politically, since the *dhamma* was contained in the *Tipitaka*, the revision led to the revival of the moral tone of the kingdom, and indicated Rama I's intention to be a righteous king.

The king also ordered the revision of the *Traiphuum*, so that its text was in accordance with the *Tipitaka*. His intentions in revising the *Traiphuum* were in line with those of King Lithai. It was meant to be a primary instrument for educating the people in Buddhist values. As we have seen already, this effectively reaffirmed the values of kingship and justified hierarchy in the established social order.

In order to purify the *sangha* and restore its prestige, the king issued a number of decrees on monastic conduct. The decrees specified the correct behaviour that monks had to observe. They laid down the relationship between the monastic community and lay society, and between the monks and civil authority. Punishments for disobedience were also prescribed (Prince Dhani 1964, pp. 1–15; C. Reynolds 1973, pp. 35–50).

In his legislation and administration of justice, the king, as did his successors, closely followed the prescriptions set out in the *Dhammasattha*. If there was any doubt about the merit of some laws, the laws were

> to be examined with regard to their agreement with the Pali cannon, and in cases where they did not agree they were to be altered accordingly, in order to restore what was believed to be the original text. (Wenk 1968, p. 36)

Rama I's own behaviour was intended to be exemplary for his officials and his subjects:

> In the morning the King used to come out to offer alms to monks on their morning rounds, after which he had a set of monks invited by regular turns to partake of food in the Audience Chamber. . . .
> In the evening the King took his meal early and then came out to the Audience Chamber to listen to the daily sermon delivered by a monk. (Prince Dhani 1959, pp. 257–58)

The king, moreover, instructed his officials and the royal household to observe regularly the five and eight precepts in the monastery (ibid.).

From the religious activities of Rama I, it can be seen that there was a shift in the conception of kingship from one of divine kingship towards that of the *dhamma raja*, or Buddhist kingship. In a sense, it reflected the Buddhist kingship of Sukhothai. From now on, Thai kingship was sacred because it symbolized the *dhamma*, the principle upon which the order of the kingdom depended, and it became less and less dependent on the Hindu myth of divine kingship.

After the death of Rama I in 1809, it could be said that the condition of the religion and the *sangha* was healthy and stable as a result of his restoration and purification of the faith and the *sangha*. He had also established a close relationship between kingship and religion which continues to the present day. The main religious tasks remaining to his successors were to maintain the prosperity and purity of Buddhism and the *sangha*, and to secure the people's adherence to the *dhamma*.

The relationship between Buddhism and kingship began to change during the reign of King Mongkut (Rama IV, 1851–68). King Mongkut had been in the monkhood for twenty-seven years before assuming the throne. As a monk he had gained a reputation for being a reformer influenced by the Mon tradition. Dissatisfied with the old practices of Buddhism the prince-monk had launched a reform programme to make Thai Buddhism as close as possible to the Pali canon of Theravada Buddhism. This involved a reform of monastic discipline, changes in details of rituals, and a redefinition of the canon. One of the most important consequences was the establishment of the new Thammayut order within the Thai *sangha*. The new order has been highly regarded ever since for its disciplinary strictness and its close association with the royal family (for King Mongkut's reform, see C. Reynolds [1973, chaps. 3–4 , pp. 66–137]).

As king, Mongkut thought of himself as essentially a man, not a "superhuman" in the way implied in the concept of divine kingship (Riggs 1967, pp. 95–105). He was very sceptical about the legendary stories which glorified divine kingship such as the *Jataka* and the *Traiphuum*. He rejected everything in religion that claimed supernatural origin. He was also very sceptical about the notions of heaven and hell, a prominent feature of the *Traiphuum* (Bradley 1966; C. Reynolds 1976, pp. 210–20).

It has also been suggested that the public image of the king from this reign onwards gradually changed from that of divine king buttressed by the Brahmanical cult and ritual to that of the leading human, the defender, and patron of the Buddhist church. The old customs and ceremonies associated with divine kingship were questioned, reinterpreted in Buddhist terms, secularized, or neglected and gradually forgotten. Buddhist rituals were introduced to replace Brahmanical rituals in royal ceremonies or superimposed upon them (Riggs 1967, pp. 99–101). However, this does not mean that the Chakri kings had lost interest in the classic *dhamma raja* concept of kingship, or that they were entirely averse to the glorification of the king as *devaraja*. As Tambiah has pointed out, King Mongkut, like his predecessors, while striving to justify and legitimate his position by capitalizing on the Buddhist concept of kingship, also relied on Brahmanical rites which glorified the king as *devaraja* (Tambiah 1976, pp. 226–27; Wales 1965). This view is shared by John Blofeld, who points out that although the ceremonies were associated with the Brahmanical cult, the context was essentially Buddhist. The two elements were in harmony, each dealing with a different compartment of life. As Blofeld puts it:

> It would be going too far to say that King Monkut permitted the Brahmin ceremonial merely because it lent splendour to royal occasions.... One turned to the Buddha to understand how to pursue the great task of liberation, and to the Hindu gods to obtain various mundane favours affecting the welfare of the individual and of the kingdom as a whole. As a pious man, who was nevertheless the king, it was his duty to pursue his own liberation and at the same time solicit the protection of the Hindu gods for his throne and his country. (Blofeld 1972, p. 41)

It is difficult to assess the degree to which Thai kingship was divorced from the Hindu cult. We can only observe that from the time of King

Mongkut, Thai kings appear to have been more clearly identified with Buddhist values then previously, but have by no means totally discarded the tradition of Hindu kingship. Brahmanical ceremonial is still used to complement Buddhist rituals in royal ceremonies today.

During King Mongkut's reign, a number of cultural, economic, and social changes were initiated. After his death in 1868, his son Chulalongkorn succeeded him and launched further "modernization" programmes (Griswold, *King Mongkut of Siam*, 1961; Graham 1939; Vella 1955; Wales 1965; Watthanaset 1957).

King Chulalongkorn was clearly concerned with the task of modernizing the country. His long reign (1868–1910) brought administrative, judicial, and financial reforms; the development of modern communication; the first stirring of political development; the growth of social services and bureaucracy; and great economic development. The administrative, social, and economic reforms carried out during his reign constituted a great leap in the transformation of the society. The king nevertheless did not neglect the traditional legitimizing functions of a Buddhist king, namely, the promotion and purification of Buddhism and the *sangha*.

Following traditional expressions of monarchical support for Buddhism and the *sangha*, the king built many new monasteries and restored the old ones. He had a replica made of the Buddha Jinnasi, the image of the Buddha which was once the pride of the Sukhothai kingdom. The replica was housed in a new royal monastery, Wat Benjamaborpit. The king's attempt to come to terms with Buddhism and to propagate it was manifested in the revision of *Tipitaka*. The revised edition was later translated from Pali into Thai and printed as a book. The translation was intended to enable the people to understand Buddhism more widely. The entire text consisted of ten volumes. The king himself paid for the publication of 1,000 sets of the book for distribution to monasteries in the kingdom and to libraries abroad. In 1874 he entered the monkhood temporarily. In 1983, he received from the Viceroy of India the Buddha's relics found at Kapilavatthu in India (Prachoom 1966, pp. 100–3). It was also during his reign that the great reform of the *sangha* was launched to unify the *sangha* organization and to systematize the *sangha* administration. This reform, as part of the attempted "modernization" of the country, was intended to bring about nation-wide integation, of which educational and provincial administrative reforms were also a part.

The importance of the concept of divine kingship continued to decline and many customs associated with it were curtailed or abolished. For example, King Chulalongkorn abolished the practice of prostration in front of the monarch. From this reign, the king's traditional duty of adhering to *Dhammasattha* was extended so that the king was no longer just an executor of traditional laws; he became a legislator with unlimited powers to change Thai government and Thai life. The change in the conception of kingship in this respect was attributed to the impact of Western notions of modern government (Vella 1955; Riggs 1967; Wales 1965).

King Chulalongkorn died in 1910 and was succeeded by his son, Wachirawut (Rama VI), who ruled the kingdom between 1910 and 1925. The new king perpetuated the traditional legitimizing function of a Buddhist. Despite the absence of significant religious acts of purification and promotion of Buddhism and the *sangha* equivalent to those of his predecessors, the political exploitation of Buddhism by this king was unmistakable. In the face of threat from the colonial powers, King Wachirawut was very concerned about national unity and felt it essential to maintain the independence of his kingdom. In order to realize this goal, he injected into Thai collective consciousness a spirit of nationalism and national allegiance. He developed a sense of nationhood composed of the nation (*chat*), religion (*sasana*), and the monarch (*phramahakasat*). These three symbolic components constituted the pillars of the Thai nation; each depended on the other and had to be preserved if the Thai nation was to survive and progress (for Wachirawut's idea of the interdependence and inter-relation of the nation, the religion, and the monarchy, see F. Reynolds [1977, pp. 267–82]). The king urged the Thai to unite in body and spirit to defend the nation, the religion, and the monarchy from the incursions of enemies, mainly Western colonial powers. In the course of defending and protecting the three institutions, the king maintained that it was legitimate if Thai soldiers killed their national enemies. As he puts it:

> For those who have to fight in war in the defence of our nation, some may think that it is against the teaching of the Buddha which prohibited killing. . . . But we are not intending to wage war against one another, but to protect ourselves. In this case, the Buddha once said that it was the duty of able men to fight against enemies who invade with the intention to take our land, to jeopardize Buddhism, and to destroy our sovereignty . . . let us make it known to the world

that we, the Thai, are determined to protect our nation, religion, and monarchy, and to preserve them as they were in our ancestors' time. . . . We shall fight with swords and guns, sacrifice our bodies as fences for protecting and preserving them. . . . It is not against the Buddha's teaching. . . . Protecting our nation is indispensable, just as we have to protect Buddhism and Dhamma. (King Wachirawut 1953, pp. 168, 193–94)

Furthermore, the king tied national independence to the survival of Buddhism. He reminded the Thai that Thailand was the last line of defence for Buddhism; he emphasized that the first and second lines (Myanmar and Sri Lanka) had already fallen and that it was now up to the Thai to make the last line stand. If they did not take this responsibility, the end of Buddhism was obvious, which would be a great disgrace for the generations of Thai to come (ibid.). Buddhism, in the eyes of the king, could provide the basic principles necessary for preserving the moral order of society, and so he encouraged the people to adhere to the *dhamma*. By adhering to the *dhamma*, the king said, people would live in peace and be happy (King Wachirawut 1925, p. 34). In order to strengthen people's adherence to the *dhamma* and Buddhism, the king introduced Buddhist daily prayers in schools, police stations, army garrisons, government departments, and even prisons and mental hospitals (F. Reynolds 1977, p. 274; Thompson 1941, pp. 368–69).

The innovation of the concept of nationhood as composed of the nation, the religion, and the monarchy by Wachirawut has continued to play a crucial role in Thai religio-political ideology. It has become the foundation of the "civic religion" of Thai socio-political life (for an elaboration on the term "civic religion", see F. Reynolds [1977, pp. 267–82]). The political exploitation of the religion in this respect has been followed by later Thai rulers, especially in the 1960s, in order to mobilize the support of Thai people for politically defined ends. More recently, the symbolic slogans of nation, religion, and activists of the 1970s provide legitimacy for their political ideologies and activities.

King Wachirawut died in 1925 and was succeeded by Prachathiphok (Rama VII, 1925–32), the last absolute monarch in Thailand. The 1932 revolution brought an end to absolute monarchy and replaced it by constitutional monarchy. Thailand then embarked on a form of government that is more democratic. However, the Thai king still plays an important, though mainly symbolic, role in Thai Buddhism. The king is now both the high protector and patron of Buddhism and the constitutional head of government. Unlike the absolute monarch for whom protection and promotion of Buddhism and the *sangha* was a prerogative, Thai kings, as constitutional monarchs, now act in accordance with the wishes of the Cabinet.

The Political Secularization of Buddhism in Thailand

The intrusion of Western powers in the nineteenth century weakened the traditional mode of government in Southeast Asia.[2] The sacral nature of government was challenged and the ideological basis of the state, which was formerly provided by religious beliefs and values, was questioned. The colonization of Laos and Cambodia by the French in the nineteenth century had the effect of weakening not only the traditional mode of government but also traditional élites. The French no longer relied on traditional mandarins whose mode of thought was deeply rooted in religious orientation. The colonial master employed French-educated indigenes whose horizons embraced Western models of government. The disruption of the traditional integrating systems caused by the intrusion of Western power and Western ideas had, as a consequence, the effect of separating the religious and political components of those systems. Under Western rule, the colonial countries were held together by vastly superior military, technological, economic, and administrative power. Yet, there were liberation movements in these countries whose leaders were drawn from both Western-educated patriots and indigenous leaders. In their struggle for independence, Western notions of equality, liberty, self-determination, and so forth were employed to legitimize their quest for independence. At the same time the liberation movement would also mobilize mass resistance by instilling into the minds of the masses a sense of the humiliation of religion and of traditional values inflicted by the colonial master.

With the demise of colonial rule, the newly independent states were faced with the full impact of a legitimacy crisis. Western notions of representative government were an important part of external attacks on traditional religious-political modes of government in Southeast Asia in the early nineteenth century. After independence, many of the newly independent countries adopted Western representative government as their model of government, while others were attracted to secular theories of authoritarianism. However, only a small group of ruling élites exposed to Western education developed a real comprehension of, and commitment to, new secular political values. The masses still remained steeped in traditional religious modes of thought and became alienated from the political process.

In a situation where people were divided into a secularized ruling élite and a largely traditional religious-oriented mass, the political leaders were confronted with a cruel dilemma. To keep up with the socio-economic and political changes of the modern world, and to live up to the expectations of modernized communities, certain aspects of the traditional culture of society had to be secularized. This is a process which is totally foreign to the traditional masses. Conflicts and tension often escalated when social and political as well as cultural secularization were imposed on them. This inevitably led to a legitimacy crisis for the ruling élite and their policies of political and administrative modernization.

In these circumstances, the leaders of newly independent countries had to turn once again to religion and society's religion-based values for assistance. National religion was invoked to initiate, explain, and legitimize the actions, political institutions, and programmes of the ruling élite. There thus came about in post-independence Southeast Asia a parallelism between new religio-political phenomena and the secularization of socio-politics. At the same time that secular political participation by the masses was being encouraged, religious interest groups, religious political parties, and religious communal groups also became prominently active in politics. Strong religion-based parties in a country such as Indonesia were found playing an important political role in Indonesian politics. For the Myanmar political élite it was convenient to mobilize Buddhism to legitimize their politically defined ends. After independence in 1948, U Nu, the Prime Minister of Myanmar, was compatible with, and supportive of, socialism, the mainstream ideology of his political party. In the hope of stabilizing his rule, U Nu sought legitimization for his government by proclaiming Buddhism the state religion of Myanmar in 1961. In Cambodia there was Prince Sihanouk and his Buddhist approaches to government and the running of state affairs, both domestic and international. In post-independence Laos political leaders of conflicting ideologies made full use of Buddhism to legitimize their claims to power. In Thailand the mobilization of traditional institutions, notably Buddhism and the monarchy, in aid of political stability has been remarkable. These phenomena are examined below.

Political Mobilization of Thai Buddhism

The second section shows that the close association of Buddhism and political authority in Thailand has been continuous throughout the nation's history. By exploiting certain values that Thai Buddhism so obviously provided, the regime could, given time, legitimize itself and build sufficient popular support to carry through the policies and modernizing plans which it envisaged.

In an age when development has increasingly become a symbol of an advanced or developed country, ruling élites have frequently mobilized traditional institutions and values to legitimize government-sponsored development scheme. Religion, a traditional source of legitimacy, can also legitimize efforts for development.

Though it is difficult to make the legitimizing function of religion explicit in today's political system in Thailand, evidence suggests that religion is still being reinterpreted and used to support rulers who are committed to development, and to legitimize change. Since the late 1950s, and especially during Sarit's era, the ruling élite made special efforts to invoke and popularize the oldest and most potent of Thai collective symbols — religion and the monarchy. These two institutions have been used to initiate, explain, and defend political actions. Of these two, Buddhism has been increasingly mobilized.

This section delineates the political mobilization of Buddhism and the *sangha* by the Thai Government to legitimize its policy of development.

The cardinal reasons for the political mobilization of Buddhism by political rulers came from the belief that national security and integration were threatened to the extent that the government's legitimacy was challenged. The threats, in the eyes of the government, were conceived as coming from the two major overlapping problems of communist subversion and lack of national integration[3] arising from regionalism (for regionalism in Thailand, see Keyes [1967]) and from the presence of ethnic minorities, notably the hill people of the north.

For many years the Thai Government tried to solve the problems of communist subversion and rural and regional dissidence through suppression and anti-communist campaigns. Only in the late 1950s did the government realize that military coercion and political repression only exacerbated the problems and further alienated dissidents. It became clear to them that the first priority was to "win the hearts and minds" of the people, that is, to secure the people's loyalty to the nation through drastic social and economic development programmes. These programmes have come to be known under the name of national development (*Kan patthana prathet*) and national integration.

In Thailand, national development has included the building up of the armed forces, road and dam construction, rural development, the expansion of education, the extension of bureaucracy, and the sponsoring of economic development schemes by ministries and departments. National integration has comprised policies for integrating the country politically, socially, and economically, ranging from appeasing and developing the relatively poor and undeveloped northeast, and spreading Thai language, religion, and custom among ethnic and cultural minorities in the north, northeast, and south, to the coercive resettlement of migratory hill peoples.

In the early 1960s the government became increasingly aware that its secular development schemes were insufficient to counter subversion and regionalism. In the course of time evidence had accumulated of its remoteness from the rural populace, and of barriers between the officials and the people. The use of Buddhism in development came to be seen as one solution to these difficulties. This new policy seems to have been based on the following presuppositions: the great majority of Thai are Buddhist; the *sangha* (the community of monks who are professional carriers of Buddhism) is held in esteem and enjoys great prestige; rural monks are influential in village affairs; and the Thai people trust the *sangha*. For these reasons the political leaders believed that the *sangha* was the best possible agent for extending welfare and national development and integration as well as mobilizing support and encouraging loyalty to the government. At the same time the *sangha* was under fairly tight government control. Through patronage the government could secure the co-operation of high-ranking monks in the *sangha* (Somboon 1977, pp. 5–21, 29–42; 1981*a*) and, as the *sangha* was hierarchically organized from state to village level, it was hoped that this would ensure loyal assistance at the village level. The argument that communism threatened Buddhism and the *sangha* no less than national interest was a powerful one. One can see how it was believed that the *sangha* might be manipulated to effect the government's political ends.

The leaders of the government during the 1960s and 1970s justified their mobilization of Buddhism in several ways:

1. The prosperity of Buddhism and the *sangha* was closely related to that of the nation and the government. Thus the monks should adjust their roles to help the government's plans for national development (Sarit 1960).
2. People were becoming materialistic and neglecting their religion. In consequence, ties of kinship and community were weakening, rendering village society more prone to communist infiltration. A reassertion of religious values would strengthen the community base of Thai society in its fight against communism (Puang 1970). The fear of communism and the need to strengthen the people's attachment to Buddhist values were dramatically expressed in 1969 by Thanom Kitthikachorn, the Prime Minister from 1963 to 1973:

   At present people in some parts of the country are threatened by communist terrorists, and some people are particularly vulnerable to the propaganda of insurgents. . . . It is obvious that the enemy wants to enslave us, to destroy our freedom, our religion, and our king. (Thanom 1969; he had in fact been advancing this kind of argument for some years [Thanom 1966])

Later, the Director of the Communist Suppression Operations Command (CSOC) elaborated on this, to the effect that to ward off the "communist danger" monks should help the government by promoting the people's morality and teaching them positive and creative *dhamma*. The monks should also promote understanding between the government and the villagers and teach the people the danger of communism (Saiyud 1970).

3. The government's policy was to follow the teaching of the Buddha that a government should promote the well-being of the religion (Mahachula Buddhist University 1972, pp. 5–9, 11).

The Thai *sangha* had responded well to political mobilization. The rationale for co-operation with the government in development and integration was as follows.

First, it was consistent with the *sangha*'s responsibility to serve society, in accordance with the Buddha's teaching that as monks depend on the material support of the laity they are morally obliged to promote the well-being of laymen. Conversely, if the monks do not contribute to the well-being of society, they will be regarded as social parasites (Phra Ubalikunupamacharn 1972, p. 12).

Second, it was pointed out that it was the government and the king who supported and protected the *sangha*, and enabled it to live the monastic life. In return the *sangha* should render every possible assistance to these institutions and be loyal to the interests of the nation (ibid.).

Third, according to Somdet Phra Wannarat,[4] there were obvious threats to Buddhism. These were the animosity of hostile forces such as communism, which opposed Buddhism, and the danger of invasion by hostile foreign countries (that is, North Vietnam, China, and the communist Pathet Lao). Furthermore, there were materialistic Thai who did not adhere to the *dhamma* and exploited their fellow countrymen. All of these jeopardized Buddhism; the *sangha*'s involvement in national development and integration programmes would help to defeat all such internal and external subversion of the faith (Somdet Phra Wannarat 1967, pp. 6–16).

Fourth, the *sangha*'s involvement in integrating the hill people was especially meritorious. Somdet Phra Wanarat asserted that the hill people had always needed the *dhamma*, but no one had taught them. The missionary monks were following the Buddha's example as well as earning merit. Moreover, merit would accrue to the government who sponsored the programme, while the hill people, being exposed to the *dhamma*, would also gain merit. Finally, the propagation of Buddhism to these people not only strengthened their morality, but also helped to ward off other undesirable forces (such as communism).

Fifth, the *sangha*'s participation in government policies, especially in the Phra Dhammatuta programme, was a means of strengthening and restoring the people's loyalties. This was strongly emphasized by Somdet Phra Wannarat:

> Through the strengthening of the people's attachment to Dhamma, the people will be loyal to the nation, the king, and the government; by adhering to Buddhism the people will better understand each other, thereby promoting national integration; through national integration people will be unified. Moreover, the monks will lift up the villagers' morale and will help them in their development. (Somdet Phra Wannarat 1969, p. 9)

Finally, the *sangha*'s involvement was necessary to maintain its status. In other words the monkhood had to change or become obsolete and thus discredit the faith. These views were promoted by some prominent monks who were the architects of plans employing monks in community development programmes (Phra Maha Prayut Payutto 1968, pp. 58–72; 1970, pp. 14–22, 56–68; Phra Maha Chai Aphakaro 1972, pp. 1–3; May 1972, pp. 19–30).

From all these considerations, the Thai Government, with the co-operation of the *sangha*, instituted a series of schemes to "win the hearts and minds" of the rural people. The basic aims of the schemes were identical. They were to use the *sangha* to promote both Buddhism and socio-economic development and thereby deter subversion and pacify rural dissent. Three of these programmes are here considered:

1. The *sangha* in the community development programme: The government programme of community development was part of the counter-insurgency measures used in sensitive areas, especially in the north and northeast, as one way of averting communist subversion and securing villagers' loyalty to the central government (Department of Community Development 1971, pp. 16–19; Caldwell 1974, pp. 13, 50–59). The objectives of the programmes were to increase rural production and income; expand rural public works; promote health, sanitation, education, recreation, and youth training; preserve village culture; and more effectively extend government services to reach the people (Department of Community Development 1971, pp. 20–21).

The implementation of the programme was based on the following three principles. First, it was to be a joint undertaking of the villagers and the government, with the initiative coming from the villagers and the government providing technical assistance and materials that the villagers could not provide for themselves. Second, community development was to stress self-help, mobilize local resources in the most useful way, assist in establishing a training ground for democracy, and create a national consciousness among the rural population. Third, and most importantly, community development was meant to change people's negative attitudes towards the government and to secure villagers' loyalty by eliminating conflicts among themselves and with the government (Phat 1975, pp. 1–9; Department of Community Development 1975).

This programme had full co-operation and support from the *sangha*.

Its rationale for co-operation was based on the assumption that

> up-country, the people put their trust and confidence in monks;
> obedience and co-operation in any activity becomes automatic
> if the request comes from the monks ... community development
> programmes are sure to be effectively accomplished with
> monastic help and co-operation. Having this in mind and in line
> with the national development policy of the government, the
> (Buddhist) University deemed it advisable to initiate projects
> for the training of monks in the promotion and co-ordination of
> community development activities, with an aim to contribute
> to the government's efforts in raising the standard of living of
> our rural population. (Mahachula Buddhist University 1967,
> p. 89)

Thus training programmes to enable monks to participate in rural development schemes were instituted in two Buddhist universities. These programmes helped train graduate monks from Buddhist universities in community and rural development, both in theory and in practice. Upon the completion of their training, such monks were sent to villages and expected to lead and advise other local monks and the populace in general in community development programmes. The ultimate goals were to raise the standard and quality of village life while strenghtening rural unity, thereby contributing to national security and integration. These goals had been clearly set out in the duties of the trained monks:

1. Their primary duty was to propagate and promote Buddhism. They were to strengthen the people's attachment to the *dhamma* by teaching them moral principles based on Buddhist ethics, and by establishing Buddhist Sunday Schools for the young, and so forth.

2. They were to teach the *dhamma* in a way that would encourage the people to participate in communal activities organized for their benefit. For example, they were to emphasize the principles of *dana* (giving) so that the villagers would be more willing to sacrifice personal interests for the sake of communal interests. Teaching the principles of loving kindness and compassion, honesty, and co-operation would promote village unity. They were to advise villagers on sanitation, public health, hygiene, and a proper diet. Finally, they were to teach local monks the

techniques of community development.

3. To promote the livelihood of the villagers, the monks were to advise them on modern agricultural technology and techniques such as new methods in farming, crop rotation, and the use of fertilizers.

4. The monks were also to instill a sense of loyalty to the nation, government, religion, and the king. One way they were to do this was by acting as intermediaries between the government and the villagers. On the one hand, the monks were to convey to the villagers the government's policies and its concern for their well-being. On the other hand, the monks were to inform the government of the villagers' needs and attitudes and advise the people on how to contact government agencies to meet their needs (for the duties of trained monks, see Somboon [1977, especially chap. 4, pp. 65–109]).

In carrying out these tasks the monks were advised to incorporate what they wished to impart into their teaching, preaching, and conversation with the villagers. Ritual gatherings and religious occasions were sometimes used to promote new government development schemes. Moreover, it was not uncommon to see some active monks not only teaching but also physically helping the villagers in constructing roads, digging wells, and erecting buildings.

2. Dhammatuta programme (*dhamma* missionary): This programme, set up in 1964, was one in which monks participated in the government's effort of national integration. It involved more direction from the government and was initiated on the assumptions that the people's attachment to Buddhism was a safeguard against communism and that those who were not adherents of Buddhism or who had only a weak attachment to the faith were a potential threat to national security and integration. Such people were vulnerable to subversive propaganda.[5] In this programme, trained monks were to strengthen the people's faith and adherence to Buddhism, to teach them correct and useful but simplified Buddhist tenets and the application of Buddhism in everyday life, including the relevance of religious practices to the development goals of the nation.

The ultimate objectives of this programme are

1. to restore Buddhism and protect the prestige of the *sangha* from

deterioration, and to save the people from demoralization and vulnerability to communist propaganda (Pin 1964);

2. to mobilize the people's loyalty to the nation, the government, and the king;

3. to create a better understanding among the people and between the people and the government, thereby promoting national integration; and

4. to strengthen the villagers' morale and help them in development.

(Somdet Phra Wannarat, the Director of Phra Dhammatuta work, in speeches given to Phra Dhammatuta monks during 1966–69; see also Pin [1968, pp. 40–41] and Somboon [1977, p. 97])

The selection of monks to participate in the Phra Dhammatuta programme was done jointly by the Department of Religious Affairs and the *sangha*'s Supreme Council of Elders (Mahatherasamkom). The Dhammatuta monks were chosen from devoted volunteers. Most of them were monk-students at the Buddhist universities in Bangkok. There were fewer volunteers from up-country.

In carrying out their assignments, the Dhammatuta monks travel from village to village in groups or separately, by foot, by car, or by bus. They stay in a village for a few days to a week delivering sermons and talking to the villagers. In their initial approach the village abbot and village headman are generally informed of the monks' arrival in advance, and they in turn inform the villagers and organize meetings. At the meeting the monks deliver a sermon or lecture on the *dhamma* that imparts specific government policies, the duties of good citizenship, loyalty to the government, nation, and the king, and teaches them about development efforts. The lectures are usually accompanied by the distribution of medicine, textbooks on the *dhamma*, and other relevant items. Films are shown about government programmes and the royal family visiting the people, opening new buildings, and carrying out state ceremonies (Somboon 1981*b*).

In the cities the monks teach the *dhamma* to prison inmates to improve their morality and prepare them to be good citizens. The Police Department has also asked the monks to teach the villagers that crimes such as manslaughter, robbery, drug trading, prostitution, and involvement in illegal lotteries not only lead to social disorder, but are also acts of great demerit (*bab*) (ibid.).

3. Dhammajarik programme: This programme's underlying suppositions were almost the same as those of the Phra Dhammatuta programme, that is, that attachment to Buddhism provides a safeguard against communism, and that those who are not adherents of Buddhism pose a potential threat to national security and integration. The Thai Government has, since the 1960s, considered non-Thai and non-Buddhist hill peoples as such a threat, and so in 1965 the Department of Public Welfare initiated the Phra Dhammajarik programme, the Buddhist mission to the hill people, and called upon the *sangha* to carry out this programme.

A senior official in the Department of Public Welfare, Pradit Ditsawat, elaborated on the main reason for using the *sangha*:

> The propagation (of *dhamma*) among the hill people would be likely to promote administrative and development aims among the hill people. This is because the integration of our people into a larger community depends upon the ties of customs and religion. (Department of Public Welfare 1965, p. 10)

The programme's main aims were to integrate the hill people into Thai culture and the national social and administrative order (ibid., pp. 10–13; Department of Public Welfare 1968, p. 28). On the one hand, this meant making them loyal to the nation, religion, and king through strengthening their belief in, or converting them to, Buddhism. On the other hand, it means strengthening the bonds that some Thai already had with the hill people.

Since 1965 the Phra Dhammajarik programme has been run as a joint endeavour of the Department of Public Welfare and the *sangha*. The government provides the necessary financial and material assistance while the *sangha* recruits the monks. By and large, the majority of the Dhammajarik monks are Bangkok-based voluntary recruits, although local monks are also chosen (Department of Public Welfare 1971, pp. 26–27).

The main task of the Dhammajarik monks is to convert the hill people to Buddhism. Their methods include teaching the hill people about religious customs and the basic tenets of Buddhism. The hill people are taught how to pay respects to the Triple Gems and make merit by giving alms to the monks, and are encouraged to take vows as Buddhists and be ordained as monks or novices (Department of Public Welfare 1965, pp. 19–20).

Apart from attempting to convert the hill people, the monks teach them good hygiene and how to develop the community. To promote good relations between the people and the government, the monks try to impress on them the government's concern for their welfare and that its policies are for their benefit. They teach the hill people elementary facts about government organization, Thai language, customs, and tradition, and their duty and responsibility towards the government and the king. The monks distribute medicine and other commodities, telling them that the gifts are provided by the government. Before and after giving them the things, the monks instruct them to pay respects to the Triple Gems (Somboon 1977, pp. 20–21). Such practices are said to be a very effective means of approaching the hill people (Department of Public Welfare 1975, pp. 6–10, 20–21).

Buddhism in Khmer Politics

Sihanouk and Buddhist Socialism

Theravada Buddhism has been the religion of the majority of the Khmer people since the fourteenth century, although Hinduism, Mahayana Buddhism and, above all, indigenous animistic practices have left their traces. In the modern history of Cambodia since the 1950s, Khmer Buddhism has continously been mobilized to achieve the political goals of the ruling élite. Prince Sihanouk was one of the leaders who was said to have made extensive use of Buddhism to legitimize his "Buddhist socialism". According to the Prince, Buddhist socialism was formulated in accordance with fundamental principles of Buddhism, which were the basis of Khmer cultural and social structure. He asserted that his Buddhist socialism was in fact based on his understanding of the Khmer way of life and culture. It was compatible with, and supportive of, the Khmer's penchant for living collectively and for relying on traditional mutual help. He stated his commitment to follow Buddhist principles in his Buddhist socialist effort to establish equality, promote the well-being of the poor in Khmer society, and to strive towards national identity. Prince Sihanouk made it clear that his Buddhist socialism was unlike other kinds of "socialism", both of the West and of the East, in that it was inspired far more by Buddhist morality and the religious traditions of Khmer national life than by doctrines imported from abroad. Thus, he claimed that his policy of political neutrality was conceived of in terms of the Middle Path in accordance with the

Buddha's teaching (for Cambodia's political social structure before the 1970s, see Chandler [1972] and Zago [1976]). In his battle against communism, Prince Sihanouk invoked Buddhism to support his campaign. According to Buddhism, he asserted, the ruler must respect the ruled and treat them with empathy and goodness. This, he said, was in contradiction to Marxism, which encouraged the weak (the ruled) to overthrow the strong, and to exercise a proletarian dictatorship, rather than find ways to co-exist. With regard to the ownership of property, Prince Sihanouk's Buddhist socialism disagreed with the idea of Marxist socialism, which encouraged state ownership rather than private ownership. The Prince also said that if his Buddhist socialism dispossessed the rich, this was achieved by persuading them of the meritorious value of giving to charity. However, Sihanouk's Buddhist socialism seemed to offer little in the way of a solution to overcome the serious political and economic crisis at the end of the 1960s. He was deposed by Lon Nol on 18 March 1970, the date which marked the end of Khmer monarchy. In October 1970, Lon Nol officially proclaimed the new republic. Prince Sihanouk acknowledged the failure of his Buddhist socialism and attributed this failure to the weakness of its theory of non-violence, of following the Middle Path, and of *Metta-Kuruna* (loving and compassion). Such methods have proved too soft to deal effectively with the country's serious problems. However, his opponents attributed his downfall to his religious misconduct. He had, they asserted, allied himself with the forces of evil; violated the teachings of the Buddha by opening a state casino in the country; and ordered the execution of his enemies from the Free Khmer Movement. The ruling élite of the new republic assured the Khmer people that the government upheld and supported Buddhism as the national religion, and respected Khmer traditions. They also placed the blame on Sihanouk for manipulating Buddhism for his own political purposes. The people were told:

> Cambodia is a country in which Buddhism is the state religion; Cambodia has also made Buddhism into a system of government, which we gave the name "Khmer Buddhist socialism", as opposed to ordinary socialism, and in particular to Marxist socialism. However, this Khmer Buddhist socialism was unfortunately unsuccessful: this admission comes from the mouth of one who was (or claims to be) its animator if not its very promotor, Prince Norodom Sihanouk, the man who is now allying himself with the

forces of evil and acting as a traitor to his country. This failure should not be taken to mean that the precepts of Buddhism are either unrealistic or impractical. On the contrary, we consider that, in the field of foreign relations, to take an example, a policy embodying the concept of the Middle Path between the two blocs, i.e. a policy of true nonalignment, is surely the best of possible approaches. Sihanouk's neutrality, however, was not a true neutrality, but one which leaned to the left. His socialism was Buddhist in name only; it was diverted from its original correct path, in other words, the teachings of the Buddha were not adhered to. The ex-dictator merely sought to use Buddhism as an instrument for his personal Machiavellian, autocratic, and despotic policy. (Ibid., p. 112)

Lon Nol and Political Mobilization of Buddhism

Although the policy of the Lon Nol government was not presented in Buddhist terms, it gave the people the impression that it respected Khmer tradition and continued the role of the government as protector and patron of the national religion. The religious roles formerly performed by the royalty were now the prerogative of the president of the republic. The *sangha* was assured of being able to maintain its prestige and status, and that the radical change of political rule was not meant to be prejudicial to Buddhism (ibid., p. 113). To assure the Khmer people of its fervent adherence to Buddhism as the traditional root of the Khmer way of life, the first government of the republic had the following words inscribed on the Republic Monument erected in front of the royal palace as the national slogan:

Buddhism teaches us to be honest, to reject selfishness and to promote mutual assistance. Above all it is a symbol of Liberty, Equality, Fraternity, Progress and Well being. (Yang 1985, p. 61)

Lon Nol himself had made it explicit to the people that he would follow the teachings of the Buddha in governing the country, and that he strongly believed in the Law of Karma and was convinced that justice and morality would prevail.

Thus was seen once again the political mobilization of Buddhism in Cambodia. Buddhism was now invoked to explain the downfall of Sihanouk in terms of his sinful deeds, and he was no longer qualified to be the ruler. The new ruling élite justified their dethronement of Sihanouk by accusing him not only of mis-management of the country's economy and inability to maintain political stability but also of committing serious crimes against the national religion (ibid.).

So Lon Nol had once more declared holy war against the Khmer Rouge and the Vietnamese (for civil wars in Cambodia, see Chandler and Kiernan 1983). He persuaded the Khmer people to believe that the war with these enemies was a war not only against aggression, but also against irreligion. He urged his people to stand firm and fight against the communists, for if their rule was ever established in the country, there would be no place for Buddhism. Monks and officials who had a good knowledge of Buddhism were mobilized to help in an anti-communist campaign to alert the Khmer people to the dangers of communism. The people were harangued with the slogan "If communism comes, Buddhism will be completely eliminated" (Yang 1985, p. 62).

Ideological conflict in Cambodia during the 1970s had thus intimately involved Khmer Buddhism and the *sangha* in the civil war. The Lon Nol regime found it natural to justify their counteraction against the Khmer Rouge in Buddhist terms. The idea that the communists were *Mara* or *Dhmil* (atheist devil) and that "there is no place for Buddhism if communism comes" provided a powerful argument which generated fear and hatred in the minds of the people. On the other hand, the Khmer Rouge, with the intention of liberating the people from the old conception of society and government and from their bondage to capitalism and colonialism, accused Buddhism of being the opium which impaired the people's talent and power both physically and mentally. The teachings of the Buddha were said to make people see life negatively and accept suffering without making any effort to improve their own fate, and perpetuating poverty and exploitation. Differences in the way of life of monks and laymen were also exploited by the Khmer Rouge to undermine the prestige and importance of the monkhood. The monks were accused of being unproductive, and are therefore social parasites. Merit-making activities such as contributing to the building of monasteries and religious places, and catering to the need of monks were represented as a squandering of the people's wealth in unproductive programmes which weakened national economic growth.

Buddhism under the Khmer Rouge

The civil war ended in April 1975 with the total victory of the Khmer Rouge. The Khmer Rouge established communist rule, imposed an iron grip in order to control the people and began making drastic changes. A new communist constitution was promulgated. Religious freedom was also recognized in article 20 which reads:

> Every citizen of Kampuchea has the right to hold any belief in religion and has, as well, the right to have neither belief nor religion. Any reactionary religion interfering with Democratic Kampuchea and its people is strictly prohibited. (Yang 1985, p. 16)

Buddhism, the former national religion of the Khmer, though not prohibited, has to undergo a radical reorientation. This involved a change of the roles and functions of the teachings, the *sangha*, and the monastery. The *dhamma* (the teachings of the Buddha) had now to be reinterpreted to support revolutionary causes and actions. The professional carriers of Buddhism, that is, the monks, were not encouraged to continue their careers. Those who remained in the monkhood had to undergo re-education and were treated as the laity. They were subjected to hard labour in the fields as well as in the construction of roads and irrigation systems. Their former religious prestige and status and privileges were repudiated. They were now to be despised as a burden on society who only "eat but do not produce". Not only were the monks thus humiliated, they were also hardly given any support either by the government or the Khmer Buddhist citizenry. It was the policy of the Khmer Rouge to belittle the religion, and finally to eliminate it. So far as the people were concerned the government made it impossible for them to support the monks. Because of the amount of work assigned to them by the agents of the government, villagers no longer had time to tend to the monks' needs. Because of poor rations and the shortage of food the villagers themselves could barely survive, and it was therefore impossible for them to make merit by offering alms to the monks. The world learnt also of the destruction and devastation of monasteries, and the burning of religious texts and statues of the Buddha.

The brutality of the Khmer Rouge as far as Buddhism and the *sangha* were concerned became legendary, and widely known throughout the world. Within a period of four years of the rule of the Khmer Rouge, Buddhism almost disappeared. If there was any saffron robe left in Cambodia, it was merely a deformed symbol of the religion, and no longer genuine Khmer Buddhism (Yang 1985, pp. 69–93).

Buddhism and the Heng Samrin Government

The invasion by Vietnam and the take-over of Phnom Penh on 7 January 1979 marked the end of Khmer Rouge rule. A government backed by Vietnam with Heng Samrin as president was installed. The Heng Samrin government's policy concerning Buddhism has been, on the surface, more positive than that of the Khmer Rouge. It has shown its concern for the controlled restoration of Buddhism. But the development of Buddhism has been closely monitored and kept subservient to the state. It is observed that the state has carefully planned and structured the size and growth of religion. Ordination is not directly discouraged but there are constraints by age. That is, a male adult under fifty years old is forbidden to enter the monkhood. This, the government asserts, is due to the 40 per cent decrease of the male population. If the number of monks swelled out of proportion, there would be a shortage of young active adults in the work-force. Devout Khmer Buddhists construes the government's policy relating to religion as a means to weaken Buddhism in the long run. In addition to allowing limited ordination, the government has indicated its intention to repair damaged monasteries and religious statues (ibid., pp. 97–100).

In contrast with the Khmer Rouge, Heng Samrin has attempted to capitalize on the reverence and loyalty of the Khmer people towards Buddhism and the *sangha*. Instead of condemning Buddhism as the opium of the people, he has highly praised Buddhism as one of the most important social and moral forces conducive to the building of a desirable society. He said:

> Buddhism was established in Kampuchea in the third century and has flourished ever since. It will last forever. People worship and observe Buddhism because they realize that Buddhism is a religion which advises people to abstain from wrong and to perform only good acts; a merciful humanitarian religion which preaches hard work, endurance, restraint, non-violence, non-exploitation, non-oppression, sound conduct, non-corruptibility, and the refusal to take bribes. This religion teaches us to live in a spirit of democracy, collectivism and harmonious unity, and to think of the interest of the majority rather than personal gain. It teaches us to know how to help ourselves and to save others from hardship. It accords well with the yearning of human society for peace and happiness. (*Foreign Broadcasting Information Service, Asian and Pacific Report* [*FBIS*], 2 June 1982)

Under the communist regime of Heng Samrin the monks were no longer officially viewed as social parasites but rather as benefactors of the country. They were praised:

A number of our Buddhist monks who strictly observed Buddhism have turned this into positive action as a contribution to serving society in ways and means which do not contravene the Buddha's regulations. In many regions, the monasteries have expanded their traditional role as centers for instilling ethics and the rules of an honest, clean and healthy life in society, and places where Buddhists are taught to strengthen unity and to preserve the mores and customs, civilization and culture, script, literature of the nation. (Ibid.)

The Heng Samrin government has made extensive use of Khmer Buddhism and the *sangha* for politically defined ends. Monks have been urged to join in revolutionary training courses where they are indoctrinated in Vietnamese and Russian communism, and where they are installed with fear and hatred for imperialist oppression and exploitation of the minds of the monks. The monks have to adapt and adjust their role and reinterpret the teachings of the Buddha to suit the revolutionary beliefs, practices, programmes, and policies of the government. Monks must keep strictly in line with government policy (*FBIS*, 7 June 1982).

Heng Samrin reminded everyone that

religion has been reborn because the country has been reborn. If the fatherland is attacked and oppressed by the enemies and perishes, religion will also be destroyed. (*FBIS*, 9 July 1984)

The monks were also reminded that the strategy for the survival of the state is as important as that of the monkhood and Buddhism. Thus, a war against the enemies of the country is the strategy for the self-preservation of the *sangha*. The monks must work hand in hand with the government to fight against the enemies of the country. They are also warned that

Buddhist monks must strictly observe religious regulations and abide by the provisions of the constitution and lines of the People's Republic of Kampuchea government. Anyone who uses Buddhism and the beliefs of our people to carry out activities to sabotage the correct lines, subvert national and international solidarity and destroy the fruits of the Kampuchean people's revolution will be punished. (*FBIS*, 5 September 1979)

The organization and administration of the *sangha* is also tightly controlled by the government. The Dhammayut and Mahanikai sects are now merged into one order. The high-ranking administrative monks are political appointees and they play an important role in revolutionary activities. However, the government exercises a heavy hand in ensuring that the monks comply strictly with the Buddha's authentic teachings and the 227 rules of conduct for monks (*vinaya*). The ordination is also closely controlled by local authorities. Monks do not have much freedom of mobility. Religious rituals and ceremonies are also subjected to control (*FBIS*, 9 July 1984).

The Preservation of Buddhism

Although Buddhism under the Heng Samrin government seems more relaxed than it was under the Khmer Rouge, a majority of the Khmer, especially those who are outside Cambodia, feel uncertain and doubtful about the policy of the communist regime towards Buddhism.[6] They are of the opinion that what the Vietnamese and the Heng Samrin government have been doing for Buddhism and the *sangha* is just stage play and a part of the regimes' political mobilization of the Buddhist Khmer.[7]

There has been a vigorous attempt by the Khmer under the leadership of Son Sann to preserve Khmer Buddhism in its original form. In their exile along the Thai border in Prachiburi, Khmer communities of about 150,000 have admirably tried to preserve their Khmer roots. Khmer traditional art and culture are preserved, disseminated, and handed down to the younger generation. Young children are trained in Khmer classical dance forms as well as in Khmer folk dance. Khmer craftsmanship is also revitalized. Masters of these arts are highly regarded and treated with respect. The training in these arts has always been kept alive whether the Khmer be in exile or in a war situation or in the jungle, as they believe that all these traditional cultural forms are part of their unique Khmer identity.[8]

Prime Minister of the Coalition Government of Democratic Kampuchea, Son Sann, evidences a strong belief that Buddhism is the foundation of Khmer culture and way of life and could provide the most vital integrating force for Khmer unification. He attributes the disintegration of the Khmer nation partly to the un-Buddhistic conduct of the Khmer. This, he has elaborated, involved the misunderstanding of the *dhamma*, a failure to remain steadfast to the teachings of the

Buddha, the pervasive presence of materialism, and the attack of communism on already weakened Khmer Buddhism. The Prime Minister sincerely believes that if Khmer Buddhism is resurrected in its original form, then the task of unifying the Khmer is not impossible. He thus actively supports the restoration of Khmer Buddhism.[9] The Research Centre of Khmer Buddhist Association in the border camp has been the organization that shoulders this important and heavy task.

The Research Centre of Khmer Buddhist Association is in charge of looking after the *sangha* organization and tending to the needs of exiled monks and novices. The administrative committee of the association helps in the organization of research and studies relating to the restoration of Buddhism. They have tried to acquire Buddhist scriptures and texts both in Khmer and foreign languages. Buddhist scholars who were forced to disrobe by the Khmer Rouge have been reordained and have become teachers of new monks and novices. About 50 acres of land was allocated to constructing living quarters for monks and novices and other religious structures for the holding of ceremonies. These buildings, though simple and inexpensive, are regarded as indispensable for religious functions and rituals. They are the centre and symbol of Khmer unity. The approximately 140 monks and novices are essential to the well-being of the Khmer population and are treated with reverence.

The attempt by the Khmer to preserve Buddhism manifests their strong will to maintain their Khmer identity. For the Khmer, Buddhism and Khmer identity are synonymous. Without Buddhism one can hardly conceive of Khmer culture and tradition. It is therefore beyond imagination that the Khmer could live under a political system whose ideology is strongly hostile to Buddhism.

Thus, whether it be Sihanouk, Lon Nol, Pol Pot, or Heng Samrin, all have attempted to use Buddhism for their own purposes and to legitimize their political control. The advantages in terms of creating national supports are obvious. However, at the same time, the purity of the Buddhist faith is compromised and the spiritual development of the population is sacrificed. The political leaders should also recognize that when they mobilize religion to legitimate their rule, they should not remould it, or it would lose its identity and sacred nature. If Buddhism is perverted and no longer accords with the people's traditional perception of it, it will cease to be a socializing and acculturating force and a unifying ideology of all classes within Khmer society.

NOTES

1. This brief account of the origin and evolution of the world, society, and Buddhist kingship is derived from Buddhist scripture, especially the *Aggana Suttanta* and *Jataka*. These works have been translated into English by various scholars and can be readily consulted in the Pali Text Society Series.
2. Before it was colonized by the French in 1863. Cambodia was a semi-independent state subordinate to its neighbours, that is, Thailand and Vietnam. For more details, see Coedes (1968) and Vickery (1977).
3. National integration here means the bringing together of various parts of the nation into an integrated whole — to the minimum value of consensus necessary for the maintenance of a socio-political order — so that the government can exert its authority throughout its realm. For an elaboration on this concept, see Asia (1967), Binder (1964), Coleman and Rosberg (1965), Zolberg (1967), and Weiner (1971).
4. He was then an influential member of the Mahatherasamakom (the Council of Elders, which is the sole executive body of the Thai *sangha*) and the Director of Phra Dhammatuta Division (Maekong Ngan Phra Dhammatuta). He subsequently became the supreme patriarch in 1972.
5. Details of their views and arguments have partly been taken up in Somboon (1981*b*, pp. 6–12). See also Prapat (1967), an offical document of the Ministry of the Interior (1967), Thanom (1969), Somdet Phra Wannarat (1968*a*, pp. 8–9), and Buddhadasa (1970, pp. x–xi).
6. Conversation with H.E. Prime Minister Son Sann on 31 January 1986.
7. Interview with Ieng Mouly, Assistant of H.E. Prime Minister Son Sann.
8. Information from a visit to a Khmer camp, Size II, in Thapaya on 1 February 1986 and April 1988.
9. Conversation with H.E. Prime Minister Son Sann on 31 January 1986.

REFERENCES

Akin Rabibhadana. *The Organization of Thai Society in the Early Bangkok Period, 1782*. Southeast Asia Program Data Papers no. 74. Ithaca: Cornell University, 1969.

Andaya, Barbara. "Statecraft in the Reign of Lithai of Sukhothai". *Cornell Journal of Social Relations* (Special Issue on Southeast Asian Studies) 6, no. 1 (Spring 1971).

Asia, Claude. *A Theory of Political Integration*. Homewood, IL: Dorsey, 1967.

Beer, Samuel H. "The Analysis of Political System". In *Patterns of Government*, edited by Adam B. Ulam. 2nd ed. New York: Random House, 1962.

Binder, Leonard. "National Integration and Political Development". *American Political Science Review* 58, no. 3 (September 1964): 622–31.

Blofeld, John. *King Maha Mongkut of Siam*. Singapore: Asia-Pacific Press, 1972.

Bradley, W.L. "Prince Mongkut and Jesse Caswell". *Journal of the Siam Society* 54 (1966).

Buddhadasa Bhikku. "A nu-mo-tana" [Appreciation]. In *Phutthasatsana Kap Sangkom Thai*, pp. x–xi. Bangkok: Sivaporn Press, 1970.

Cady, John F. *Thailand, Burma, Laos and Cambodia*. Englewood Cliffs: Prentice Hall, 1964.

Caldwell, J. Alexander. *American Economic Aid to Thailand*. Massachusetts: D.C. Health, 1974.

(Phra Maha) Chai Aphakaro. "Kan Prubprung botbat khong Phrasong" [The adjustment of the *sangha*'s roles]. *Kalapruk* (Bangkok) 1, no. 1 (1972): 1–3.

———. "Phrasong kap kan Phatthana thongthin" [The monks and community development]. *Buddachak*, no. 26 (May 1972), pp. 19–30.

Chandler, David P. *The Land and People of Cambodia*. Philadelphia, 1972.

Chandler, David P. and Ben Kiernan, eds. *Revolution and Its Aftermath in Kampuchea*. New Heaven: Yale University Southeast Asia Council, 1983.

Chaophraya Thiphakarawong. *Phrartcha Phongsawadan Krung Ratanakosin Rachakan thi Nung*. Bangkok: Klang Witthaya, 1962.

Charnvit Kesetsiri. "Buddhism and Political Integration in Early Ayudhya, 1350–1488". *Journal of the Faculty of Archaeology* (Silpakorn University) 4, no. 4 (April 1974).

———. *The Rise of Ayudhya*. Kuala Lumpur: Oxford University Press, 1977.

Chitt Phumisak. *Botwikhro Wanakam Yuk Sakdina*. Bangkok: Chomrom Nangsu Sangtawan, 1974.

Coedes, George. *The Indianized States of Southeast Asia*, edited by Walter Vella. Translated by Susan Brown Cowing. Kuala Lumpur: University of Malaya Press, 1968.

Coleman, James S. and Carl G. Rosberg, eds. *Political Parties and National Integration in Africa Political Culture and Political Development*. Princeton: Princeton University Press, 1965.

Damrong Rajanubhab. *Laksana Kanpokkhrong prathet Sayam tae Boran*. Bangkok: Ministry of the Interior, 1959.

David E. Apter. *Politics of Modernization*. Chicago: University of Chicago Press, 1969.

Department of Community Development. *This Is Community Development in Thailand*. Bangkok: Community Development Press, 1971.

_____ . *Functions of Department of Community Development*. Bangkok: Community Development Press, 1975.

Department of Fine Arts. *Tamnan Munlasasana* [History of origin of Buddhism]. Bangkok, n.d. [believed to have been written in the 1940s].

_____ . *Tamnan Prakat Muang Nakhornsithanmarat* [History of Nakhornsithammarat]. Bangkok, 1962.

Department of Public Welfare. *Raingan kitkan khong Phra Dhammajarik* [Report on the activities of the Phra Dhammajarik programme]. Bangkok, 1965.

_____ . *Report on the Propagation of Buddhism*. Bangkok, 1968.

_____ . *Raingan kan Phoeyphrae Phuttha satsana nai mu Chaokhao* [Report on the propagation of Buddhism among the hill people]. Bangkok, 1971–75.

(Prince) Dhani Nivat. "The Old Siamese Conception of the Monarchy". *Journal of the Siam Society* 36 (1947).

_____ . "The Reconstruction of Rama I". *Journal of the Siam Society Selected Articles* 4 (1959).

_____ . *Monarchical Protection of the Buddhist Church in Siam*. Bangkok: World Fellowship of Buddhists, 1964.

Durkheim, Emily. *The Elementary Forms of the Religious Life*. London: George Allen and Unwin, 1971.

Graham, W.A. *Siam in Transition*. Chicago: Chicago University Press, 1939.

Griswold, A.B. *King Mongkut of Siam*. Ithaca: De La Mare Press, 1961.

Griswold, A.B. and Prasert na Nagara. "A Declaration of Independence and Its Consequences". *Journal of the Siam Society* 56, no. 1 (1968): 29–92.

_____ . "The Inscription of King Rama Gemhen". *Journal of the Siam Society* 59, no. 9 (1971): 179–228.

_____ . "King Lodaiya of Skuhodaya and His Contemporaries". *Journal of the Siam Society* 60, no. 10 (1972): 21–152.

_____ . "Epigraphy of Mahadhammaraja I". *Journal of the Siam Society* 61, no. 11 (1973): 71–181.

_____ . "Kingship and Society at Sukhodaya". In *Change and Persistence in Thai Society*, edited by Skinner and Kirsch. Ithaca: Cornell University Press, 1975.

Iaming and P. Phitsanaakha. *Somdet Phrachao Taksin Maharat*. Bangkok, 1956.

Jaywickrama, N.A., trans. *The Sheaf of Garlands of the Epochs of the Conqueror*. A translation of *Jinakalamalipakarnam of Ratanapanna Thera*. London: Pali Text Society, 1968.

Keyes, Charles F. *Isan: Regionalism in Northeastern Thailand*. Data Paper no. 65. Ithaca: Cornell University Press, 1967.

Kriangsak Pisanaka. *Thai Ha Yuk*. Bangkok: National Library, 1969.

Ling, Trevor O. *The Buddha: Buddhist Civilization in India and Ceylon*. London: Temple Smith, 1973.

_____ . "An Introduction". In *Political Buddhism in Southeast Asia: The Role of the Sangha in the Modernization of Thailand*, by Somboon Suksamran, pp. x–xi. London: C. Hurst, 1977.

Lingat, R. "The Evolution of the Conception of Law in Burma and Siam". *Journal of the Siam Society* 38 (1950).

Lipset, Seymour M. "Some Social Requisites of Democracy: Economic Development and Political Legitimacy". *American Political Science Review* 53 (1959): 86–87.

(King) Lithai. *Traiphuum Phra Ruang*. Bangkok: Klang Witthaya, 1966.

Mahachula Buddhist University. *General Information*. Bangkok: Mahachula Buddhist University, 1967.

_____ . *Kam prasai khong Chomphon Thanom kittikhachorn*. [Field Marshal Thanom Kittikhachorn's speech]. Bangkok: Ratchaborphit Press, 1972.

Malinowski, Bronislaw. *Magic, Science and Religion*. New York: Doubleday Anchor Books, 1954.

Mendelson, E. Michael. "Buddhism and Politics in Burma". *New Society* 1 (1963).

_____ . *Sangha and State in Burma: A Study of Monastic Sectarianism and Leadership*. Ithaca: Cornell University Press, 1975.

Ministry of the Interior. Official document on the Dhammajarik monks and the hill people. 15 January 1967.

Phadnis, Urmila. *Religion and Politics in Sri Lanka*. London: C. Hurst, 1976.

Phat Bunyarataphan. *Community Development in the Country*. Bangkok: Community Development Press, 1975.

Phraya Prachakitkornchak. "Phongsawadan Yonok" [History of the north]. In *Prachumphongsawadan chabab Hosamut haeng chart* [Collection of chronicles]. National Library edition. Bangkok: Department of Fine Arts, 1964.

Pin Mudhukanta. *Report to His Majesty the King on the Purpose of Phra Dhammatuta Programme. Official Document of the Department of Religious Affairs*. Bangkok: Department of Religious Affairs, 1964.

_____ . *Nae nam Phra Dhammatuta* [Introducing the Dhammatuta programme]. Bangkok: Religious Affairs Printing House, 1965.

_____ . "Kwam pen ma khong Phra Dhammatuta" [Development of the Phra Dhammatuta programme]. *Phra Dhammatuta* I (1968): 40–41.

Prachoom Chomchai, ed. and trans. *Chulalongkorn the Great*. Tokyo: Centre for East Asian Cultural Studies, 1966.

Prapat Charusatien. *Rath lae kana Song* [State and the *sangha*]. A message from the Minister of the Interior to the Dhammatuta monks on the Opening of Orientation. Bangkok: Ministry of the Interior, 1967.

(Phra Maha) Prayut Payutto (now Phra Rajavaramuni). "Problems, Status and Duties of the Sangha in Modern Society". In *Visakha Puja B.E. 2511*, pp. 58–72. Bangkok: Sivaporn Press, 1968.

_____ . "Botbat khong Phrasong nai Sangkom thai" [The *sangha*'s role in contemporary Thai society]. In *Phutthasatsana kap Sangkom thai*

Patchuban [Buddhism and contemporary Thai society]. Bangkok: Sivaporn Press, 1970.

Puang Suwannarat. "Tatsanakati thor Botbat khong Phrasong nai kan Patthana Chumchon" [Attitude towards the *sangha*'s participation in community development]. A letter from the Under-Secretary of the Ministry of the Interior to the Secretary-General of Mahachula Buddhist University, 4 August 1970.

(Phra) Rajavaramuni. *Dictionary of Buddhism*. Bangkok: Mahachula Buddhist University, 1975.

_____. *Social Dimension of Buddhism in Contemporary Thailand*. Bangkok: Thai Kadi Research Institute, Thammasat University, 1983.

Reynolds, Craig J. "The Buddhist Monkhood in Nineteenth Century Thailand". Ph.D. thesis, Cornell University, 1973.

_____. "Buddhist Cosmography in Thai History with Special Reference to Nineteenth Century Culture Change". *Journal of Asian Studies* 35 (1976): 210–20.

Reynolds, Frank E. "Civic Religion and National Community in Thailand". *Journal of Asian Studies* 36 (1977): 267–82.

Riggs, F.W. *Thailand: The Modernization of a Bureaucratic Polity*. Honolulu: East-West Center Press, 1967.

Saiyud Kerdphon. "Tatsanakati thor kan mee suan ruam Patthana chumchon khong Phrasong" [Attitute towards the monks' participation in community development]. Official document, Communist Suppression Operations Command. 31 July 1970.

Sarit Thaanarat. "San Khong Nayok Ratthamontri thung Thi Prachum samantana Phra Kanathikan thua Ratcha-anachak" The Prime Minister's message to the administrative monks' from all provinces. 18 April 1960.

Satuan Suphasophon. *Phraputtha sasana kap phra Mahalsat Thai*. Bangkok: Klang Witthaya, 1962.

Siddhi Butr-Indr. *The Social Philosophy of Buddhism*. Bangkok: Mahamakut Buddhist University, 1973.

Smith, Donald E. *Religion and Politics in Burma*. New Jersey: Princeton University Press, 1965.

Somboon Suksamran. *Political Buddhism in Southeast Asia*. London:

C. Hurst, 1977.

————— . *Political Patronage and Control over the Thai Sangha*. Singapore: Institute of Southeast Asian Studies, 1981*a*.

————— . "Religion, Politics and Development: The Thai Sangha's Role in National Development and Intergration". *Southeast Asian Journal of Social Science* (University of Singapore) 9, nos. 1–2 (1981*b*): 54–73.

————— . *Buddhism and Politics in Thailand*. Singapore: Institute of Southeast Asian Studies, 1982.

Tambiah, S.J. *World Conqueror and World Renouncer: A Study of Buddhism and Polity in Thailand against a Historical Background*, pp. 226–27. Cambridge: Cambridge University Press, 1976.

Thanom Kitthikachorn. "Kam Prasai Khong Nayok Ratthamontri nuana nai okat ngan anusom sip kao phi khong Mahachulalongkorn rajuvidyalai" [The Prime Minister's speech on the nineteenth anniversary of Mahachula Buddhist University]. 18 July 1966.

————— . "Sang Khong Nayok Ratthamontri thung Phra Dhammatuta" [The Prime Minister's message to the Dhammatuta monks]. 8 January 1969.

Thompson, Virginia. *Thailand: The New Siam*. New York: Macmillan, 1941.

(Phra) Ubalikunupamacharn. "Owart thor Phra Dhammajarik" [Address to the Dhammajarik monks]. In *Report on the Propagation of Buddhism among the Hill Tribes*. Bangkok: Department of Public Welfare, 1972.

Vella, Walter F. *The Impact of the West on Government in Thailand*. Berkeley: University of California Press, 1955.

Vickery, Michael. *Cambodia After Ankor*. New Haven: Yale University Press, 1977.

Von der Mehden, Fred. *Religion and Nationalism in Southeast Asia: Burma, Indonesia, the Philippines*. Madison: Wisconsin University Press, 1963.

(King) Wachirawut. *Phra Phutthachao Tratsaur Arai*. Bangkok: National Library, 1925.

————— . *Thetsana Suia Pa*. Bangkok: Kurusapha Press, 1953.

(Somdet Phra Maha Samanachao Kromphraya) Wachirayan Warorot. *Pramuan Phraniphon*. Bangkok: Mahamakut Buddhist

University, 1971.

Wales, H.G.Q. *Ancient Siamese Government and Administration*. Reprint ed. New York: Paragon Boon Reprini, 1965.

(Somdet Phra) Wannarat. "Phra Owat hai kae Phra Dhammajarik" [Address to Phra Dhammajarik]. *Raingan kan Pheoyphrae Phutthasatsana nai mu chaokhao* [Report on the propagation of Buddhism among the hill tribes in north Thailand]. Bangkok: Department of Public Welfare, 1967.

————. "Nam Dhamma sue Prachahon" [Bringing *dhamma* to the people]. *Phra Dhammatuta* 1 (1968).

————. "Phra Owat hai kae Phra Dhammatuta" [Address to Phra Dhammatuta]. *Phra Dhammatuta* 1 (1969).

Watthanaset, S. *Kiatthikhun Phra Mongkut Klao*. Bangkok: Thai Watthana Phanit Press, 1957.

Weber, Max. *The Religion of India: The Sociology of Hinduism and Buddhism*. New York: Free Press, 1958.

Weiner, Myron. "Political Integration and Political Development". *Political Modernization*, edited by C.E. Welch, Jr. California: Wadsworth, 1971.

Wenk, Klaus. *The Restoration of Thailand under Rama I*. Tucson: Arizona University Press, 1968.

Woodward, F.L. *The Book of the Gradual Sayings*. Vol. III. Pali Text Society. Oxford: Oxford University Press, 1933.

Yang Sam. "Changes in Khmer Buddhism from 1954 to 1984". Mimeographed. A research report submitted to the Social Science Research Council. Indochina Studies Program, 1985.

Zago, Marcello. "Contemporary Khmer Buddhism". In *The Cultural, Political, and Religious Significance of Buddhism in the Modern World*, edited by Heinrich Dumoulin. London: Collier Macmillan Publishers, 1976.

Zolberg, Aristide R. "Patterns of National Integration". *Journal of Modern African Studies* 4 (December 1967): 48–67.

Singapore: Buddhist Development in a Secular State

TREVOR LING

The Buddha in Singapore

Chinese Temples

Any specific "beginning" of Buddhism in Singapore is very difficult to discern clearly against the general background of the Chinese temples and their various practices. Immigrants from southern China came to Malaya long before the founding of the Settlement by Sir Stamford Raffles in 1819, migrating "westwards and southwards from their homes in search of knowledge and in quest of the exotic products of the tropics" (Song 1984, p. 1).

> They did not at first attempt to form permanent colonies, but always at the end of each trip returned home in their junks when the monsoon changed [from northeast to southwest]. (Ibid., p. 3)

Later, they began to form colonies, at Penang and Melaka, and then, with the founding of the Settlement of Singapore, quickly began to establish themselves on the island. As Raffles himself wrote in June 1819:

My new colony thrives most rapidly. We have not been established
four months, and it has received an accession of population
exceeding 5,000 — principally Chinese. (Ibid., p. 7)

The relatively minor place held by the Buddhist element in Chinese
popular religion may be seen from the general religious practices of
the Chinese settlers, in so far as the nature of their practices can be
deduced from the furnishings of the earlier temples in Singapore.

The building and maintenance of a Chinese temple in Singapore
would have required a considerable degree of practical and financial
co-operation from a number of people. Readiness for this kind of co-
operation would in turn indicate some already existing shared social
identity. In the circumstances prevailing in the early nineteenth century
in Singapore, such solidarity existed, if at all, among people of common
dialect and from the same Chinese province. Lee Poh Ping has shown
that the

> solidarity arising from common dialect origin was probably one
> factor contributing to trust between the Chinese merchants and the
> petty merchants in the entrepot economy. (Lee 1978, p. 46)

Lee identifies the basis of this social solidarity even more specifically in
that "many organisations proliferated in Singapore from a common
territorial and, also, blood origin", and not from a community of
common dialect only. For example,

> Hokkien speakers from the prefecture of Chang-chou had their own
> association, the Chang-chou Association, which excluded other
> Hokkien speakers. (Ibid., note 24)

Lee gives further examples of this kind. Such an association would
require some sort of permanent building which could cater for the
Association's basic needs, and it seems that such needs were very
conveniently met by a Chinese temple.

A notable example in Singapore of a temple which performed this
dual function is the Hokkien temple known as the Thian Hok Keng or
in Mandarin, Tian Fu Gong (Temple of Heavenly Blessing) in Telok
Ayer Street. This served the Hokkien community both as a temple and
as a *hui-kuan* (or community hall). In its latter role it included such
"functions as the support of education and cultural activities", helping
members in the search for employment, and, when appropriate, even
a certain amount of political action. Lee adds that the characteristic form

of good works for prosperous members "in order to gain recognition from the Hokkien community for their leadership" was to have contributed to the building of a Chinese temple (ibid., p. 46). The temple in Telok Ayer Street, one of the oldest streets in Singapore, was at that time on the waterfront. Hence, it was "dedicated mainly to T'ien Hou, the seafaring goddess" but "with Kwan Yin and Kwan Ti as subordinate deities" (Yen 1986, p. 11). The inclusion of Kwan Yin, the female Bodhisattva, indicates the major devotional concern of the Buddhist element in Chinese religion in Singapore at that time. The building of the temple on that site, which was completed in 1842, replaced

> a small waterfront joss-house, where sailors and immigrants gave offerings and thanks at the shrine of Ma Cho Po (Mother of Heavenly Sages) for a safe sea passage. (Beamish and Ferguson 1985, p. 53)

Thus, the major donation for the building of the Tian Fu Gong temple came from a Hokkien merchant, Tan Tock Seng (Yen 1986, p. 185), who had migrated to Singapore from Melaka soon after 1819, and had become one of the leading figures among the Hokkiens. His was the largest donation towards the cost of the building of Tian Fu Gong, and he eventually became the Principal Director of the Management Committee. The temple was, and still is, primarily a place of *Chinese* religion rather than in any recognizably special sense a *Buddhist* temple. Everything about it emphasizes its Chinese character. "All the building materials were brought from China, as well as the major statue of Ma Cho Po" (Beamish and Ferguson 1985, p. 53). It is clear, therefore, that there was from the earlier days a close link between the Chinese temples and clan associations, and that there was a strong sense of identification with China and Chinese culture even to the extent of importing from China materials for the making and furnishing of the temples. In this way, the earliest temples in Singapore reflect the range of Chinese popular religion at that time, and therefore include some elements of a Buddhist nature, most notably the honour given to the Bodhisattva, Kwan Yin.

By 1881 the Tian Fu Gong served also as the meeting place for a society known as Lo Shan She. One of the activities of the Lo Shan She was the holding of "regular lectures on the first and fifteenth of every lunar month to expound the Sixteen Sacred Maxims of Emperor K'ang-hsi" (Yen 1986, p. 292). The audiences at these lectures are said to have been "mainly merchants and intellectuals of Chinese-educated background", and the Sacred Maxims dealt largely with such matters as

> filial piety, loyalty to the clan, propriety and thrift, law-abidingness, emphasis on agricultural work, appeasing neighbours and fellow-villagers, repudiation of false doctrines and exaltation of right learning.

It may be noted that most of these have a strongly *Confucian* rather than Buddhist character. For "the cultural nationalists" the purpose such lectures were intended to serve was "to arrest and reverse the growing trend towards Westernization" (ibid., p. 292) and to combat the undermining of the principles on which the Chinese clans were organized, for it was seen that this could lead eventually to the loss of traditional Chinese values, and even, it was feared, the loss of Chinese identity. As the long-term purpose of the lectures was to combat the various heterodoxies which were undermining traditional Chinese culture (and Confucianism in particular), it seemed that the best policy "was to re-assert the Confucian moral values" (ibid., p. 293). How far the promotion of Chinese culture, seen as essentially the promotion of Confucian values, can be regarded as consistent with the promotion of *Buddhist* values is debatable. Nevertheless a Buddhist element was present in the traditional Chinese temple, as in Tian Fu Gong, in the form of the Bodhisattva, Kwan Yin. There was at least this degree of coexistence in Chinese tradition between Confucian and Buddhist elements.

Some of the recent temples, however, have tended to be more specialized, in the sense that one temple may give somewhat greater importance to one cult than to another. Whereas in the earlier period in Singapore it was, on the whole, unusual for a Chinese temple to be regarded, for example, as exclusively Taoist or exclusively Buddhist, this is now not so clearly the case, and it may be an indication of what appears to be a growing *tendency* (and it is only a tendency) for Chinese temple-goers to differentiate consciously between "Buddhist" and "Taoist" identities. In one temple in 1987 (Feng Shan Si, in Mohammed Sultan Road) the present writer asked a group of work people associated with the temple, who were sitting resting, whether the temple was reckoned to be Buddhist or Taoist, as it could not be clearly determined from the variety of the cultic statues. The question precipitated a spirited argument, some declaring: "It's Buddhist", and others hotly denying it: "No! No! It's Taoist!". This temple has been described elsewhere as "syncretic" (Lip 1986, p. 90). On balance, however, it might well be considered now to be more Buddhist than "Taoist", and certainly more Buddhist than some of the *older* Chinese temples in Singapore. Another factor which may possibly have strengthened the tendency among Chinese Singaporeans to distinguish between "Taoist" and "Buddhist" is that in the 1980 census of Singapore these were two in a list of possible religious identities between which citizens had to *choose*.

What has happened to make possible this growing religious differentiation among Chinese people in Singapore may be seen also as a reflection of a growing ethnic *confidence* among Chinese Singaporeans. Yao Souchou in a recent article has drawn attention to the *symbolic* and *political* dimensions of ethnicity. He has argued that "at the core of what may be called the cognitive or personal and public domains of ethnicity" there lie not purely economic or social class issues but issues of a psychological and historical nature:

> In the changing drama of one's lifetime, the underlying values in models of ethnicity give a sense of emotional constancy and perhaps provide a simple panacea for existential anxiety. This is particularly important in a highly fluid, socially and economically competitive urban situation. (Yao 1987, p. 171)

In such a situation, the "cultural and religious values that constitute ethnic membership become morally self-evident" (ibid.). And for the Chinese immigrants in nineteenth century Singapore these cultural and religious values were demonstrated in the construction and furnishing of their temples, which, as we have noted, were also places of Chinese associational activities and functions.

The older Chinese temples in Singapore are all alike in this comprehensiveness, or catholicity as far as all aspects of Chinese religious culture are concerned: Taoist or Buddhist, and often with a Confucian element as well. It may therefore be suggested that in the "highly fluid, socially and economically competitive urban situation" of early nineteenth century Singapore, what provided the Chinese with "a sense of emotional constancy" were the "cultural and religious values that constitute *ethnic* membership" (ibid.); these were the values which were exemplified in the *Chinese* temple, rather than the more specifically Buddhist temple.

Yen Ching-hwang (Yen 1986, p. 11) observes that although Tian Fu Gong was not the first Chinese temple to be established in Singapore, nevertheless it "became the centre of religious activities for the entire [Chinese] community for sometime". He notes that it

> was founded by the leaders of various dialect groups in 1838, and was dedicated mainly to the T'ien Hou, the seafaring goddess, with Kwan Yin and Kwan Ti as subordinate deities. (Ibid.)

But he notes also that in Melaka the earliest Chinese temple was dedicated to the Bodhisattva, Kwan Yin, " the embodiment of the infinite quality of pity of Shakyamani Buddha", and the the Kwang Fu Kung temple in Penang, founded in 1799 was also dedicated to the Bodhisattva, Kwan Yin, and that the "funds for the construction of the temple appear to have been collected among all Chinese" in Penang. In Singapore, however, the Tian Fu Gong temple which "became the centre of religious activities for the entire [Chinese] community for some time . . . was dedicated mainly to T'ien Hou, the seafaring goddess, with Kwan Yin and Kwan Ti as subordinate deities" (ibid.).

That the Chinese temple Tian Fu Gong which was the centre of religious activities for the Chinese community in the early period of Singapore's history was dedicated not to the Bodhisattva, Kwan Yin, but to the seafarers' goddess, T'ien Hou, is a fact which Yen suggests reflected the relatively lesser importance of the Bodhisattva compared with the greater importance of the seafarers' goddess, in so far as the Chinese in Singapore were concerned. He suggests also that many of the junk owners who frequented the port of Singapore were among those who donated towards the construction of the Tian Fu Gong:

> They seem to have believed that the prosperity of Singapore and the benefits they derived from it were due to the power of the seafaring goddess, and thus constructed the temple in dedication to her

— *rather than* to the Bodhisattva, Kwan Yin, to whom, on the other hand, the Chinese of Melaka and Penang had dedicated their temples, respectively, as Yen points out (ibid., p. 11). The fact that Chinese junk owners in the the ports of Melaka and Penang should have preferred to dedicate their temples to the Bodhisattva, Kwan Yin, whereas in Singapore the junk owners preferred the goddess of the sea, may be taken as an indication "that there were more Chinese in Singapore

connected with sea voyages and trade than in Malacca and Penang",
because of the fact that Singapore had become "the leading British port
in Southeast Asia after its founding in 1819" and "had a thriving trade
with many parts of the world" (ibid., p. 12).

Such is the general historical background of Chinese temple
Buddhism in Singapore. What now have to be noted are the more recent
developments of different types of Buddhism in Singapore which is
perhaps best characterized as "associational Buddhism".

The *Dhamma* in Singapore

Growth of Associational Buddhism

The second of the three constituent elements of what has collectively
come to be referred to as "Buddhism" is the *dhamma*, that is, the body
of doctrine regarded as having been taught by the Buddha. Since all
three of these constituent elements are to be respected and revered,
concern for the study and proper understanding of the *dhamma* is as
important as reverence for the Buddha and for the community of
Buddhist monks. In Singapore there has in recent years been a notable
growth of interest in, and concern for, the proper study and
understanding of the *dhamma* by lay people. In some cases this
awakening of concern has been due to efforts made by certain Buddhist
monks to revive the teaching of the *dhamma*. An equally important factor
in Singapore in the past has been a growing readiness on the part of
some of the citizens of Singapore to engage in the study of Buddhist
doctrine. Indeed there are indications that the numbers of such lay
people are greater than can be met from the small number of teachers
available. Various organizations have, however, begun to grow in
response to this need. What follows is an account of some of these and
of their characteristics, membership, and activities.

In a paper published in 1971 (*Proceedings . . .*), Joseph Tamney
describes what he saw at that time as the failure of Mahayana Buddhism
in Singapore. By this was meant its failure to attract a new generation
of young Chinese Singaporeans; his findings were based mainly on
data derived from a survey of students at the National University of
Singapore. In a subsequent paper published in 1978 ("Chinese Family
Structure . . .", in *Asian Profile*) he developed his general conclusion that
in Singapore the retention or non-retention of religious beliefs was

related to social stratification, and that non-retention of Buddhist identity was associated with upward social mobility (p. 217). Such, at that time, was Tamney's perception of the "failure" of Mahayana Buddhism in Singapore, namely, its failure to retain young upwardly mobile adherents.

However, by 1988 a new kind of interest in Buddhism can clearly be seen in Singapore. It represents an interest in *Buddhist ideas* and their application in personal practice. It would not be inappropriate to characterize one of its chief elements as a growth of interest in *Buddhist philosophy* among younger Singaporeans who have a background of secondary, and in many cases tertiary, education. With this goes a readiness to acknowledge that the acceptance of a Buddhist identity should be based on something more than occasional or even routine visits to a Chinese Buddhist temple and the performance of the usual ritual actions. It is not without significance that a similar trend can be observed in Malaysia, mainly among the Chinese, where it has led to the formation of a vigorous movement known as the Young Buddhists of Malaysia, consisting largely of young professional people, who from time to time organize Malaysian national conferences concerned mainly with Buddhist philosophy and ethics, as well as local programmes of talks and seminars. In Singapore too this trend has led to the forming of Buddhist associations of various kinds. While it is possible to see at the time of writing in 1989 that there is in Singapore a movement which can justifiably be called "associational Buddhism", it is worth noting that this is not entirely of recent origin. Marjorie Topley, in a paper published thirty years ago, drew attention to an early form of the return to a more philosophical emphasis within Chinese Buddhism in Singapore in the institution of the *sen lin,* or "Forest of Laymen", formed in 1934, one of the aims of which was "to purify Buddhism in Singapore" (Topley 1956, pp. 70–118; 1979). In the early stages of the development of this movement it does not appear to have been particularly concerned with Buddhist philosophy. The movement found support among a number of already existing Chinese temples and vegetarian restaurants:

> Many of its ordinary members and some of the committee members are uneducated women of peasant origin who manage either their own vegetarian halls or the halls to which they have been appointed by officials of their religion. (Topley 1979, p. 179)

There was also a tendency for the early Singapore Federation of

Buddhists, which emerged from the Forest of Laymen movement in 1950, to lay great stress upon its Chineseness and the contributions made by the Chinese to Singapore's development (ibid.).

As Topley points out, Chinese religious organizations in Singapore at that period were notable for the way in which they overlapped and interpenetrated one another (as no doubt they still do to some extent). Another outcome of the Forest of Laymen was the Qi Shi Lin, in Kim Yam Road, where lay Buddhist devotees at the end of the decade of the 1950s were meeting, some regularly, some occasionally, for the chanting of Buddhist scriptures (ibid., p. 166). This is now known as the Singapore Buddhist Lodge and is one of the busiest and most crowded of lay Buddhist associations in Singapore. The following brief account of its activities will provide an illustration of the nature of associational Buddhism in Singapore.

The Singapore Buddhist Lodge

Situated off River Valley Road, in Kim Yam Road, the Lodge is now a large complex of buildings, still surrounded by fine large trees. There is an appropriateness in the use of the English word "lodge" in this connection, for not only has it the meaning of a "temporary abode", as when it is used in connection with Freemasonry and similar associations, but also because its root (in old French) indicates an "arbour", a hut in a wood or shady place ("a *lodge* in some vast wilderness"). Something of the same kind of location was adopted by the *earliest* Indian Buddhists, who were urban dwellers withdrawing to the seclusion of the forest (ibid., p. 166). But here the Lodge exists in fairly extensive grounds within what is now a central urban area of Singapore. At the weekends, and especially on Sundays, the whole place presents a lively scene. In the main building lay devotees gather in considerable numbers[1] for the chanting of Buddhist *sutra* (verses). Above the lofty hall there is an upper floor containing offices and a well-stocked library of Buddhist literature, some in Chinese, some in English, and much of it at a serious academic level. It is noteworthy that while it is mostly the middle-aged and older people who chant in the hall, it is the younger ones, including secondary schoolchildren, who use the library. Such use by schoolboys and schoolgirls is often connected with the Buddhist Studies programme, which was one of the options available in Religious Studies in Secondary 3 and Secondary 4 at the time of writing.

The Singapore Buddhist Lodge appears to have been one of the earliest examples of what now may be more generally referred to as Buddhist associations. The word "association" for this form of Buddhism can be recognized as corresponding with the Chinese word *hui* in general meaning: an assembly, a meeting, a union or association, but not necessarily or usually of a religious kind. There is to some extent a correspondence in function. The use of the term with reference to a certain kind of Buddhist practice certainly distinguishes the groups that are so described from the general run of casual Chinese Buddhist temple-goers. One of its chief characteristics is that adherents to this form of Buddhism have a serious interest in what can in general terms be described as a more *philosophical* formulation and presentation of Buddhist ideas and practices. Of such associational Buddhism there are various examples in Singapore at present. In addition to

1. The Buddhist Lodge

there are at least twelve other associations or societies (but the list cannot be claimed to be exhaustive). They are

2. Grace Lodge, Punggol (in the north of the island);
3. Buddhist Library, Hoa Nam Building (Foch Road);
4. Mahaprajna Buddhist Society, Foch Road;
5. Phor Kark See, Bright Hill;
6. Buddhist Union, Jalan Senyum;
7. Buddhist societies in tertiary educational institutions: (a) National University of Singapore; (b) Nanyang Technological Institute; (c) Singapore Polytechnic;
8. Singapore Buddhist Federation;
9. Singapore Chinese Buddhist Association;
10. Dharma Cakra Society, 40 Jalan Eunos;
11. Dharmafarers: Friends of Buddhism Singapore;
12. Singapore Buddha-Yana Organisation (formerly Singapore Buddhist Youth Organisation);
13. Singapore Buddha Sasana Society (Tibetan in origin), Topaz Road.

All of these have in common the fact that they are constituted by recognizable, continuing bodies of members, and that their concern is with a type of Buddhism *other than* that of the occasional practice by individuals of temple rituals, which is the main feature of traditional "Chinese-temple Buddhism". It is important to establish this point, as from time to time the distinction is consciously made by those who represent some aspect of the newer, growing form which is here referred to as associational Buddhism.

But even with associational Buddhism in Singapore, two somewhat different emphases can be discerned. In one there is a primarily philosophical interest. This is not merely an intellectual interest in ideas as a kind of pleasant diversion but in Buddhist *philosophy*, that is (as the word itself indicates), *a love of wisdom*, both for the sake of acquiring it and of living by it. In this case what is in view is a particular *kind* of exposition of what "wisdom" consists in: in this case, it is the Buddhist exposition of it (or more precisely, the Mahayana Buddhist exposition). For it was the "Great Vehicle", the *Mahayana*, that was so clearly and unmistakably concerned with questions of a *philosophical* kind (as philosophy is generally understood). On the other hand, while the Theravadin tradition of scholarship, whose texts were in Pali, was concerned with the analysis of the material and sensory universe, and the complexity of possible inter-relations of all the parts, it paid so much attention to analysis, and to the analysing of the analysis,[2] that any immediate *practical* relevance, in terms of the ethical and meditational life of real Buddhists, was virtually lost to sight. Hence came about the Mahayana claim that unlike the Theravadin and other similar traditions, theirs was the great (*maha*) vehicle (*yana*) which could carry the vast majority of ordinary people eventually to salvation, whereas the Theravadin school and others of that time which were like it would be able to accommodate safely only a very small number: theirs was therefore a "little" (*hina*) "vehicle" (*yana*). It was mainly the Mahayana form of Buddhist teaching and practice which captured and has retained the attention of Chinese people from the earliest days until now, and it is mainly this tradition which characterizes the concerns of associational Buddhism, as it is found in Singapore at the present time.

Grace Lodge, Punggol

The northeastern coast of Singapore is broken up into a number of broad peninsulas, each separated from the other by inlets of the sea. On one of these is Punggol; its location gives it a somewhat isolated character, and one which is not at all unsuitable as a place of retreat. Nevertheless, Punggol is a newly developing area, and development in Singapore can be rapid. Grace Lodge might be described in very general terms as a "Buddhist Centre", and in *principle* not unlike the Buddhist Lodge in Kim Yam Road. The most prominent part of the very new, splendid building is the large hall in which congregational chanting of Buddhist *sutra* takes place, and this can (and in fact does) accommodate up to 500 people, sitting or standing in rows across the width of the hall. Those who take part in the chanting qualify to do so by having "taken refuge": that is to say, having at some time performed the ceremony of affirming faith in the Buddha, the *dhamma* (his doctrine), and the *sangha* (his community). The visible sign of this is the robe which is worn by everyone who takes part in the chanting in the hall. It was emphasized by one of the Buddhist nuns of Grace Lodge that the wearing of such a robe represents membership "of the Buddhist community" in general: not necessarily *membership of Grace Lodge*. About the exact size of the membership there was some uncertainty. The sense of Buddhist "association" or identification which is being encouraged and fostered at Grace Lodge is much more than local; it is in principle a conscious identification with all other "confessed" Buddhists everywhere (that is, those who have "taken refuge"). There could, therefore, be said to be a stronger sense of identity with *all* confessed Buddhists elsewhere than could be claimed to be the case with the traditional Chinese Buddhist temple-goer who performs an individualistic ritual which, while it may be common to all such temple-goers, does not so directly and consciously constitute and promote a sense of universal *Buddhist* identity.

Regular participation in such common ceremonies is maintained more readily at Grace Lodge by means of the register of members, and the sending out of a monthly broadsheet (eight pages in the month of Vesak) containing not only news of the Lodge's activities but also general articles which clearly are intended to have an educative Buddhist function. These include articles for children as well as for adults. This monthly broadsheet is distributed also to other Buddhist associations of various kinds in Singapore, and is used to invite "other Buddhists" to the "functions and celebrations" which take place at Grace Lodge. Another aspect of the strongly associational character of the Lodge's functions and activities are what might be called the weekend "retreats" which are held when a public holiday follows, or precedes, a Sunday, thus making possible an overnight stay at the Lodge, between two full days of "retreat": that is, a programme of talks and *sutra*-chanting.

Those who attend and participate vary considerably in age as well as in other ways, such as that of formal education. Not all are necessarily fully committed. A young man who described himself as a free-thinker confessed that he was "very interested" by what he had seen and heard at Grace Lodge, and "felt he had to learn more about Buddhism". In terms of religious identity (as far as the Singapore census of population was concerned) he said he would probably at present put himself down as having "no religion", but he *might* put himself down as Buddhist since he used to visit Buddhist temples, but added "I should have to learn more about it". When asked *how*, he replied, "by reading more books". But in his case evidently it was the existence of this assemblage of old and young who had, basically, affirmed *their* faith in the Buddha, the *dhamma*, and the *sangha* which had impressed him. This was his third visit, and he had come in the first instance in response to an invitation from his employer, who also was present that day. As for his mother and father and family, some, he said, were Taoists (his parents), some of the others were Buddhists, and one a Christian. It was his sister, herself a Buddhist, who began to "teach" him "something about Buddhism". She had taken him first of all to the Buddhist Lodge in Kim Yam Road. Then he discovered that his employer was a Buddhist, although he had only recently become one "about three or four years ago".

A young woman, evidently about to become a mother, said she attended the Lodge fairly regularly although she lived in the Tampines area. (This is a distance of about four miles in a direct line, but more nearly nine by road, owing to the shape of the northwest coastline. She described Tampines as "far off".) Others came regularly to the Lodge from distant parts of the island such as Jurong and Seletar. She added that not only on Sundays but also on Saturday and Tuesday evenings at 8 p.m., some attended regularly for *sutra*-chanting. She and her husband were among those who attended the Lodge when it was at Telok Kurau, her husband having introduced her to the Lodge about a year before. Her parents also had been attending for some time, but her brothers did not, as they were Taoists. Like the young man she mentioned specially the *sutra*-chanting on the first Sunday of every Chinese lunar month, when large numbers attend, and when "you get to eat a vegetarian meal as well". On Kuan Yin's birthday, and on Vesak Day the Lodge was always very crowded.

This can only to a limited extent be said to reflect an interest in a *philosophical* form of Buddhism (although that *is* present), but it is clearly a very much more *associational* form of Buddhism than that which has come to be regarded generally as "Buddhism" in Singapore, that is: the conventional rituals of Chinese temples, which may vary from more to less Buddhist in character.

The Buddhist Library

An important form of associational Buddhism in Singapore (and one of its earliest forms) is the Buddhist Library (for details, see Mok [1986]). This is in fact something more than a library: it is a centre of activities of various kinds connected with the presentation and teaching of Buddhist philosophy and ethics. It was founded in 1981 as the Buddhist Research Society. Its founder was the Venerable Dhammaratana (ibid., pp. 10 ff.), a Sinhalese monk who had been impressed by the work of the Venerable Dhammananda in Kuala Lumpur. By the time a survey of its membership was made five years later in 1986 there were some 800 members. In April 1988 the membership was reported to be around 3,000. The Library has a regular programme of lectures and talks on Buddhist subjects as well as devotional sessions conducted by a Buddhist monk.

Its founder, the Venerable Dhammaratana, was a native of Sri Lanka, born in a village near Colombo and ordained as a novice at the age of thirteen into the Kotte Chapter of the prestigious Sinhalese Buddhist Order, the Siam Nikaya. At the age of thirty-three he was invited by the Sinhalese Mangala Vihara in Singapore to assist in the administration of that temple, and after only a further short period in Sri Lanka he returned to Singapore in 1973 to become the Assistant Resident Monk at Mangala Vihara, where he remained for two years. There followed yet another period in Sri Lanka, and after four years he returned to Singapore in 1977 to become head of the newly formed Tisarana Buddhist Association. This was a movement of an ecumenical Buddhist kind, concerned with the propagation of Buddhism. In Dhammaratana's view this included direct missionary activity, the promotion of serious Buddhist studies, and the practice of meditation. Dhammaratana had perceived that there was in Singapore at that time no place where such activities were being pursued or promoted. Out of these perceptions came the founding of the Buddhist Research Society in 1981, and from that, eventually, the setting up of the Buddhist Library, which was officially opened in July 1983.

An important point to be made in this connection is that while it was a Buddhist monk of Sinhalese origin who saw the need, and was responsible for the founding of the Buddhist Research Society, the response came largely from the *Chinese* Buddhist residents of Singapore. In 1986 Chinese members of the Society made up 96.2 per cent of the total, and 89.5 per cent of the members identified themselves as Buddhists (ibid., p. 99, tables 7, 8). (The largest other religious category was "no religion", 6 per cent.) Talks are given in either English or Mandarin, in the latter case there may also be a Hokkien translation. As far as age is concerned, two-thirds of the members are between twenty and forty. In terms of education 60 per cent had reached secondary or pre-university level, compared with 18 per cent of the general population; and 32 per cent had received tertiary education, compared with 2.7 per cent of the general population (ibid., p. 97, table 4). The majority of the members were *not* regular temple-goers: only 40 per cent visited a temple often; the other 60 per cent said they visited temples "only occasionally", or "infrequently", or "not at all" (ibid., p. 113, table 30). To summarize these characteristics it can be said that the majority of the members of the Buddhist Library are young (in their twenties and thirties), predominantly Chinese, and in terms of education mostly with secondary level education and above, with almost a third of the members educated at tertiary level. As we have noted, virtually 90 per cent identify themselves as Buddhists, yet less than half of them visit Chinese temples at all regularly. There is thus a noticeable degree of correlation among the Chinese in Singapore between level of education and type of Buddhist practice, that is, either traditional Chinese temple Buddhism on the one hand, and what may now be described as associational Buddhism on the other.

The Mahaprajna Buddhist Society

In the Society's own words:

> Some time in August 1985, a group of Buddhists decided to form a Buddhist Society to express their faith in the Buddha's Teachings and to practise and propagate the Dharma. The Society was formed in October 1985 with a Buddhist monk, the Venerable Hou Zhong, as its adviser and guide, and set out its two main objects as being (1) "to promote moral education through the propagation of the true spirit of Buddhism" and (2) to enhance the standard of

Buddhism by providing for the welfare and by financing the education of monks/nuns approved by the Society. ("Objects")

The Society, in its publications makes clear that it is a *lay* Buddhist society, which is nevertheless guided and led by members of the Buddhist *sangha*. It is therefore "not a totally lay Buddhist organization or a wholly *sangha* organization" (interview with Venerable Zhi-Ru, 17 April 1988). Its leader the Venerable Hou Zhong, writing in December 1985, expressed the hope that its members would "aim to be cultured and morally cultivated" ("Objects").

The founding of this Society in 1985, with the aim of promoting *moral education* through the propagation of the true spirit of Buddhism, came at a time when the subject of moral education in secondary schools in Singapore had become a prominent topic of discussion and planning, especially with regard to the programme of teaching for pupils in Secondary 3 and Secondary 4. The plan, set up in 1982, was to offer a number of options at that level. Eight options were decided upon, each one dealing separately with a major religious tradition, one of which was Buddhist Studies. By 1985 the Buddhist material had been prepared and written by academic specialists in Buddhist studies in consultation with the Singapore educational planners, and the whole subject of Buddhism was beginning to be considered, in secondary educational circles at least, in ways which were to some extent new, certainly as far as popular ideas and culture in Singapore were concerned at that time. It may therefore be more than a coincidence that the Mahaprajna Buddhist Society came together in its earlier form in the year 1986.

But this was not the only factor involved, as one of the founding members, now a Buddhist nun, made clear:

> My family used to be more Taoist than Buddhist, and I never paid much attention to [my mother's religion], until she started going to the Buddhist Lodge to do chanting. And some of my family members accompanied her when there were some ceremonies going on. After that we became *interested* in Buddhism, but wanted to know more about the doctrines.[3]

At that time a Buddhist monk from Taiwan was giving some talks at the Buddhist Lodge, and she began to attend those talks. When the demand for more regular instruction classes arose, a place of meeting had to be found. For a time the classes were held in the attic of a temple in Upper Thomson Road. The result of these classes was the decision to form a Buddhist society on a more regular basis, and to invite the Taiwanese monk to take charge of the instruction. The Mahaprajna Buddhist Society was formed in early 1986.

The Society soon began to flourish. Its *dhamma* teaching programme, at four levels (Introductory, Beginners, Intermediate, and Advanced), is comprehensive, as far as Indian and Chinese Buddhism are concerned, each of these levels having twenty-four two-hour units of teaching which are open to members of the Society. Chanting sessions are another feature of the Society's programme, when Mahayana *sutra* are chanted in either Mandarin or Hokkien. These are intended to have a threefold value: spiritual enhancement, Buddhist cultivation, and the creation of a sense of unity among the members. By the end of 1987 the Society was in need of a new centre to expand its programme as well as to meet the demands of an expanding membership.

The Society's leaders and members identify themselves with the Mahayana tradition of Buddhism. But they do not perceive themselves as over against the Hinayana tradition; the intention is that members should "get a full overview of what Buddhism is about".[4] This is a characteristically Mahayana point of view, since the essence of the Mahayana ("Great Vehicle") is its *inclusiveness* rather than exclusiveness, or claims to exclusive possession of Buddhist truth. As for *formal* relations with other Buddhist bodies or organizations in Singapore these are minimal; informally such relations are open and, as far as the Society is concerned, are good. The Society has a "religious" adviser or specialist; a monk from Taiwan, who "is very committed to the Society". He acts similarly as adviser to the Buddhist Societies of the Polytechnics (Singapore and Nanyang), mainly as a result of contacts with Polytechnic students who attend the Mahaprajna Society. Some of the members are at an early stage in their careers, having, in many cases, just set up a family; some are still pursuing tertiary education. The reason given for the predominance of this type of membership is that "the kind of classes we hold require reading, report-writing, and research; it's quite academic"; it was considered that other types of people might find it too difficult for them to take part in the classes. These others would, however, "come for different activities, the chanting and the Saturday night talks". In fact, both types of members attend the latter, since "you just have to sit and listen" (that is, no homework is required). The numbers attending have grown; in 1985 the average size of the classes was twenty, in 1988 this had risen to fifty. As the religious adviser speaks Mandarin and conducts the classes in Mandarin, these are more popular than the class in which English is used. All the members of the Society are Chinese.

A point which is strongly emphasized by the leaders of the Mahaprajna Society is the importance in Singapore of distinguishing clearly between Buddhism and Taoism. A phrase which recurs in what they say concerning the Society is the importance of promoting "the true spirit of Buddhism". This emphasis is not intended as a criticism of any other Buddhists, but, they say, in order to emphasize the importance of distinguishing between Buddhist and Taoist practices. "Buddhism," said one of them, "is a religion, but a religion different from Taoism, because it has to do with a way of life." The attitude towards conventional Buddhist worshippers at a temple such as Tian Fu Gong (in Telok Ayer Street), which has some clearly Buddhist features together with others of a more Taoist nature, was that those who worshipped there might be regarded as Buddhists, but that it was hoped that they would eventually come to understand fully "what Buddhism is about". That was the purpose of the Society: to try to educate people in the meaning and the practice of Buddhism.

The Singapore Buddha Sasana Society (Sakya Tenphel Ling)

Another example of a Buddhist association or society which has come into existence in Singapore within the past thirty years is the Singapore Buddha Sasana Society. This had its origin in what was then called the Singapore Buddhist Youth Circle, founded in 1959. In 1965 it was renamed the Singapore Buddha Sasana Society. Its Executive Council, as well as the membership, consists mainly of young people, and these appear to be predominantly young professional people. In 1979, after twenty years of the Society's existence, a permanent headquarters was established in Topaz Road. This was made possible by the efforts of the members and their friends, who had contributed and obtained donations for the building fund. The Society's affairs are in the hands of a youthful executive council consisting of fifteen of the members, all of whom are Chinese. There is a resident monk who is a Tibetan, the Venerable Lama Tashi Tenzin La. However, the Society emphasizes that it places "proper emphasis on both Theravada and Mahayana teachings". The general aim of the Society within its Singapore context according to its president, Michael Yang, has been "to present Buddhism in a form that is suitable for a modern progressive society and yet remain faithful to our very ancient roots".

The Society's activities provide clear evidence of their broad inclusive attitude in Buddhist matters. This is in itself an illustration of the *comprehensive* Mahayana approach. The week's activities by the second half of the 1980s consisted of the following: on Sundays, talks in Mandarin or English on a broad range of Buddhist subjects; some of the speakers are monks, some are laymen. At 9 a.m. on Sundays, an act of devotion, or *puja*, is carried out, and at 11 a.m. a programme of chanting of Pali *sutra*, taking refuge (in the Buddha, *dhamma*, and the *sangha*), and the taking of the moral precepts. A passage of a devotional nature is read out by one of those present and this is followed by meditation. The proceedings end with the singing of Buddhist hymns.

On Wednesday evenings and Friday evenings there is chanting of a Tibetan text followed by meditation on what has been chanted. The Tibetan practice of prostration is used on Friday. The general emphasis of the Buddha Sasana Society is thus characteristically Mahayana in that it includes a variety of forms and traditions of Buddhist devotion.

Buddhist Societies in Institutions of Tertiary Education

Associational Buddhism in Singapore, it has already been demonstrated, in general terms, is to a considerable extent (although not entirely) the expression of interest among the younger, English-educated section of Singapore's population in Buddhist teaching. Such interest may extend also to devotional practice. This becomes particularly clear in the case of the Buddhist associations in institutions of tertiary education in Singapore at the end of the 1980s.

The National University of Singapore Buddhist Society was formed at the beginning of the decade (1981). Its inception was due to what is said to have been "a feeling of need" for such a society where young Buddhists could come together to share their experiences in the *practice* of Buddhism. At the beginning of 1989 the society was said to have 160 members, although more than that number attended its meetings. The Society's regular programme consists of lectures and talks, and small-group study of Buddhist teaching and practice, the groups being formed on a Faculty basis (Arts, Science, Social Sciences, and so forth). Membership is open to the adherents of any religion; the only requirement is that of being a registered student of the National

University of Singapore. The majority of the members are Chinese, together with a few Indians, but no Malays. Of the members it was estimated that about 20 per cent were students who had recently been attracted to Buddhism. The main reason given for the interest of first- and second-year students in particular was the Buddhist Studies programme in schools, at Secondary 3 and Secondary 4 levels, a programme which began in 1985/86. First-year students provide the largest proportion of NUS Buddhist Society members, whereas second- and third-year students, it was claimed, have more academic work on their hands, and therefore not so many registered as members. It has also to be allowed that interest may have waned after the first year. Certainly those who remain as members into the senior years (third year and fourth year Honours classes) are committed to the Society and help in the organization of its activities. Some of these also belong to Buddhist organizations in Singapore outside the university, such as the Buddhist Library, Singapore Buddhist Mission, Phor Kark See (temple), and the Buddhist Lodge.

Corporately, the NUS Buddhist Society is associated with other Buddhist organizations in Singapore, and particularly with the Buddhist societies of other institutions of tertiary education: the Nanyang Technical Institute, the Ngee Ann Polytechnic, the Singapore Polytechnic, and the Institute of Education. These four, together with the NUS Buddhist Society, form the Tertiary Buddhist Fellowship. Associated with this organization is the Singapore Buddhist Graduates' Fellowship (registered in 1988), which exists to help the five tertiary education societies. In 1989 there was a meeting once a month in the Hilton Hotel to hear a talk and transact its business.

Ngee Ann Polytechnic Buddhist Society

The Buddhist Society at Ngee Ann Polytechnic was registered as the time of the founding of the Polytechnic in 1974. Before that, it had existed, although unregistered, at the Ngee Ann Technical College. Its objectives, as stated by its President (Ms Choo Boon Noi) are to propagate Buddhism within the Polytechnic campus, and to correct misconceptions concerning Buddhism. There had been a growth of interest in Buddhism among Polytechnic students in recent years, in Choo Boon Noi's view following the introduction of the Religious Knowledge programme in secondary schools. Another factor, in her view, was the generally tolerant attitude associated with Buddhism, which was seen by students as attractive in contrast with some other traditions. All the members were Chinese, although there had in the past been one or two Eurasians and some Indians.

The Society is a member of the Singapore Buddhist Federation and of the Tertiary Educational Buddhist Fellowship but had no links with non-Buddhist religious associations, nor any with the (Japanese) Nichiren Buddhists, who "reject the basic Buddhist teachings", defined by Boon Noi as belief in the four Noble Truths, the five precepts, and the attainment of *nibbana* as the ultimate aim. The Society's activities included meetings for the teaching of Buddhist *dhamma* and for meditation, with chanting in Pali before and after the classes. There were also said to be lectures and talks, participation in book fairs, visits to old people's homes, and visits to Buddhist temples of various different traditions, such as Thai, Tibetan, Sri Lankan, and Chinese. It was reckoned that more than a few of the members made their own visits to temples for their personal devotions. In Boon Noi's estimation there was a revival of Buddhism in Singapore "especially in quality". In particular, Chinese younger people were now able to differentiate between Buddhism and Taoism.

Buddhist Cultural Diversity

Among these various Buddhist associations there is considerable variety with regard to the kind of Buddhist teaching and practice which each has adopted. For example, "the Ananda Metyarana Buddhist Youth Circle concentrates all its activities around Ananda Metyarana Buddhist temple under the guidance of the *Thai* monks" whereas those who attend the Tibetan temple, Sakya Tenphel Ling, engage in the rituals of *Tibetan* Buddhism, and are directed by a monk who is ordained in the Tibetan order. In such ways Chinese Singaporeans come into contact with various forms of Buddhism which are not the traditional forms of Buddhism in China. While Singaporean society is strongly Chinese in many of its cultural aspects it is not purely and simply Chinese, but Singaporean. For Chinese forms of Buddhist learning and practice developed in China as appropriate forms in which Buddhism expressed itself within traditional Chinese culture, whereas Singapore's citizens are exposed to cultures and traditions other than those of their ancestors, whether these were Chinese or Indian or any other. There is no compelling reason in Singapore for Chinese young people or their parents to confine any interest in Buddhism they may feel to purely Chinese Buddhism, that is to say the form which succeeded in establishing itself in China, long ago. On the other hand, there is no reason why it should be confined to forms of Hinayana Buddhism, such as Sinhalese or Thai, as being in any more marked degree *authentically* Buddhist. The whole long history of Buddhism suggests that the appropriate form of Buddhist ideas and practice in a cultural context such as that of modern Singapore is yet to emerge, and is perhaps even now in the process of emerging. Certainly it does not necessarily have to regard the cultural pattern of Buddhism which took form within the Indian cultural context, strongly shaped as this was by the surrounding Brahminical influences, as being in every cultural situation the most appropriate. Gautama the Buddha was of the Sakya clan, and the evidence suggests that the Sakya and their culture had affinities outside those of Brahmanically dominated Indian society, and from beyond the frontiers of that part of Asia which has, since their time, come to be known as Indian.

The *Sangha* in Singapore

The Central Importance of the Buddhist Sangha

The Buddhist *sangha* is an essential constituent of the various different cultural forms of Buddhism in Southeast Asia. In essence, the word *sangha* (as the *company* of Buddhist monks) may refer to either the local body of monks or to the *universal* Buddhist monkhood. The generally accepted way of referring comprehensively, in Asian contexts, to what in English is generally called "Buddhism" is: the Buddha, the *dhamma* (or *dharma*), and the *sangha*,[5] that is, the Enlightened One, his Doctrine, and the Community; the community, that is, of monks, by whom the doctrine is preserved, taught, and practised.

The *sangha* is thus an essential and integral feature of Buddha *dhamma*, or, in more familiar terminology, "normative Buddhism". Where there is no *sangha* (if this is a more or less permanent state of affairs) there cannot properly be said to be Buddhism in the full, normative sense. Even where, as in some non-Asian countries, lay people have, after much reading and study, taken it upon themselves to teach the Buddha *dhamma* (as, for example, did Christmas

Humphreys in England), and some of the hearers have begun to follow the teaching (the Buddhist Way, or *Buddha Marga*), the resultant situation cannot, in terms of classical Buddhist usage, be correctly described as the establishment of Buddhism in that country as long as no form of the *sangha* has been established, with its members living in accordance with the rules and provisions of the *vinaya*, that is, the code of conduct, discipline, and communal association for Buddhist monks, or *bhikkhu*.[6]

In Singapore, Buddhists constituted 26.7 per cent of the population in 1980. This was the second largest religious category, the largest being Taoists, with 29.3 per cent. Nevertheless, in Singapore, Buddhist monks are far less evident generally than they are, for example, in Bangkok or Yangon, even when allowance has been made for the fact that in Singapore Buddhists are a smaller percentage of the total population than in Myanmar and Thailand. In Singapore fewer young men, even of Buddhist families, are likely to enter the *sangha* for the customary short period in early manhood, and this too is in contrast with the practice in Myanmar and Thailand. A period of absence by a young man from his normal employment for the purpose of fulfilling the requirements of compulsory military service is normal in Singapore; a period of absence in order to gain Buddhist merit by donning the robes of a monk for a period would be somewhat abnormal, even for the 27 per cent Buddhists (Department of Statistics, Singapore, *Census of Population, 1980, Singapore*, p. 4). Another relevant consideration is that the majority of Singapore's Buddhists adhere to the Mahayana tradition, unlike those of Myanmar and Thailand where the Theravadins constitute the majority, among whom the practice of merit-making through temporary membership of the *sangha* is commonly regarded as of greater importance than it is by the adherents of most Mahayana Chinese forms of Buddhism. For whatever reason, it is rarely that one sees a Buddhist monk in public places in Singapore, compared with in Yangon or Bangkok.

Another aspect of institutional Buddhism in Singapore, when compared with mainland Southeast Asian countries such as Thailand and Myanmar, is the relatively small number of Buddhist *monasteries*. This contrasts sharply with the large number of Buddhist *temples*. It also reflects the lesser importance which is attached to monastic life by Chinese Buddhists in Singapore compared with the attitude in the predominantly Theravada countries of Southeast Asia. It is possible that this is partly due to the fact that in areas of Chinese culture generally somewhat less attention is given by Buddhists to the importance of monastic life and institutions than is the case, for example, in Myanmar, Thailand, and Sri Lanka. It appears that in Singapore too Buddhist monastic life has had a position of, at best, only minor importance, and, until recently at least, seems to have counted for relatively little in the Singapore Buddhists' evaluation of these matters. This lack of concern may be interpreted as a consequence of the general Chinese disinclination to allow healthy young men to shut themselves away from the normal life of home and family, even for the relatively short periods that are customary in Myanmar and Thailand. It may well be seen also as indicative of the high priority given to economic considerations in Singapore: in this case, economic production. In the matter of the supply of Buddhist monks, moreover, Singapore can be said to be *under*-productive, in that monks have to be invited from Taiwan or elsewhere, both as teachers and for the performance of Buddhist professional functions.

But at this point it is necessary to add "at least until recently". For there are beginning to be signs of a heightened valuation of the permanent *sangha*. Nevertheless, in the matter of the availability of monks in Singapore for the performance of specialist functions it appears still to be necessary sometimes to invite monks from Taiwan and elsewhere.

From the foregoing brief outline of the shape and extent of Buddhism in Singapore it would appear that it has not, at least until recently, conformed to the normative pattern found elsewhere in Southeast Asia today, and traditionally also in China, that is, the accepted pattern of three main elements: the Buddha, the *dhamma*, and the *sangha*, the "triple gem", "the three refuges".

Sangha *and* Sasana

A traditional way of summarizing the *teaching*, which is popularly referred to as "Buddhism", is that of the three *Pitaka*. Broadly, *Pitaka* may be translated as "basket" or "collection". There are three (*Tri*) of these, so the whole is referred to as "the *Tri-pitaka*" (Pali: *Tipitaka*). The three are (1) the *Vinaya Pitaka*, the collection of teaching concerning the Buddhist *sangha* and its disciplines; (2) the *Sutra Pitaka* (Pali: *Sutta*), the collection consisting of discourses and stories, mainly attributed to the Buddha; and (3) the *Abhidharma Pitaka* (Pali: *Abhidhamma*), the collection concerning the more complex aspects of Buddhist doctrine and meditational practice. The first and third are the concern mainly of Buddhist monks, rather than lay people. The second, the *Sutra Pitaka*, which consists of stories of the Buddha, and stories told by the Buddha, is the major source of Buddhist teaching and guidance for lay people and the *sangha* alike.

Buddha Sasana

The process whereby the teachings of the Buddha, and the Buddhist way of understanding and living are apprehended and practised is referred to as Buddha *sasana*, a term which is broadly translated as "Buddhist rule of life" (possibly, in modern terminology, "Buddhist life-style"). In Buddhist tradition this entails, among other things, appropriate, and to some extent reciprocal, *interaction* between monks and laymen: for the laymen, in terms of rendering of service and financial support, and for the monks in terms of teaching and advising. It is in this connection that the practice of Buddhism by lay people has traditionally, in the Buddhist milieu, been seen to require the presence of a permanent *sangha*, that is, a body of Buddhist monks. In Southeast and East Asia, such has been the case in Myanmar and Cambodia and Thailand and Tibet. Wherever this kind of arrangement exists and functions, the Buddha *sasana* is said to flourish.

In Singapore it appears that the *sangha* is less characteristic a feature of local Buddhism than is normal elsewhere in modern Southeast Asia. Two observations on this apparent abnormality may be offered. First, much of what is *seen* in Singapore as "Buddhist" practice will be found in the temples, where lay people may be observed in front of Buddha statues making ritual gestures of reverence. This will seem to consist mainly in the waving of joss-sticks and perhaps repeating quietly some ritual formula. On the whole this is more characteristic of Chinese, Mahayanist practice, although it has its parallels with Theravadin (that is, Hinayanist) practice, in Sri Lanka especially. But the absence from such a scene, in almost all cases in Singapore, of a Buddhist monk, is not so characteristic of Theravadin Buddhist temples in Sri Lanka, or Myanmar, or Thailand. In Singapore Buddhist "monks" (or *bhikkhu*) are likely to be seen only in the larger, more recently developed temples such as Shuang Lin Si (1909) in Jalan Toa Payoh, Long Shan Si (1926) in Race Course Road, and Phor Kark See in Bright Hill Drive.

The Singapore Buddhist Sangha Organisation[7]

However, in Singapore, the *sangha* certainly now exists in the form of an officially registered organization: the Singapore Buddhist Sangha Organisation (SBSO). It was registered in 1966 and has it headquarters in Phor Kark See (a temple founded in 1925); membership of the organization is open to all ordained Buddhist monks in Singapore. In March 1989 the SBSO had fifty-eight members. Certain conditions of membership are laid down: a candidate must be recommended by a member, and must provide written evidence of his identity, such as a certificate from his temple or his superior, and evidence that he is a permanent resident of Singapore or the holder of a work permit or visitor's stay permit. Those monks who do not have "permanent residence" in Singapore and who need permits are mainly from Thailand, China, and a few Tibetans. Monks in this category usually come on short visits only, and therefore may not seek or require membership of the SBSO.

Besides the help given by the SBSO to monks from outside Singapore further help may come from the organization known as the Singapore Buddhist Federation (SBF). This includes not only monks but also Buddhist laymen of Singapore, and consists mainly of Chinese Buddhists. The Federation is older than the Sangha Organisation, and the language used in its formal meetings is Mandarin. However, some Chinese Buddhist monks in Singapore speak only Chinese dialects, so the use of Mandarin by the Federation may to that extent limit the participation of such monks in its affairs. On the other hand, the Singapore Buddhist Sangha Organisation's meetings are conducted in English and in Thai, so that the extent of participation of Singapore *Chinese* monks in the SBSO's affairs would appear to be limited to those who speak English (or, possibly, Thai). Generally, this means that only a Buddhist monk who speaks *both* Mandarin *and* English will be able to participate in the affairs of both the SBF and the SBSO; the overlap of such Mandarin- and English-speaking monks appears to be relatively small.

Sangha and State in Southeast Asia

In Buddhist history in India and Southeast Asia there is a tradition of co-operation and mutual support between the Buddhist *sangha* and the state. In India this tradition can clearly be seen from the time of

Emperor Asoka, even though the close relationship was lost in a later period with the re-assertion of the influence of the Brahman priesthood.

In Myanmar (Taylor 1987, pp. 50–57) the role of the *sangha* was for long periods subject to the power of the Myanmar kings, which included the power to purify the *sangha* if it became corrupt and failed to exercise discipline over its members in the way that Buddhist tradition required. In such cases, as Robert Taylor points out, "it was the right, even the duty, of the king to intervene and purify the membership and practices of the religious order" (Taylor 1987, pp. 56 ff.). This tradition of royal control and purification of the *sangha* broke down, however, with the British invasion of Myanmar in the nineteenth century, the capture of Mandalay, the royal capital at that time, and the deportation of the Myanmar king into exile, in India. The Buddhist *sangha* then became a force antagonistic to the government established by the British, and remained so throughout the period of British rule, and continued when in 1942, British rule was displaced by the Japanese, who for three years became the political rulers of Myanmar until their defeat by the Allies in 1945. A further brief period of British rule followed until on 4 January 1948 Myanmar became once again a state ruled mainly by the Myanmar. But in Myanmar the traditional relationship between the *sangha* and the government had remained broken throughout a long period and has proved difficult to re-establish.

In Thailand the integration of the *sangha* and the state was a more gradual process, but it can be clearly seen with the establishment of Theravada Buddhism in the fourteenth century; a similar development took place in Cambodia, but this too has in recent history been disrupted by Vietnamese invasion and the escape into exile in refugee camps in Thailand of many of Cambodia's Buddhists.[8]

In general, it may be concluded from this rapid review of relations between the *sangha* and the state in Southeast Asia that the continued well-being and strength of Buddhism in any given country depends to a very large extent on the nature of the relations between the *sangha* and the government of the country concerned.

Sangha *and State in Singapore*

Unlike Myanmar and Thailand throughout most of their history Singapore is a secular state. The word "secular" in this context does not imply that the state necessarily stands in opposition to institutional forms of religion practised within its realm but that no one form of religion enjoys any special relationship with government. This contrasts, for example, with the case of Britain, where by virtue of their ecclesiastical office certain English bishops have, by right, seats in the House of Lords, and where there is, in theory, a state Church, the Church of England, *by law established*. Such also is the case, with certain differences in detail, in Thailand. And until the British invasion of Myanmar and the carrying away captive into India of the Myanmar king, between whom and the *sangha* there was a traditional close relationship, such had been the case in Myanmar. In Singapore, a secular state, on the other hand, no special relationship exists between the government and any of the institutional forms of religion practised by Singaporean citizens, including the Buddhist *sangha*.

Moreover, the Buddhist *sangha* is a much less publicly prominent feature of the Buddhism of Singapore than it is elsewhere in Southeast Asia. On the other hand, it is important to take into account the number of flourishing Buddhist societies and associations that are found in Singapore, these consisting principally of Buddhist lay people. From the point of view of a sociological analysis of religion this may be at least equally as significant a feature of Singaporean Buddhism as the visibility of monks in public places in Bangkok and Yangon. Their growth in Singapore raises an important question: What is the significance, from a Buddhist perspective, of the growth in Singapore of these associations of lay people which are largely, though not entirely, independent of the professional Buddhist community, the *sangha*?

NOTES

1. Probably 200 or 300 on an average day.
2. A Buddhist philosopher, the late Edward Conze in his comparisons of the Mahayana and Theravadin (Hinayana) systems, used rather mischievously to describe the Theravadin *abhidhamma*, or philosphical books, as a cross between the mathematical complexities of a large company balance sheet and Bradshaw's railway timetable. He used to add that it was *not only* the dense complexity that they had in common.
3. Information from the Buddhist nun who is resident at Grace Lodge.
4. That is, the celebration of the Buddha's birth, and of his Enlightenment,

and of his entry into *nibbana*.

5. The Sanskrit prefix *san* (Pali: *sam*) carries the same broad meaning as the prefix *syn* and the Latin *com* or *cum*, that is, "together", or the idea of the association of more than one with another; so that here the basic idea is that of a "community", a shared life.
6. Literally, "sharesmen", each of whom is entitled to a "share" — either in the common life, or the share of the food reserved by householders (or laymen) for the monks.
7. The present writer is greatly indebted to the Venerable Kwang Phing, resident monk at Kong Meng San Phor Kark See Temple, Bright Hill Drive, Singapore, for his kind help with information on the Singapore Buddhist Sangha Organisation.
8. Even in the severely deprived conditions of a refugee camp within the Thai border, Cambodian Buddhist monks have succeeded in maintaining something of their characteristic concern not only with Buddhist rituals but also with Buddhist learning. In a visit to the large refugee camp at Site 2, the present writer was impressed by the extent of the library they had contrived to collect, and also with their enthusiastic participation in the two-day seminar on aspects of Buddhism which had been arranged with the assistance of the Adenauer Foundation in Bangkok.

REFERENCES

Beamish, Jane and Jane Ferguson. *A History of Singapore Architecture: The Making of a City*. Singapore: Graham Brash, 1985.

Department of Statistics, Singapore. *Census of Population, 1980, Singapore: Release No. 9: Religion and Fertility*. Singapore: Graham Brash, 1980–81.

Lee Poh Ping. *Chinese Society in Nineteenth Century Singapore*. Singapore: Oxford University Press, 1978.

Lip, Evelyn. *Chinese Temples and Deities*. Singapore: Times Books, 1986.

Mok, James. *The Buddhist Library and Its Social Matrix*. Academic exercise, Department of Sociology, National University of Singapore, 1986.

Song Ong Siang. *One Hundred Years History of the Chinese in Singapore*. Singapore: Oxford University Press, 1984.

Tamney, Joseph. *Proceedings of the Eleventh International Conference for the Sociology of Religion*. The International Association for the Sociology of Religion, 1971.

_____ . "Chinese Family Structure and the Continuation of Chinese Religions". *Asian Profile* 6, no. 3 (June 1978).

Taylor, Robert. *The State in Burma*. London: C. Hurst and Co., 1987.

Topley, Marjorie. "Chinese Religion and Religious Institutions in Singapore". *Journal of the Malayan Branch of the Royal Asiatic Society*, no. 29, part 1 (1956), pp. 70–118.

_____ . "Religion and Social Realignment among the Chinese in Singapore". In *The Study of Chinese Society*, edited by Maurice Freedman. Stanford: Stanford University Press, 1979.

Yao Souchou. "Ethnicity: The Symbolic and Political Dimension". *SOJOURN: Social Issues in Southeast Asia* 2, no. 2 (August 1987): 169–77.

Yen Ching-hwan. *A Social History of the Chinese in Singapore and Malaya, 1800–1911*. Singapore: Oxford University Press, 1986.

Index

Contributors

Peter A. Jackson is Executive Officer of the National Thai Studies Centre at the Australian National University.

Trevor Ling is Emeritus Professor of Manchester University, and a Visiting Fellow at the Institute of Southeast Asian Studies, Singapore. He was formerly a Visiting Professor in the Department of Sociology at the National University of Singapore.

Somboon Suksamran is Professor of Political Science at Chulalongkorn University, Bangkok.

Tin Maung Maung Than is Research Fellow of the Institute of Southeast Asian Studies, Singapore.